COLOURS

COLOURS

IRELAND – FROM BOMBS TO BOOM

HENRY McDONALD

MAINSTREAM
PUBLISHING
EDINBURGH AND LONDON

First published in Great Britain in 2004 by
MAINSTREAM PUBLISHING COMPANY (EDINBURGH) LTD
7 Albany Street
Edinburgh EH1 3UG

ISBN 1 84018 774 3

Lyrics to 'Wasted Life' by Stiff Little Fingers reproduced
by kind permission of Complete Music Ltd.

A catalogue record for this book is available from the British Library

Typeset in Avant Garde and Garamond
Printed and bound in Great Britain by
Antony Rowe Ltd, Chippenham, Wiltshire

This book is dedicated to the memory of my
co-author, cousin, friend and mentor Jack Holland,
who died in New York earlier this year.

Acknowledgements

I am indebted to the following, who were either inspirational in their ideas, practical in their help or, in the case of loved ones, patient and tolerant in putting up with the frustrations, moods and egotism of the writer.

Alternative Ulster magazine's staff and friends, Ivana Bacik, Dr Sean Barrett, Professor Paul Bew, Paul Burgess, Kelvin Boyes, Robin Bury, Anto Clarke, Tony Crowe, Jim Cusack, Paul Donnelly, Stephen Downey, Jeff Dudgeon, Dr Bryan Fanning, Brian Finnegan, Maggie Fitzgerald, the residents of the Fountain Estate, several officers in the Garda Siochana who for obvious reasons prefer to remain anonymous, Tommy Gorman, Graham Gudgin, Jimmy Guerin, Kim Haugton, Terry Hooley, Ian S. Kennedy, Conor Cruise O'Brien, Malachi O'Doherty, Bobby McConnell, Paul McCambridge, Ken McCue, Paul MacDonnell, Seamus McDonagh, Chris McGimpsey, Anthony McIntrye, John McManus, Liz McManus, Yvonne Murphy and her magnificent staff at Belfast's Linenhall Library Political Collection, John O'Farrell, David Norris, the Lupu family and their many friends and supporters in Dublin's Romanian community, Glenn Patterson, Victor Patterson, the many officers of the Police Service of Northern Ireland who cooperated in this and previous books, Richard Poots, Ken

Reid, the residents of Shandon Park, Newry, Dr Peter Shirlow, the Northern staff of the *Sunday World* newspaper, Mick Wallace and Li Xuan.

To all those I might have overlooked I offer my profound and sincere apologies.

Finally, to my family a deep hug for all those nights and days when I wasn't there.

Contents

Preface

This is more than just a memoir; it is an exercise in time travel.

The time machine I use here has only two gears: one to reverse into the past of my childhood and youth, the other to go forward to the present. Such a journey takes the reader through the startling changes (for better and worse) that this island has witnessed over the last 35 years. This breeze through space and time will hopefully map out the shifting landscape of Ireland between two centuries. If anything, the flashbacks and the comparisons between then and now will show that the pace and depth of change in Ireland has been nothing short of revolutionary.

The 'revolution', however, particularly in the Republic, has not been of the type envisaged by the student radicals of the late 1960s, the dreamers of the 1970s or the angry young men and women, of whom I was one, of the 1980s. To search for an overarching theme for this book, I would suggest it lies in the struggle to break off what James Joyce described as the 'nets' of family, religion and nation. Whether it is the battles over freedom against the Catholic Church's authority or the personal conflicts of the author himself trying to break away from the tribe, the major theme remains the same: the triumph of the individual over the collective.

For three and a half decades, the world's media trained its attention on the terrorist 'war' raging in Ireland's north-east six counties. Behind

11

a screen of gunsmoke and fire, beyond the macho men in the woollen masks toting their rifles and laying their bombs, stands another narrative, a hidden Ireland. That 'other nation' of ordinary individuals struggling to cope with the pressures of life at the end of one century and the start of another is the story of this book.

Despite the constant use of the first person, I have endeavoured to avoid the self-indulgence and self-obsession associated with other 'laddish' memoirs; hence the move in most chapters from the personal anecdote to larger intricately connected themes. Each chapter focuses on a thematic question, on the basic building blocks of our existence: man's tendency to sub-divide into factions; the tensions between sexuality and morality; the search for a utopian future; and the individual's evolutionary drive for wealth and riches.

It is also the story of the writer himself and how these changes affected him and those around him. I do not, as Lenin is reported to have said about Trotsky, associate history with myself. Nor are there any prescriptions or solutions offered to the remaining problems that blight Irish life, such as sectarianism in the North or the existence of a gangland sub-culture in the South. I would not be arrogant enough to try to, let alone assert that I do, speak for a certain age group who grew up, endured and survived Ulster's Troubles. The views expressed here are mine alone, which I fully stand by.

I am equally blessed and cursed with a strong recall for events that have marked my life over the last 35 years. I have mined from memory many of the incidents from the 1970s and '80s recounted throughout this book. Equally useful, too, has been the advice, recollections and stories from others who also lived through these momentous times. All of that which is dredged up from my personal story actually happened, although it is seen at times through the dark and often kaleidoscopic filter of times past.

So fasten your safety belt, sit back and relax as you are taken on a trip across space and time in a tour of an island at the western edge of Europe that has undergone a profound and revolutionary transformation, all seen through the eyes of a man on the edge of middle age looking back with shock and awe over how all this came about.

Henry McDonald
Belfast
12 June 2004

Prologue

Every little boy who plays cowboys and Indians wonders if one day he will ever get his hands on a real gun. My boyhood dream of holding a 'grown-up' weapon came true even before my First Holy Communion and I pointed it into my mother's back.

It was a .38 snub nose revolver which belonged to the legendary Official IRA figure Joe McCann, who was staying in our house in the Markets area of Belfast on and off between the end of 1971 and early 1972.

At that time, McCann was an on-the-run, a roaming gunman for the still-at-war Officials and one of the British Army's most wanted republicans in Northern Ireland. Handsome, physically courageous and immaculately dressed, often dyeing his hair from black to blond over our kitchen sink in 1 Eliza Street, McCann, even before his death at the hands of undercover soldiers, had become an overnight hero for the Northern Catholic youth. In the early hours of 9 August 1971, when over a thousand men were arrested and interned without trial, he and his comrades had engaged the British Army in a gun battle in our street. McCann's image, in silhouette, kneeling and holding an M1 Carbine rifle underneath a Starry Plough flag, in front of a fire blazing from an Inglis Bakery lorry that his unit had hijacked and then used as a makeshift barrier to prevent British troops from entering Eliza Street, became famous across the planet. It captured the spirit of resistance and defiance that men such as McCann were prepared to show in the face of the summary British injustice of Internment. The iconic photograph was later used in the 1980s by U2 on the front of one of their early albums and is still regarded today as one of the most widely recognised images from the early Troubles.

'Big Joe' used our home as a safe house where he could change into his many disguises, rest on our sofa in between 'jobs' and get fed while all the time eluding the British Army and the Royal Ulster Constabulary. One early afternoon, he rapped on our door along with another man called Sean and asked my mother for shelter. I was sent outside to sit on the windowsill and watch out for passing army and police patrols whilst McCann and his comrade sat down to a lunchtime meal, a cholesterol-laced Ulster Fry. Occasionally, I could come back inside and report to McCann on what I had seen, especially if there were any suspicious-looking characters or outsiders milling around the Markets. I suspect now that Big Joe had actually sent me on the mission simply to ensure that he and Sean got to devour their fry-up in peace.

During one of my sit-reps to Big Joe, I noticed that our portable sky-blue-coloured record player, which lay on the bottom shelf of a television table, had been flicked open. I went over and lifted it up, and inside on the turntable discovered there were two guns, Big Joe's revolver and a .45 automatic pistol belonging to Sean. The two men saw me stare in fascination at these real-life weapons and McCann leaned over and whispered something into Sean's ear. McCann then went across the room to the record player, fished out the pistol, released the catch for the chamber and took out all six bullets from the gun. Suddenly, he ordered me to stand to attention, told me to pull a grey school jersey I was wearing up over my face and handed me the .38. I was to go in and hold up my mother, who was washing the dishes in the tiny kitchen of our home contiguous to the yard belonging to Mooney's Bar in nearby Cromac Street.

The moment she felt the sensation of cold steel on her back, my mother froze, dropped a cup into the sink and then turned around. She screamed as much out of anger as terror at McCann and Sean over the sight of her only son with a jumper pulled over his face pointing a .38

revolver at her. Snatching the pistol from my hand, she ran into the living room and started shouting at the two men who were buckled over, choking with laughter.

My parents had a single condition for McCann and his comrades whenever they sought refuge in between 'operations' or while on the run: no guns in the house. Not only had they broken the house rules but the two desperadoes had also seemingly armed her child. She finally calmed down only when they stopped howling and McCann showed her the six bullets in the palm of his hand. Their young 'recruit' was then ordered not to speak about this ever again and sent outside once more to scan the streets for more dodgy-looking characters.

Little boys, of course, find it desperately hard to keep secrets. So, a couple of hours after Big Joe and Sean left our house, I rapped on the door of Billy McCormick, who lived further down Eliza Street. When we sat down to play toy soldiers in his living room, I boasted that I had just held a real handgun given to me by the legendary Joe McCann. Billy said he didn't believe me and accused me of making it all up. I didn't bother trying to convince him it was true and we returned to our mock war with the Airfix infantry.

Other boys living in Eliza Street back then, even younger than I, also got to play with real weapons. One afternoon in 1972, just before Joe McCann was shot dead, twin brothers living right beside Billy's house ran into Eliza Street brandishing the best toy machine guns we had ever seen. They were in fact genuine Thompson sub-machine guns that were hidden in the house and under the control of the boys' father, a leading Official IRA gunman in the Markets. The twins were darting about street corners, chasing each other as well as us with the guns, mimicking the rat-a-tat-tat sound of a machine gun firing. Our game with the Thompsons didn't last long, though, because someone must have tipped off the local IRA. A number of men came around the corner from McKenna's Bar, a favourite haunt of the Officials, to take the machine guns away. We were, after all, dicing with death. In the shadows, the twins, Billy and myself could have been mistaken for gunmen by British troops who would have fired on us. Without the Brits, we still could have been shot and killed because my mother later told me that the two Thompsons were fully loaded when the brothers found them hidden in their house and decided to play war games outside.

These episodes were part of our lives during what was, in reality, wartime. The Markets in the early '70s, like many other areas around Belfast, resembled a war zone. There were frequent gun-battles, drive-by shootings, bombs exploding outside bars and men shot down by gunmen in the street. At night, the streets were patrolled by British soldiers who had their faces blackened with boot polish. They moved nervously through the Markets, pointing their rifles at people, pubs and houses, and sometimes the area would be illuminated with spotlights trained from the British military base, which had once been a Protestant church, near Cromac Square.

When the Brits weren't around, the two factions of the IRA took to the streets, sometimes to fire on British Army positions or loyalist gunmen up in Donegall Pass, or, more often than not, to fight with each other. The rival paramilitaries and their political adjuncts competed for space around all the walls of the Markets. The Officials plastered the area with the famous silhouette of Joe McCann on Internment morning along with the slogan 'Soldier of the People'; the Provos printed up their own propaganda posters declaring that they were the 'People's Army'. As well as OIRA (Official IRA), PIRA (Provisional IRA) and, later, INLA (Irish National Liberation Army), there were bewildering acronyms like UTP (Up the Provos), UTS (Up the Sticks – slang for the Officials) and again later UTE (Up the Erps – street-speak for the INLA). From the bar to the playground, there were discussions, arguments and fights over which republican faction was right. These debates and rows naturally intensified after the Officials declared a ceasefire in May 1972.

My memories of my own childhood are peppered with incidents involving snipers, feuds, car bombs and raids by the British Army on our home. 'Get off the streets' was a constant battle-order barked out to local children when violence was about to break out. In 1972, there was a gunfight involving both Officials and Provisionals against the loyalist UVF, which had occupied the largest giant gas tank towering over the Markets. I can still see the OIRA gunmen poking their rifles around the corner of McKenna's and taking pot shots at the UVF snipers holed up in the gasworks. When the shooting war erupted, Owen Mullan and I had just came out of his house after staging a paramilitary funeral. Owen's two goldfish had died and we buried them in his backyard, putting their corpses inside a matchbox covered with strips of green, white and orange material. Our final salute to the fish was to fire our cap guns over their makeshift little coffin. The second we went out to Stanfield Street, the sound of gunfire echoed all around us. People fled in all directions as the loyalist snipers rained their bullets down on the Markets.

Potential death and destruction came even closer three years later when the same loyalist terror group left a car bomb outside our door. The car was a light-blue Cortina and it was abandoned shortly after teatime on a Friday night. *It's a Knockout* had just ended on television and *The Good Old Days* was about to start when the bomb went off. The force of the explosion threw my father and me across the living room. We hit the floor and were showered in glass, the sound of the blast reverberating in our ears. Miraculously, neither of us was injured even though the bomb exploded just a yard or two from our front window. The incompetence of the UVF bombmaker who placed the device in the car probably saved our lives. (Twenty years later when I was sitting down in a Shankill Road pub with the UVF high command to discuss a book on the organisation, I mentioned the car bomb that had been left directly outside my old home. 'If your man had have been a better engineer, I wouldn't be here today,' I joked, attempting to break the ice and eliciting a laugh from the men sitting across from me.)

Our house also became a target for the Provisionals during several feuds involving the two IRA factions between 1971 and 1977. On one occasion, a Provo gunman accompanied by several women broke into our home and held us hostage. They had been looking for a young OIRA activist whom they had threatened to kidnap during one of the feuds. We were rescued by another Official (now a member of the Social Democratic and Labour Party), who calmly walked into our house after the Provo invasion and sat with us until the PIRA gang's nerve broke and they left.

We lived right beside Mooney's Pub, which stretched over two bars between Cromac and Eliza Street. In the early Troubles, Mooney's was also targeted by the loyalists. One balmy summer evening, my sister Cathy and I were playing outside Mooney's side door at the top of Eliza Street when a white Cortina drove by. I noticed it made several journeys up and down Cromac Street over a couple of minutes. The reason it attracted my attention was because there were two large orange-coloured cushions in the back window. It must have been the third time the car drove country-bound up Cromac Street when there was a rattle of gunfire. Cathy and I dived for cover into the doorway of Mooney's Lounge, while adults outside on their way to the pub hit the ground. No one was killed in the shooting but a couple of men were wounded in the leg. We had had another brush with death, yet half an hour later we were back outside, Cathy swinging around the lamp-post with a piece of rope, me kicking a football up against the entrance to Mooney's backyard imagining I was Bob Latchford scoring a hat-trick for Everton at Anfield.

As 1 Eliza Street had been used as an election headquarters for the Officials in 1973, as well as being a safe haven for the likes of Joe McCann, we also drew the attention of the army and police. The occasional searches and raids on the house often produced moments of high farce. Despite my parents' rule that no guns be brought into their home, the British Army got it into their heads that we were storing weapons. So in 1977, they hit the house along with several uniformed RUC officers. When they called, we were throwing a birthday party for my paternal granny, Mary, who was enjoying a vodka and tonic in our living room. Although she informed the soldiers and policemen that it was her birthday, they insisted that she, like the rest of us, would remain under house arrest.

The Brits who arrived at our house had a policy of taking a Military Policeman with them who would body-search each of the troops involved in the raid. They did this to show they were not about to plant weapons around the house. The soldiers also piled up their SLR rifles in our hallway under the picture of the Pope, so those under house arrest could see them. On the night of the birthday-party raid, Granny Mary had been too busy re-filling her glass with a generous measure of vodka to notice the troops doing this. So, when she eventually spotted the neat triangle of SLRs, she let out a yell. Then she started berating my father, asking him why he hadn't listened to her and stayed away from politics, before turning on my mother and blaming her for bringing 'them guns' into the house. For a second there was silence, and furtive glances were exchanged between soldiers and policemen. Had this old lady let out an important secret? Did she know something about guns in the house? A moment later, when they realised which weapons she was talking about, the soldiers and police burst out laughing while the senior

Military Policeman assured Mary that they were their guns and no one else's.

These few incidents singled out above were some of the many bizarre moments that punctuated an otherwise normal and, dare I say, idyllic childhood. Amid the shootings and bombings, the riots and demonstrations, and the mass paramilitary funerals, I was a happy kid. For there was always time for soccer tournaments, Subbuteo contests in friends' parlours and the weekly trips to the shop at the bottom end of Eliza Street for *Shoot* football magazine and, later, Marvel's *Amazing Adventures of Spiderman* and *The Incredible Hulk*.

But never will I get sentimental or misty eyed about those formative years spent in the maelstrom of incipient civil war. Far too many people, some of whom were close friends of our family, lost their lives needlessly in wanton and horrible acts of violence. The 'armed struggle' that wreaked so much havoc in our area and beyond was a criminal adventure that would never result in the goal of the lost Republic. Those blood-soaked times were truly, to borrow a line from the Markets-born poet Padraig Fiacc, 'nights in the bad place'.

Yet even in those dark nights there was constant light. Floodlit football regardless of the season was free for boys in the Markets. After dusk, the lights were turned on at the back of the Inglis Bakery mill, bathing the upper end of McAuley Street in surreal orange light. There was enough illumination to play in the area from where, in the early hours of the morning, huge lorries would come roaring out laden with bread and all the other baked products for little bakeries and mini-markets across Northern Ireland. When the lorries were still in their loading bays, we would turn up to play five- or seven-aside soccer late into the night, using the gates as goals.

There were 26 pubs, several light industries and a couple of stables housing horses trained for trotting races; it was an area resembling a busy market town rather than an urban slum. Though there was, of course, dire poverty and appalling social conditions. When Mooney's Bar closed down next door, our house became riddled with so much damp that the city council condemned it as unfit for human habitation. We did not get our first inside toilet until our new home was ready in 1981, the same year our family was able to use a modern bathroom. The flight of factories and businesses after 1969 led to mass unemployment and a hollowing-out of the area's commercial heart,

Cromac Street. However, this did not detract from the sense of social cohesion and solidarity that pervaded the area through the worst days of the Troubles.

This world has gone forever. Life in the place where I grew up has become atomised, with the present generation retreating into their own privatised little worlds. Up to 60 per cent of the housing stock today is owner-occupied, with houses being put on the market for more than £100,000. Local people are hoping to sell up and move further out towards the rural edge of prosperous south Belfast. Those left behind escape from the drabness of their world through alcohol, drugs and the near-religious cult of Glasgow Celtic. Where once political allegiances preoccupied the youth of the Markets, Celtic is the twenty-first-century badge of identity.

Industries have disappeared to be replaced by the service sector, with buildings belonging to telecommunications giants like British Telecom and international hotel chains such as the Hilton and Marriott clustered around the area. Educational attainment remains extremely low even compared to other traditional working-class communities. A large underclass, including many young men of working age, lives permanently off state benefits and sees no need, let alone duty, to find a job.

In the Markets of the '70s and '80s, the area was electrified with political disagreement, debate and argument that could end up being settled at the barrel of a gun. It is one of the greatest paradoxes of the peace process that while the era of feuding and factional fighting on the republican side is mercifully over, in its place there is a social vacuum. You either have the supporters of Sinn Féin and the IRA, who follow their leadership blindly and without question through ideological U-turn after ideological U-turn, or, like the majority living in places like the Markets, the others who are disinterested and indifferent about politics. It was surely a fitting symbol of these times that a new slogan was daubed on walls around the Markets at the end of 2002. 'Free Wee Mo' kept appearing on the old gasworks wall and outside the local scrapyard. The demand for freedom did not concern a local republican jailed unjustly by an oppressive British state but instead a fictional character in the soap opera *EastEnders,* who had just been imprisoned for killing her abusive husband. Where once the walls were covered in the maxims of revolution and defiance, in the twenty-first century, the graffiti concerns the fortunes of a made-up heroine on a trashy television programme.

Whenever I look back on life in the Markets during wartime, I am constantly reminded of that haunting remark made by Marlon Brando near the end of *Apocalypse Now*. Brando, as Colonel Kurtz, faces his soon-to-be assassin Willard (played by Martin Sheen). The half-crazed commander of the renegade army on the Cambodian–Vietnamese border recalls his childhood travels along the Ohio River and his past life in the United States. 'It all feels,' Brando tells Sheen almost in a whisper, 'like a thousand centuries ago.' Returning to the Markets of the twenty-first century, my own memories and the many ghosts that swirl around there create that same sensation evoked by Colonel Kurtz, of an ancient world that is fading fast into the mists of time, disappearing like smoke evaporating into thin air.

CHAPTER ONE

Red Army Blues

In the autumn of 1978, I joined the 'Red Army', much to the disgust of my socialist father and the alarm of a loving, if over-anxious, mother.

I grew up surrounded on one side by portraits of the Sacred Heart of Jesus and the busts of Marx and Lenin on the other. The antique bookcase given to my dad by a publican as a present for years of custom at his bar contained the works of the communist founders as well as neatly stacked brown leather-bound volumes containing the rantings of the North Korean dictator Kim Il Sung. Close by, stuffed behind clocks and candlesticks above the fireplace, were old copies of the *St Martin de Porres* magazine, a pocket-sized Catholic publication dedicated to the black saint of the Brazilian poor, which, among other things, contained children's pages, including a pen-pal club for young believers that helped put me in touch with other Catholic kids from as far away as Cork and Kerry. In our dark cavernous hallway, where each night my parents would lay down a six-foot-long and four-inch-wide piece of wood, a first line of defence against potential assassins breaking down our front door, hung a portrait of Pope John XXIII.

Every Friday teatime, the communists would be let into this sanctum to sell their *Unity* paper with its red star and hammer-and-sickle masthead while they chatted comradely to my parents underneath the smiling visage of the Vicar of Christ. Upstairs on the second floor, in one of our two attics, a portrait of Our Blessed Lady dominated the room, one of her fingers protruding from beneath a royal-blue chador-like garment, pointing accusingly at my sister and me every time we dared venture to the top of the house to play. Yet one floor below, strewn on the carpet on either side of my parents' bed and on top of their cabinets and dressing tables, were the classics of Marxist-Leninism: Lenin's *What Is To Be Done?*, Marx's *Das Kapital* and the *Communist Manifesto*, as well as biographies of Trotsky by Isaac Deutscher and an edition of the prophet of permanent revolution's writings with a foreword by Lionel Kochan.

Oddly, this incongruous domestic dichotomy never produced an argument or a fight. Historical materialism and the mysteries of the faith were equally part of the mental furniture at 1 Eliza Street. Only once did the presence of proletarian internationalism in the parlour cause discord at home. It happened one midweek evening in the late '70s when Father McCrea, one of the parish priests, called to the house. Fr McCrea was known as the 'whispering priest' because of his tendency to say Mass and administer Holy Communion in a whisper that betrayed a painful shyness in front of his flock at St Malachy's Chapel. A pious and devout cleric, there were rumours (never substantiated) that he had been tortured while preaching the gospel in Red China. He arrived shortly after teatime and, after being welcomed into the front living room, struck up a conversation with my father. My only memory of the encounter is that the priest picked up a book my father was reading and started to lecture him about the evils of communism. The tirade only lasted for a few minutes and then Fr McCrea was on his way, bidding us good night. He never came back. I can only guess that my father strategically placed the socialist tome there to ward off the bothersome priest. If that was his intention, it certainly worked.

The original Red Army – *the* Red Army – we worshipped at 1 Eliza Street was the force that had, in Churchill's words, 'torn the guts' out of the Nazi war machine, liberated Russia and Europe from Hitler and sacrificed themselves by the millions to destroy the fascists. Every time during my childhood when there was a Second World War film on television, usually starring Audie Murphy or John Wayne single-handedly massacring the entire Japanese Army, my father and mother would remind me that it was in fact the Red Army who had actually won the war. Looking back, it was hardly surprising that the first box of Airfix toy soldiers I bought from the Model Shop in central Belfast were grey plastic Russian infantry troops who would be put to heroic use as I recreated Stalingrad and Leningrad on our staircase and behind the back of our black leather sofa in the front room. One of the cherished presents from my childhood, which I still hold onto today, was an authentic Red Army belt given to me by a half-pissed Communist Party member from east Belfast during one of those Friday-night paper sales.

But the 'Red Army' I signed up to in the last few months of 1978 was one my father would never be happy about. I was introduced to this force at the very end of my first year at St Malachy's College, one of Northern Ireland's principal Catholic grammar schools. Most of my friends came from the school's vicinity, the nationalist working-class redoubts of north Belfast. One morning close to exam time, I was having my breakfast, preparing for school, when the eight o'clock news came on the radio. There had been a riot the previous evening at Solitude, the home of Cliftonville FC. The violence involved local fans and supporters of Glentoran, the east Belfast side. There had been clashes at the end of the game and a pitch invasion with rival supporters fighting it out on the turf. After the pitch was cleared, there was further trouble outside the ground between fans and the RUC. It all sounded exotic and exhilarating, almost like the soccer violence endemic at English grounds and made infamous in the 1977 *Panorama* documentary that followed the hooligans of Millwall and the fortunes of larger-than-life thugs like Harry the Dog. When I went to school, the classroom was abuzz with talk about the riot at Solitude. Some of my best friends had actually been there, including Michael Crawford, the boy who would first introduce me to the Red Army. Michael and others also clarified that the mayhem had a sectarian edge: that the Cliftonville fans were Catholics while the Glenmen were Prods. But, because it was the end of the season, I had missed the chance to see Solitude for myself.

Over a summer dominated by the World Cup in Argentina, illuminated by the silky skills but cynical gamesmanship of Kempes, Luque, Passarella *et al.* and the injustice inflicted on the elegant but luckless Dutch team in the final, Solitude took on the allure of the Forbidden City. I promised myself that, come August, I would take up Michael's offer and attend the opening game of the new season.

When I told my parents I wanted money for the match, they exploded in rage. My father lectured me about 'tribalism' and 'sectarianism', such things that divided the working class and diverted the people from the class struggle. 'People will always be led by bells and bombs,' he often said to me before heading out for the bookies, another temporal opiate of our class. Sectarianism, like religion, was the curse of the masses, and sectarianism in soccer (the people's game, after all) was the worst of all. It was only then that I first understood his and my uncle Sean's constant invective about the 'Provos' being 'Celtic supporters with Armalites', Catholic avengers rather than 'real' republicans.

There were other less ideological objections to my desire to join the new Red Army. Solitude is situated at the edge of the Waterworks, a manmade lake under the shadow of the Cavehill Mountain at the northern geographical end of the city. The space between the ramshackle stadium and the north shore of the waterway is a sectarian divide separating the mainly Catholic Lower Cliftonville Road and the Protestant Westland, a post-war housing estate. It was not until I attended my first game that I realised I had been there before, three years earlier on a two-day sleepover at Liam Murray's house, another friend who turned out to be one of the Cliftonville FC's most loyal and lifelong dedicated fans. Instantly, I recognised the Waterworks and the Westland, recalling a balmy evening in the summer of 1975 when Liam and I watched from his bedroom as rival Protestant and Catholic gangs, emboldened by flagons of Woodpecker cider (evident from the many empty bottles around the lake the next morning), exchanged missiles and insults across the watery divide. Even back then, the Cliftonville area had acquired the reputation for being a dangerous place to be, especially at night. The Cliftonville Road, the main route to Solitude, had been a hunting ground for loyalist killers, notably the Shankill Butchers – the UVF-aligned gang who abducted any Catholic male they could bundle into a car, beat senseless, transport to a loyalist pub, club or 'safe house' and torture until the point where a bullet in the back of the head was a relief from the hours of sadistic torment.

Cliftonville Road, just like the Short Strand – the only Catholic enclave in east Belfast and a ten-minute walk from the Markets – was, to use my parents' phrase from the time, 'a death trap' to be avoided at all costs. The second I mentioned that I wanted to follow Cliftonville, I was reminded of the Shankill Butchers, the ultimate bogeymen for young post-pubescent Catholics living in Belfast during the 1970s. Under no circumstances would I be allowed to attend games at Solitude, not just because of the behaviour of some of the fans but also due to the obvious danger of falling victim to the loyalist killer gangs roaming that part of the city seeking out fresh Fenian prey. The stadium and the ground would be out of bounds, they warned me. I would never be a 'soldier' in the Red Army . . . at least that's what they thought.

But when you are 14-going-on-18 you are genetically obliged, as the cult British actor Keith Allen once informed Boyzone's front man Ronan Keating on a Channel 4 music programme, 'to say fuck off to your parents'. My first big 'fuck off' was to defy their ban on me travelling to Solitude. So, every alternating Saturday from late 1978 to 1980, I sneaked out of 1 Eliza Street with the intention of getting to the home game. Eventually, this deception would extend to away matches as well.

The subterfuge began with me telling my parents I was off to see my cousins, Fred and Pat Bell, who usually visited my paternal grandmother Mary on Saturday lunchtimes. Granny Mary owned a confectionery/newspaper shop with her second husband Paddy McSherry at the top of Cromac Street, close to where the Markets ends and the loyalist Donegall Pass begins.

Fred and Pat were in on the game. After I had gone through the shop, we all went upstairs and sought out our red-and-white scarves, which Fred had secreted in a back room of my granny's living quarters. The three of us lifted up our shirts and T-shirts, and tied the scarves around our midriffs, for security reasons that will soon be explained. Then we came downstairs and informed Mary we were heading into town to buy records or meet friends. And so the 'rat run' began.

Our route march from the shop to Solitude was marked with potential danger. At any time we could run into gangs of Linfield fans (the only one of the big teams whose supporters thronged the city centre on match days) and risk being beaten up, stabbed or worse. Well outnumbered and still relatively young, we happy few devised a strategy to avoid such confrontations. Our journey began along Ormeau Avenue, down Alfred or Adelaide Street then left up Bedford Street behind the back of Belfast City Hall. That way, suspicious Linfield men, especially those disgorging from Shankill Road buses facing the City Hall, could not be sure whether or not we had just come from the Markets. There were times when we would amble past knots of Linfield supporters, our hearts beating and our skin soaked with sweat around the area covered by our Cliftonville scarves. We were cut off from the rest of the Red Army like an isolated unit of recon scouts making its way through enemy territory, stealthily avoiding observation or contact with a numerically larger foe.

The rat run got easier once we crossed Wellington Place in the heart of Belfast's commercial district and made our way into Queen Street. We were now tantalisingly close to a safe haven, Castle Street, a thoroughfare clogged up with Falls Road black taxis, seedy pubs, cheap knockdown price mini-markets and amusement arcades – the key link from the city centre to republican west Belfast.

The entrance to Castle Street was blockaded by a series of security gates built by British Army engineers to act as stop-and-search centres in order to prevent Provisional IRA operatives from smuggling in firebombs aimed at destroying the department stores of central Belfast. Most young Catholics resented passing through these barriers, where they could be subjected to full body searches and have their personal details checked by soldiers and/or police officers. P-checking, as it was known, could be intrusive and at times downright humiliating. But billeted on the Queen Street/Castle Street barrier there was a female Civilian Searcher aged somewhere between her late 30s and early 40s, who made the hazardous journey all the more worthwhile. She had long blonde hair pinned up under her black peaked cap with the crown ensign on the front, a pointed nose like Sophia Loren and sharp cheekbones. Although she was not conventionally beautiful, this searcher in the peaked cap and leather knee boots became the object of my earliest teenage sexual fantasies. Every other Saturday, I would move from the male to the female line of the about-to-be-frisked, offering my puny body to her for inspection. Her stern reaction was always the same: 'Get to the other side.'

Temporary respite for the next leg of the rat run was provided at the Yankee Doodle, a cavernous amusement arcade illuminated by the flashing of gaming machines, Space Invaders, Asteroids and a US diner-style jukebox. On the wall was a collection of '70s Americana: the Fonze, Elvis in Las Vegas and Starsky and Hutch. Guarding the door to the Yankee Doodle was an overweight bouncer called Tommy, who had jet-black, Teddy boy-style slicked-back hair and a Mexican bandito moustache. The place reeked of fried onions and a rancid matter that passed for meat shoved inside hamburger baps on sale beside the money-changing booth. The air was always thick with cigarette smoke and filled with the bleeps and whirring of the slots and the games competing with the constant click-click of pool balls knocking together over scoured and scraped green baizes. But despite the dilapidated atmosphere, the Yankee Doodle was a welcome resting place for those of us who had dodged the Linfield hordes and were now about to venture across another one of Belfast's most precarious thoroughfares at the height of the Troubles.

The Red Army's west Belfast brigade, along with its isolated units from the outposts of the Markets, Lower Ormeau, the Short Strand and other Catholic enclaves, gathered up at the top of Castle Street between lunchtime and two o'clock in preparation for the route march across Millfield. Millfield was another favourite hunting ground for sectarian assassins, particularly the Shankill Butchers. Given that it links the Falls Road to the nationalist Unity Flats and the New Lodge, and that it stretches past the bottom of the Shankill, anyone ambling, drunk or sober, late at night across Millfield risked being picked up and murdered at the hands of the Butchers. It was also the only real route from Castle Street to the main roads of north Belfast leading towards Solitude.

Generally, there was little trouble as the Red Army crossed Millfield while being escorted by RUC Land-Rovers and lines of riot police in order to prevent clashes with loyalists from the Shankill. But I can recall several hair-raising occasions when we crossed after the escort had gone, in smaller numbers than the 'crowd', and were charged by groups of Linfield fans from either the Shankill itself or Brown's Square, a small Protestant area cut off from the Greater Shankill. Some of those leading the chase, such as Lenaghan and 'Fat Doc', became legendary hate figures. The latter, who came from the Lower Shankill estate and was a boyhood pal of the young men who later formed the nucleus of Johnny Adair's notorious 'C Company', had a reputation even among

Linfield supporters for his vehement detestation of Catholics, especially Reds fans. I can remember Fat Doc launching one-man charges on lines of Cliftonville supporters crossing Millfield, hurling beer bottles and bricks in our direction. This often ended with him being surrounded and kicked senseless by a group of Reds fans before the RUC 'cavalry' intervened. (Fat Doc later became a general dogsbody for the Ulster Defence Association (UDA) in the Lower Shankill and later died from excessive drinking.)

Having successfully made it past the Shankill, the troublemakers in the Red Army (and they were more numerous than some would now care to admit) turned their attentions towards other easier targets. On the New Lodge and Antrim Roads, these were British Army and RUC mobile patrols on security duty for match day. Attacks on the security forces often turned into full-scale riots, with plastic baton rounds being fired, sometimes indiscriminately, into the mass of the Cliftonville support making its way towards the Cliftonville Road. Although the riots were infrequent, they seemed to intensify from about 1980 onwards, when the first hunger strike erupted at the Maze prison. It was while walking across Millfield one Saturday en route to Solitude, rather than at a political demonstration or on television, that I heard the words: 'Smash H-Block'.

There were also other targets for the mob that had latched onto the club in the halcyon days of the Red Army. While I readily admit I took part in stone throwing against soldiers, cops and opposing team buses, I am glad to say I played no part in the attacks unleashed on a house on the Antrim Road. Gerry Fitt, the then Social Democratic and Labour Party (SDLP) MP for west Belfast, had at one time been a nationalist folk-hero in Belfast and beyond. A docker by trade, Fitt had come from the same Republican Labour background as my mother and played a prominent part in the Northern Ireland civil rights movement.

Having helped topple the unionist junta at Stormont, Fitt went on to become a minister in the doomed power-sharing government with Brian Faulkner of 1973–74. Fitt had always been more labour than republican and had opposed the Provisional IRA's terrorist campaign. He became the Provos' enemy number one after refusing to support the PIRA and INLA prisoners' campaign for the restoration of political status at the Maze prison. Thus began, from around 1979, a vicious personal propaganda assault on Fitt and his family. Along the Falls

Road, the Sinn Féin graffiti artists painted slogans such as 'Fitt is a Brit', their ire translating into violence directed at Fitt and his family outside their home on Belfast's Antrim Road. Following a bonfire to commemorate the eighth anniversary of Internment without trial which began back in August 1971, a gang of IRA supporters managed to break into Gerry Fitt's house and threaten him and his chronically ill wife. The MP only managed to eject the drunken protestors angry over his stance on the H-Blocks by pointing his personal firearm at them. A month later, after a Cliftonville–Glentoran clash at Solitude, a group of returning Reds fans turned their attentions on the Fitt home. Although the bulk of the 2,000-strong support walked past the house without incident, a vocal and menacing minority started hurling stones, bricks and bottles at the door. Holed up inside was a terrified Anne Fitt and her 17-year-old daughter Geraldine – Gerry Fitt was in the Republic that day on party business. I can still recall my face burning with shame as I stood there and watched the mob bombarding the Fitt home with missiles, chanting, 'Fitt is a Brit, Fitt is a Brit' at the top of their lungs. In that instant, I thought about my mother back at home and how she had marched with Fitt and other leading lights in the civil rights movement during the late 1960s.

When I returned that Saturday evening, pretending as usual that I had been in town with my cousins, she was watching the news report about the mini-riot outside the Fitt household. 'Fascist thugs,' were the only words she uttered, her fury not just directed at the mob that had rampaged outside Gerry Fitt's house but also towards the son who had once expressed his desire to join this 'herd'. The supreme irony of Cliftonville fans attacking the Fitt home was that just six months earlier the MP had actually defended the Reds supporters after a local derby with Linfield at Windsor Park. On 30 April 1979, Fitt had repudiated claims in the press that Cliftonville hooligans were responsible for damage caused to houses in the Roden Street area of south Belfast. 'I would like to make it quite clear that the residents in the area, the RUC and the military deny vehemently that it was Cliftonville supporters who were responsible for the wrecking . . . any attempt to lay the blame on Cliftonville can be repudiated,' Fitt told the *Belfast Telegraph*.

The disgraceful scenes outside the Fitt home failed, however, to blunt my desire to follow the Red Army across Northern Ireland. For the true test of the 'soldier' was to venture into the enemy's lair, to where the Fenians were never supposed to go. Cliftonville fans were about to go on a sectarian safari, touring parts of the Province young working-class Belfast Catholics had never dared visit since the Troubles erupted ten years earlier. In the 1978–79 season, Cliftonville's centenary year, we would travel to places normally out of bounds for the 'Fenian scum'. Those journeys would produce some of the most memorable but terrifying incidents over the winter and spring of that season.

In early 1979, we travelled by bus to Newtownards for Cliftonville away at Castlereagh Park. We had just missed the official supporters' coach and had to make do with the lunchtime service from Oxford Street station in central Belfast. Paddy O'Byrne, a St Malachy's friend from Ardoyne, and I boarded the vehicle. Before we got on, we had agreed in the station café that we would conceal our scarves in our coats. The journey would take us across the River Lagan, along the Albertbridge Road and then onto the Newtownards Road – the loyalist heartlands of east Belfast. There were about a dozen of us on the bus and there seemed to be a consensus about the scarves. They would remain out of sight until we got to Newtownards. One of the last to board the vehicle was Sean 'Webber' Devlin, an old nemesis of mine from primary school days. Webber had a reputation for violence and volatility. He had been a bully at school and once tried to stab me with a pair of mathematical dividers. Suddenly, I was his best mate. For some inexplicable reason, he had latched onto me and my companions at the away games. When I saw him walking along the aisle of the Newtownards bus that lunchtime, my heart sank. O'Byrne and I ended up in the back of the bus with Webber, who kept singing into my ear to the tune of Chas 'n' Dave's obnoxious song 'Rabbit Rabbit' – 'Hen, Hen, Hen'.

After crossing the River Lagan, the bus passed up the Albertbridge Road, halting at traffic lights at the junction of the Newtownards Road. To our left was the Albert Bar, with a group of older loyalist men, some in their 40s and 50s, standing outside. The second we stopped, Webber pulled the red-and-white scarf out of his coat and started waving it at the loyalists. In an instant, beer glasses and bottles were bouncing off the windows. Then a larger group charged out of the pub armed with pool balls and snooker cues. The windows imploded. The storm outside blew up a blizzard of little shards of glass that slashed our faces and hands. We dived in unison onto the floor as the pool balls flew through the air, all except Webber. When I looked up towards the door of the bus, I could see a man using a snooker cue to try and wrench open the automatic doors, while all around us elderly women passengers screamed. The driver put the bus into first gear and pushed the vehicle through the red light, almost crashing into cars country-bound along the Newtownards Road. By the time we sat up again, bloodied and shaken, the old dears had turned their venom on us, branding us 'Fenian scum' for having put them and the driver at peril. Webber, meantime, was lying on his side at the back seat, laughing demonically while pointing to my face, obviously amused at the sight of the blood pouring from the tiny pin-prick wounds. He was the only one on board who seemed to be enjoying himself.

We took our revenge for the ambush on the good people of Newtownards. We smashed shop windows and damaged parked cars en route from the town's bus station to the ground. In one shop close to Castlereagh Park, Webber led the charge and the survivors of the bus attack stole anything they could get their hands on. The most popular booty of the day was boxes of Yorkie bars, which we took to the ground and distributed among the Cliftonville travelling support. Some Yorkies ('good, rich and thick, spunk on your dick,' we sang to the tune of the Yorkie ad on television as we doled them out) even ended up on the pitch. Everyone in red and white seemed to be munching on the chunky chocolate. Cliftonville, by the way, lost 2–0.

(Webber later 'graduated' from the Red Army hooligans to a real 'army' – the Irish National Liberation Army, to be precise. During the 1981 hunger strike, he was pictured in an INLA propaganda news-sheet, masked and holding a revolver at a republican show of strength in an entry off Friendly Street in the Markets. Fifteen years later, the Provos shot him dead just yards away from where he once posed with the gun for the INLA. The Provos accused him of drug dealing. His mother denied this, arguing that the IRA had nursed a grudge against her son for over a decade.)

Coleraine, winter 1979. An interminably long journey from Belfast's Central station to the north-west punctuated by a series of 'incidents' at every railway station our train halted in. Reds fans from the Markets slipped away from the RUC escort each time the train stopped. They jumped down onto the platform, ran to the nearest wall, wrote their names and then UTP (Up the Provos) on it and, for good measure, booted the nearest teenager or adult male in sight just as their train was pulling out. When we arrived at Coleraine, we were met by a reception committee of very badly dressed Culchies, the type of people who still dressed like and hero worshipped Status Quo. All long hair and thick locks, Wrangler jackets and bell-bottom jeans. And this was 1979! There was one particularly vocal braying barnyard character who stood out from the Coleraine crowd because of his flaming red hair. He kept abusing us as we were led into the town by a line of weary-looking RUC officers. 'Hey, lads,' he said to the cops, 'make sure ya take them gypsies to the chippy 'cos it's the last decent feed they'll ever get.'

To which we replied in unison: 'Go home and shag your sister . . . go home and shag your sister.' Had we touched a raw nerve? He lunged forward and tried to break through the phalanx of strapping, ruddy-faced country cops around us. How we laughed as he was trailed away into the back of a battleship-grey police Land-Rover, and then launched into another chorus of 'Go home and shag your sister.'

Ballymena, December 1979. Close to Christmas, the season after Cliftonville's Irish Cup triumph. We drew 1–1. But the highlight of the match was when the Reds fans were allowed into Ballymena United's brand new all-seater stand, in those days an unusual luxury for Irish League football. When the match kicked off, there was the usual sectarian abuse exchanged across a two-deep line of cops in the middle of the new stand. Then some seasonal cheer dampened down the bigoted passions. A trio of Cliftonville fans had blown up an inflatable Santa Claus and tied a red and white scarf around his neck. When the plastic St Nicholas was held aloft, the entire crowd, including eventually the Ballymena supporters, broke into song: 'One Daddy Christmas, there's only one Daddy Christmas, one Daddy Christmas, there's only one Daddy Christmas.'

St Patrick's Day, 1979. The 'crowd' sang 'Hail, Glorious St Patrick, dear saint of our isle' at the City End of the Oval. We had travelled across the Queen's Bridge, along the Bangor–Holywood dual carriageway and back into the heart of loyalist east Belfast for the Irish Cup semi-final against Larne. The main trouble at the game occurred above head height. A young loyalist climbed onto the rafters from the

Dee Street end carrying a large plank of wood. Pursued by cops, he leapt nimbly over the beams holding up the roof that straddled their part of the terracing and ours. During the chase, the Cliftonville fans chanted, 'Fall, fall, fall.' But the attacker made it as far as the empty terracing, the no man's land between the Reds and the Larne fans. Before he got the chance to place the plank over the Cliftonville supporters, he was nabbed and dropped the wooden block onto the empty space below. The game ended 2–2. Four days later there was an evening replay back at the Oval on a freezing cold night with blizzards and heavy snow. Just before we got inside, we were bombarded with abuse from little old loyalist ladies who lived around the City End. One old dear ran from her house with a shovel full of hot coal and tossed the burning embers in our direction. I remember the coals hissing and dying in the snow close to our feet as we lined up to pay into the Oval. Cliftonville scraped home to the final with a John Platt penalty.

Windsor Park. Cliftonville v. Linfield, one week before the Irish Cup final. Prior to the game, the Blues paraded the League Championship trophy around the ground. The Linfield players took special pleasure in displaying it in front of the Red Army on the Spion Kop. We hurled every insult imaginable at them and called Peter Rafferty, the Linfield centre-half, 'a dirty baldy bastard'. After the verbal abuse came the stone throwing, shortly before kick-off. Red fans used their skills, honed at various riots against the cops and the British Army, to good effect. Rocks and bits of broken-up terracing glided across no man's land, over the heads of the line of riot police holding back the Linfield masses in the north stand, and rained down on Blue heads. Attending his first ever Cliftonville match was one of my oldest and closest friends, Adrian McCartan. Aidy had come from Brighton to stay with his sister in west Belfast shortly after Easter. His family had been driven out of the city during the early 1970s after a loyalist mob attacked his home on the Woodstock Road in east Belfast. (There is another Joe McCann connection here. He and his men came over to the McCartan household on the loyalist Woodstock Road to protect the family in early 1971, as they had just come under sectarian attack.) Our fathers had been friends before us and prior to the Troubles I can remember happy summer days playing outside in the McCartans' large garden, driving around in Aidy's pedal-powered toy tank, wearing an authentic square-head Nazi helmet on my head as we re-enacted every war film we had seen. A decade on, it felt like we were in a real war zone rather than a football match. We were flanked on either side by riot police wearing steel helmets and Perspex visors. They carried plastic shields and thick batons, and several officers were pointing plastic-bullet guns in our direction. Only a couple of hundred yards beyond the bottle-green flak-jacketed lines of the RUC on either side of us were thousands of men baying for our blood, who sang songs in praise of the Shankill Butchers, the UVF and the UDA.

Aidy stood out among the Red throng. He wore a workman's black donkey jacket and blue and yellow tartan bondage trousers and DM boots. What really made him noticeable, though, was his natural flaming hair, bordering between ginger and strawberry blond, which was spiked up with soap several inches into the air. When he stood on top of one of the crush barriers to deliver a two-finger salute to the south stand, a section of the Linfield support turned on him and started chanting: 'Oh, spot the loony, spot spot spot the loony bin.'

During the game, which Cliftonville lost 2–0 (sweet revenge for the Blues after we defeated them 4–3 in the first round of the cup), I lost Aidy somewhere near the back of the Spion Kop. When the Red Army was escorted out of the ground, another riot broke out between the fans and the RUC. Parallel disturbances erupted on the other side at Olympia Drive, where the cops started firing plastic bullets at Bluemen trying to break through to us. The Red side of the trouble spread across the M1 motorway, onto the Donegall Road and then the Falls Road. The violence became chaotic and wanton. Cars and ambulances on the motorway were stoned; army jeeps and RUC Land-Rovers were bombarded with bottles, and gangs of marauding hooligans jumped onto buses on the Falls, kicking out windows and smashing up seats. Somewhere near Beechmount in the middle of the Falls Road, I spotted Aidy hanging out of the back window of a double-decker, his boots bouncing off the back wheel. I remember Cliftonville supporters from the Markets and the Short Strand asking me: 'Hey, Hen, is that that mad-looking cunt you were with at the match?' I was proud to answer in the affirmative.

Irish Cup final day, 28 April 1979. Aidy was getting excited while I tried to calm my nerves shooting pool and playing Asteroids inside the Yankee Doodle. He kept enthusing about the previous Saturday's aggro. Although he had witnessed (and probably partaken in) soccer violence back in England, the clashes at Windsor before, during and after the final had the potential for violence of even greater velocity. Aidy had been taken by his older brother Peter to Chelsea's notorious Shed during the 1970s and had watched ferocious battles between rival London hooligans. He had been to several Brighton–Crystal Palace derbies at the Goldstone Ground, where there had been outbreaks of stone throwing and fist fights between the two sets of supporters. But for the return of this native, back to his real home in Belfast after years in exile, the aggression, menace and danger attached to following the Red Army into the enemy's lair exceeded all of that.

For the occasion Aidy wore a new leather biker jacket decorated on the back with a satanic drawing – the pentangle and the devil as half-human/half-goat – as well as the legend in Latin above, 'Rex Mundi'. I wore an upside-down crucifix pinned to the breast pocket of a torn school blazer, a black jumper with holes in it, khaki-coloured army trousers and the standard-issue DM boots. Our blasphemous 'good-luck charms', as we called them, drew the ire of pious old ladies in Falls Road black taxis who shouted at us to 'Take off that cross, ya wee bastards', as we swaggered up towards the junction of Donegall Road. On our way down towards the motorway, Aidy elbowed me to move out of the mass of red and white heading for Windsor. We sneaked off up one of the last side streets before the M1 began and Aidy produced a joint from a zipped pocket, a perfectly rolled cylinder of Rizla paper and tobacco sprinkled with Lebanese gold. The two of us puffed on the joint as we sauntered across the M1 past traffic cops holding up a line of city-bound vehicles so the Red Army could pass.

Emboldened by both Dutch and Lebanese courage, we were among the first to try and scale the fence near the goalmouth. I fell off near the top, half-stoned and almost completely drunk on the Merrydown cider we had guzzled down earlier in the Yankee Doodle's toilets. Aidy, who was taller and stronger than me, made it over the barrier and onto the pitch. There were brief hand-to-hand, feet-to-groin and head-to-head battles between knots of rival supporters, including large numbers of Linfield fans who had turned up to get at the Fenians and maybe even support Portadown. The Red Army assault troops who leapt onto Windsor's turf were eventually chased off by riot police. At this stage, it seemed the final would be cancelled, as trouble was erupting on every corner of the Spion Kop. Although bottles, cans and flag poles were officially banned, and every fan was searched going into the stadium, missiles of all varieties were still smuggled into the ground and continually rained down on the RUC lines, the pitch and, with infrequent accuracy, the north and south stands. The ingenuity of the Belfast rioter was not and should not be underestimated.

Eventually, Cliftonville's manager, Jackie Hutton, came out of the dressing-room, approached the Spion Kop and made an appeal for calm. Strangely, Hutton, who was deeply respected by the entire support, even the hardcore hoolies, succeeded. The violence abated and the teams were able to march onto the park.

There was, however, one last act of defiance the Red Army performed before kick-off. When the police band maintained the annual tradition of playing 'God Save the Queen' as the teams lined up, we rebelled en masse. Older men on the Kop went through the crowd ordering us to 'sit down, sit fucking down', which we gladly did. It must have been the first time in the history of Irish League soccer that an entire section of the 'national' stadium had sat down for the British national anthem.

The game itself started disastrously when Portadown striker Jim Campbell scored after only 90 seconds, provoking a chorus of 'You're gonna win fuck all, you're gonna win fuck all, you're gonna win, you're gonna win fuck all', to the tune of 'Those were the days, my friends'. By the final minute, however, the sides were level at 2–2, with some Cliftonville fans already getting up to leave the Kop before the crush at the whistle. Ironically, it was a former Portadown player, Tony Bell, who cracked home the winner at the other end of the ground with just seconds to go. The Spion Kop erupted as we danced and jumped with joy.

Seaview, 14 May 1979. A second trophy for the Reds in a historic year. We won the Co. Antrim shield away at Crusaders, albeit 3–1 on penalties. The UDA had warned the Red Army to stay away or face the consequences, but in another gesture of newly found Catholic defiance the fans turned up in their thousands. The atmosphere on a warm early summer's night was brittle and threatening. A young loyalist from the Tigers Bay area known as 'Steegy Big Nut' ran on from the Crusaders' end armed only with a stone in his hand and a loyalist Vanguard flag in the other. Steegy, a well-known character to Catholic teenagers in north Belfast, was remarkably light on his feet as he dodged a hail of stones and bottles from the Shore Road end where the Red Army was penned in. He managed to direct the single stone he gripped into the crowd, striking a Cliftonville supporter in the face. The fans directly behind the goal were in a relatively safer position than the Reds hemmed up to the right side of the terracing beyond the corner, who were subjected to a barrage of playing darts as well as deadlier home-made Chinese-style circular steel darts that whizzed across no man's land in the compact little stadium on Belfast's Lough shore. Returning home in triumph up along Glandore Avenue, we got our revenge for the attacks both on Cliftonville supporters and players by smashing windows of Protestant homes and damaging their cars. Then, for the want of no one else to turn on, the walk back from Seaview to the relative safety of the Antrim Road ended in the inevitable riot between fans and the RUC.

Seaview, 21 August 1979. The chance for Crusaders to avenge the Co. Antrim shield defeat turned into one of the biggest policing operations in the history of world football. Up to 1,000 RUC officers were drafted in to police the Irish League clash. Word had already reached the Red Army early that evening that we were making history. A *Belfast Telegraph* report written by the indomitable journalist Deric Henderson, now editor of the Press Association in Ireland, was required reading before and after the historic tie. 'Violence and tension during and after soccer matches in Belfast is now the biggest football policing problem in the UK,' Henderson wrote. The statistics he reeled off still have the power to shock even today. Three times more police were deployed in and around Seaview than were at Ibrox for the previous Saturday's Rangers v. Celtic game; there were ten times as many police officers on duty for Crusaders v. Cliftonville than at the Arsenal v. Manchester United match at Highbury; and there were fifteen times more than at Liverpool's first home game of the season against West Bromwich Albion. Even the cops from across the Irish Sea were stunned at policing levels for Cliftonville games. One Superintendent William Porteous of the Strathclyde force, who had to deal with Celtic–Rangers games and all the security headaches they entailed, expressed amazement over the pressure on the RUC. 'We have the religious bigotry here as well, but definitely not on the same scale,' he told Henderson. 'It's been like this for years. We can cope with 300 men, but 1,000? I find that hard to believe.' Reading these reports gave the '79ers, the first recruits to the Red Army, a perverse sense of pride. We were now, after all, the league leaders in the UK, possibly European, maybe even world, soccer violence. We were more trouble than Celtic, Rangers, Man Utd and Arsenal all put together. We were the record breakers of football hooliganism.

Even at the height of the Red Army's power, however, we were living under the delusion that we were the most important force on the terraces in the land. In truth, we were merely an aberration, a brief interlude in the bigger soccer war in Ulster. Even now, more than two decades after I discharged myself from Solitude service, disgusted over the sectarianism and the pro-IRA sentiment of a section of our support, it is still a surprise to learn that Cliftonville was only of secondary concern to the fans of Belfast's Big Two.

To outsiders, it may seem perplexing that the two sides that command the support of the urban Protestant working class maintain a rivalry fiercer and more enduring than that which they display to the only team in the city with a large proportion of Catholic support. Long before Cliftonville attracted a substantial fan base, the bitterness between Linfield and Glentoran matched the hatred of the Old Firm in Glasgow or City versus United in Manchester. Ian Kennedy, one of the directors of Straight Forward Productions, a leading independent Northern Ireland film and television company, started supporting Glentoran in the early 1960s. Kennedy can recall trouble between Glens and Blues fans prior to the Troubles. The bitterness between the two sets of fans was so intense that Linfield supporters turned up for Glentoran's finest hour, the 1968 European Cup clash with Benfica.

'There were several hundred Blues fans at the Oval that night to cheer on Eusebio and company. They came partly to see the great Portuguese players that set the 1966 World Cup alight but also they came to the Oval just to see the Glens get stuffed. When Benfica scored, hundreds of them cheered at the City End,' Kennedy remembered. Benfica's Linfield mercenaries went home deeply disappointed, though, as their east Belfast rivals pulled off an incredible 1–1 draw against the European superstars.

Hooliganism at Big Two derbies increased dramatically during the early 1970s. Peter Shirlow, now a doctor of sociology at the University of Ulster and a respected chronicler of sectarian attitudes in the

Province, started following Linfield as a schoolboy in the '60s. Shirlow blamed the increase in violence at Blues–Glens games on two factors that had a cataclysmic impact on the Protestant community: the 'proletarianisation' of the support base and the intensification of sectarian hatred from 1969 onwards.

'For a start, the Prod working class was still living in an age of deference when I started going to games. Most families went to their local church; the fan base was tied to forces of social conservatism. Men like my father wore shirts and ties to the game on Saturday. And although men like him were privately sectarian, they would never show it in public – it was poor form. On the rare occasion when someone barracked a rival player for being a Catholic, you would hear things like, "Hi, boy, mind yer language", and so on. Even the lower-middle class went to the games, the schoolteachers, the chemists, the local grocer, etc. I remember turning up to Windsor in my grammar school uniform because I had played hockey or rugby earlier that day. But then the Protestant proletariat took over. It seemed to start in the mid-1970s. A rougher crowd of youths from places like the Shankill Road were coming to the games, boys like Fat Doc. They sang sectarian songs and no one was going to check them. When we played the Glens, they were very abusive to the Catholic players in the Glentoran team. The Glens, in turn, hated being taunted as "Fenian lovers". The Linfield fans called the Oval "the Vatican City" because so many Catholics played there. We were the super Prod team and there were songs we sang to prove it.' Shirlow recalled the Linfield taunt to the Glens: 'No Fenians on our team, on on the Linfield team.'

The Red Army's emergence in late 1978 was a complete shock to the smug superiority of the established soccer duopoly, he said. 'My earliest memories of Cliftonville and their fans were old men with blankets wrapped around their legs sipping tea from their flasks. The old Reds men would talk about their day out at the golf, the bowls or the cricket. In addition, there were about 100 Protestant Cliftonville fans from the loyalist Torrens area. It was their club and I can remember being at Solitude seeing Cliftonville fans wearing Rangers shirts and scarves to the games.'

The arrival of the Taig upstarts shocked Shirlow and his generation to the core. Demographic changes in Belfast had transformed the Cliftonville area from being a redoubt of the Protestant lower-middle class, as well as the city's Jewish community, into a Catholic stronghold. And now they had a football team to follow almost 40 years after 'their' last soccer side, Belfast Celtic, had dissolved amid allegations of sectarian intimidation and inter-board squabbling. After almost a decade cowering in fear of loyalist murder gangs, young Catholics from north Belfast were emerging publicly from their ghettos and striding cockily through Protestant bastions across the North. For those in the Protestant community reared on a mentality of communal superiority and social smugness, the barbarians were suddenly at the gates.

'Then *they* came,' Shirlow recalled. 'I remember vividly, it was the Irish Cup first-round game at Windsor. It was like something out of that film *Zulu*. There were rumours about these new Cliftonville fans, the so-called Red Army. We had yet to encounter them in large numbers. And then that Saturday afternoon in January *they* arrived. About one thousand of them came over the horizon like in the film and marched onto the Spion Kop. That day there was a real sense that something was changing – that *they* were here in the heart of Protestant Ulster. Our reaction on the terraces in the old north stand was interesting: it was a mixture of shock and outrage. There were the obvious sectarian comments: "Here come the soap dodgers" or "Hey, Fenians, this is not the dole office." But it was a pivotal game in Irish League history.'

While the Red Army may have been a new X factor in Northern Ireland football, the enmity between the two Protestant-supported teams remained as bitter and explosive as ever.

'We still hated the Glens more. To us, Cliftonville were and are irrelevant compared to Glentoran,' Shirlow emphasised.

Why then do working-class Protestants, some of whom belong to the same Orange lodge, social club or loyalist paramilitary grouping, hate each other more than Catholics when it comes down to their soccer allegiances?

Shirlow contended that the rivalry is rooted in an inflated sense of collective-self, in the idea of social superiority.

'We are the Irish League; they [Glentoran] are merely the pretenders. We have support all over Northern Ireland, from Belfast to Lisbellaw in Fermanagh, from Derry to Dungannon. Linfield is the "national" side, Glentoran are purely an east Belfast phenomena with some pockets of support in east Down. They are the usurpers against the Super Prods.'

The obvious sectarian distinction (that Glentoran always played Catholics, while a de facto ban on Catholics pertained at Windsor Park) has, however, blurred. Since the late 1980s, Linfield have recruited Catholic players from both sides of the Irish border, including Dessie Gorman, who hailed from Dundalk, the Co. Louth town where Blues fans went on the rampage during a UEFA Cup tie in 1979. The absence of the we-don't-play-Fenian jibe has not, however, watered down the bitterness between the rival supporters. If anything, the enmity has sharpened since the Troubles wound down and the Protestant working class turned in on itself, with loyalist paramilitary organisations launching several turf wars in unionist areas.

Even intellectuals like Dr Shirlow are prone to irrational outbursts when it comes to the Linfield–Glentoran divide. Although he resides in an east Belfast middle-class suburb, within walking distance of where this book is being written, Shirlow has refused to acknowledge that he is in fact living in the Glentoran heartland.

'I don't live in east Belfast and even if NASA sent me photographs from space satellites and said, "Look, your house is in the east", I would still say I live in south Belfast. I'm not living with the Rats.'

Educated and normally sane supporters from the other side of this divide also descend into irrationality the second Linfield is mentioned. Paul Donnelly from the Cregagh, the housing estate where George Best grew up, was educated at Queen's University Belfast and was regarded as one of its most progressive, anti-sectarian students' union officers in the late 1980s. A rarity in Ulster politics, he is a Protestant socialist. Donnelly nonetheless excludes Blues fans and players from his otherwise universal leftist belief in the brotherhood of man.

'My father actually supported the Blues because he came from what is now the Lower Shankill estate. But personally I couldn't stand them. I hated the fact that they were associated with the unionist establishment. The allure of the Glens was that they were different, even their colour – green.' Donnelly said he was proud that Glentoran played Catholics and, up until the advent of the Troubles, after which the Oval became dangerous for them, attracted a small but significant Catholic support.

Territorialism and inter-working-class jealousy also lay at the heart of the Glens–Blues schism, Donnelly pointed out. Linfield attracted the overwhelming support of football fans on the Shankill Road. 'The Shankill saw itself as the elite of loyalism and unionism. It was on the frontline in the war against nationalism, whereas east Belfast had virtually no Catholics living there. The Shankill, I think, resented that east Belfast somehow got it relatively easy. The Shankill had to deal with republicans from the Falls on one side and Ardoyne on the other. East Belfast, as my granny used to always say, was "treasure island" by comparison. The working-class Prod who supported Linfield would often say to their east Belfast counterparts – "We've got lots of Taigs on our side of the river and you haven't" – the Blues thought they had to be the best Prods.'

Donnelly became a marked man for a hardcore segment of the Linfield support in the 1980s during derby matches. He would bless himself in the Catholic way when Glentoran ran onto the pitch, just to annoy the Blues. 'I was told there was a bounty on my head.'

Paradoxically, as relations between the Blues and Glens fans worsened in the 1980s, with riots outside their respective grounds, players assaulted (including this writer's first cousin, a Catholic from the Ormeau Road who played in defence for Linfield) and hatred solidified, relations between the fans of both those clubs, Glentoran in particular, and the remnants of the Red Army improved dramatically.

By the early 1990s, a healthy, iconoclastic fanzine culture had emerged on the local soccer scene, with true, dedicated supporters taking charge. The Reds fanzines even had guest Glentoran correspondents such as ODG – Ordinary Decent Glenman. On the terraces and stand at Solitude, new ad hoc groups were formed such as Cliftonville Against Sectarian Bigotry and Hatred. CASBAH had links with a gang of skinheads who formed their own organisation to combat the image of all skins being neo-Nazi, white supremacist, boorish thugs. Skinheads Against Racial Prejudice included several Cliftonville supporters from west and south Belfast who were dedicated to bringing the skin cult back to its original roots, to its worship of ska and reggae and the ideals of the two-tone anti-racist philosophy.

The bonds between Cliftonville and their two big-city opponents were strengthened further after the IRA and loyalist ceasefires. So much so that, by 1999, Linfield were able to return to Solitude after a 29-year security-force ban on the Blues playing at Cliftonville's stadium. On that historic match day, Linfield supporters filing into the opposite end of the ground from the Reds' beloved Waterworks end, aka the Cage, were greeted by a banner with a simple message: 'Welcome to Solitude'. Another echoed the same sentiment in the Irish language. The first of the Blues to tread on Solitude's terracing were met with applause from the Red end of the ground. It was an extremely touching as well as historic moment in the history of war-torn north Belfast. It was an episode in which the Reds fans that were there can take enormous pride.

Cliftonville's diminished but fanatically loyal and genuine supporters had certainly endured some 'wartime' experiences in the years leading up to the ceasefires. In 1992, hundreds of fans narrowly survived a UDA grenade attack on the Spion Kop at Windsor Park, which the loyalist terror group said had been aimed at 'republican scum'. Even after the IRA and loyalist cessations, the team's followers continued to be the target of loyalist extremists. In 1996, Cliftonville buses were ambushed outside Portadown's Shamrock Park, where I had been arrested 16 years earlier for indecent exposure during a drink-fuelled Boxing Day. Near paralytic with booze, I urinated directly in front of a female RUC officer. The gaffe landed me in the back of a Land-Rover with threats from her colleagues that they would throw me out in the middle of one of the Co. Armagh town's loyalist housing estates and shout 'There's a Taig.' I soon sobered up! Portadown was, and continues to be, one of the most dangerous journeys for the Cliftonville fan.

There was no such rapprochement between the Glentoran and Linfield hardcore throughout the 1990s. The songs they still sing about each other reflect that enduring nihilistic hatred. Two Glentoran tunes stand out as particularly nasty. One to the tune of 'In my Liverpool Home' illuminates the ever-present inter-working-class snobbery and contempt between loyalist east and north-west Belfast.

'In your Shankill Road slums, you hoke in your dustbins for something to eat, you find a dead rat and think it's something to eat, in your Shankill Road slums.'

Richard Poots, a Glentoran fan from Newtownards, has his own favourite song for the Linfield supporters: 'I go down the pub, I drink ten pints, I am getting plastered, I drink ten more and then go home, beat up the wife, I'm a dirty Linfield bastard.'

Pootsy expresses the views of many Glentoran fans in their contrasting attitudes to Linfield and Cliftonville. 'Every Glenman hates Linfield but not every Glenman hates Cliftonville. If you ask me who do I hate more, Cliftonville or Linfield, it's definitely Linfield. If you ask me who do you hate more – Celtic or Linfield? The answer is still Linfield. If Linfield were in the European Cup final, God forbid, against Celtic I would support Celtic.'

One of the unreported casualties of the seemingly everlasting mutual loathing between the Glens and Linfield faithful is the Northern Ireland international side. It is the great unspoken truth of Northern Irish soccer, one which local football commentators and pundits prefer to ignore. And yet it is one of the most popular discussion topics on the chatrooms and bulletin boards of independent Glentoran websites. Whilst there is an obvious dearth of Catholic support watching Northern Ireland, due partly to fear of being recognised and beaten up, partly because most Northern nationalist soccer fans prefer the Republic of Ireland, there is also a significant segment of Glentoran fans who refuse under any circumstances to watch the national team at Windsor Park. Pootsy has articulated the views of the Glentoran refuseniks who will not pay to watch international games at Windsor.

'How would Arsenal or Liverpool fans feel if every England home game was played at Old Trafford and a proportion of the gate receipts from the national team went to Manchester United? That is the situation Glenmen are in over here. I would rather go to Cyprus or Albania to watch Northern Ireland than get the bus across Belfast to see them at home playing in Windsor Park. I'm not giving my money so some of it can go to those Blue bastards.'

Both Donnelly and Shirlow accept the notion that the survival of this particular intra-Protestant divide into the twenty-first century has become a metaphor for the wider schisms tearing the loyalist working class apart.

'I don't think you can exaggerate that idea at all. A lot of the old rivalry was based on economic status – generally the Glens were the shipyard workers and plane makers, the Shankill Blues were the linen and engineering workers from the other side of the river. Football merely reflects what is going on in the working class. Protestant society since the peace process has been racked by uncertainty and the people have turned against each other. So it's a fair point,' Donnelly admitted.

The soccer split slicing through urban working-class Protestant society in the North is by no means a neat cleavage. There is no UVF team, no UDA-backed side. This was brutally evident six months after a murderous feud exploded on the Shankill Road in August 2000 between the UVF and UDA. One man was stabbed and another badly beaten during a row in an east Belfast loyalist social club off the Newtownards Road. The UVF leadership investigated the incident, fearing that the stabbing had been part of the backwash from the previous summer's shooting war with the UDA, that another bout of feuding had spread to the east of the city threatening the fragile peace between the two paramilitary movements. To the loyalist high command, there was astonishment that these two barroom gladiators turned out not only to be UVF activists but members of the same battalion and even company. The terror group's second-in-command, a lifelong Linfield supporter, searched for the reason behind the near fatal fall-out.

'These guys were comrades who had been in the movement for years. The fight wasn't over politics, women or money. After they were questioned by the organisation, it turned out that the scrap came down to football – one of them was a Glenman, the other was a Blues fan. Incredible as it seems to outsiders, that's why they fell out.'

In the absence of outright terrorist war against their republican foes, two new fronts have opened up for the urban Ulster loyalist. The first concerns their external enemy, fought out over the narrow ground of north, west and now east Belfast, along the sectarian interfaces. Soccer has become a catalyst in these territorial struggles. Police officers patrolling those parts of the city where Protestant and Catholic redoubts intersect will tell you they dread the Glasgow Old Firm derbies more these days than Cliftonville v. Linfield or Glentoran. Celtic–Rangers clashes broadcast on television in the early twenty-first century have ended in short bursts of unrest breaking out along Belfast's many ethnic mini-borders. The foot soldiers' uniform in these battles includes the replica Rangers and Celtic shirts. Indeed, so concerned was the latter club about the TV news pictures showing rioters in the famous green and white hoops assaulting police, troops and loyalists from Portadown to Belfast's Limestone Road, that Celtic issued an appeal in 2002 that no one intent on causing mayhem on Northern Ireland's streets should wear the side's colours.

The second combat zone has broken out on the loyalist home front. Since the ceasefires and the Good Friday Agreement of 1998, working-class loyalists have turned on each other with a viciousness unimagined during the Troubles. The brawling and the barracking between loyalists at the Oval and Windsor Park therefore can be seen as pageants, mock-battles for the real and murderous power struggles going on between competing paramilitary forces in Protestant Ulster.

The Red Army's veterans and their successors view all this with a mixture of bewilderment and amusement. Some make the same mistake of the republican movement and gloat about the crisis of identity afflicting the loyalist proletariat and its ever-burgeoning underclass. This attitude is encapsulated in a slogan a minority of Cliftonville fans adopted following the Good Friday accord. They have taunted Linfield, Glentoran, Portadown and other Irish League sides with a chant to the tune of 'Bread of Heaven': 'You're not British anymore, you're not British, you're not British, you're not British anymore, you're not British anymore.'

Of course, the taunting used to be much more offensive and extreme. Back in 1979–80, some of the songs of the Red Army celebrated recent IRA atrocities from the incineration of Protestant civilians at La Mon House to the assassinations of MPs and members of the British Royal Family. The cup-winning season and the year after coincided with an upsurge in Provo and INLA mass murder. When the INLA blew up the Conservative's Northern Ireland spokesman and Colditz escapee Airey Neave in March 1979, the republican songsters were quick off the mark. To the tune of 'Yanks are coming', the Cage soon started singing: 'Airey's here, Airey's there, Airey's every fucking where, nah, nah, nah, nah, the nah, nah, nah, nah.'

Six months later, the Provos placed a bomb on a fishing boat used by Earl Louis Mountbatten, who was holidaying off the west coast of Ireland. The device placed on board by Thomas McMahon killed Mountbatten, 82-year-old Lady Brabourne and two teenagers, Nicholas Knatchbull and Paul Maxwell. The atrocity occurred on the same day that the Provisionals blew up 18 British soldiers at Warrenpoint. The new season was barely a few weeks old when I first

48

heard outside Solitude the latest ballad in praise of bombers, this one to the tune of 'Old Macdonald'. It went: 'Lord Mountbatten had a boat, e-I-e-I-oh, and on that boat there was a bomb, e-I-e-I-oh . . . with a boom boom here and a boom boom there, here a boom, there a boom, everywhere a boom boom . . . '

Much of this moronic gloating over the destruction of fellow human beings was in reaction to the equally repulsive sloganising from across no man's land at the Oval, Windsor, Seaview, Shamrock Park, etc., all about the 'heroic' exploits of murderers like the Shankill Butchers as well as other equally cruel and ruthless loyalist gangs. Some Protestant fans, notably outside Shamrock Park, would run their forefingers slowly across their throats, mimicking the cut-throat killers just as we were being escorted into the ground. None of that can ever excuse the cold-hearted murder of young boys and an old defenceless man just out for a spot of fishing off the western seaboard of an island held in great affection by him. Nor can the chants of the loyalist knuckleheads provide any justification for the tee-heeing over the victims of republican terrorism. To do so is to engage in one of Sinn Féin's most stomach-turning propaganda tricks – the use and abuse of moral what-aboutery.

I look back now with a real sense of shame when I see myself marching along the dual carriageway to the Oval or across the M1 singing those disgusting tunes. This shame is compounded by the knowledge that I was guilty of a second act of betrayal. Not only did I trick my parents for the best part of two and a half years, I also deceived some good friends. Because from 1979 to late 1981 I led a double-life. On those Saturdays when the team were away, when I just couldn't be bothered or when the season had shut down for the summer, I spent my time hanging out with my other tribe – the punks. Many of those I went to gigs at the Harp and Pound with, drank with down at The Fountain, made 'pilgrimage' up to Good Vibrations with, even made love with, were Protestant kids from places with names that normally struck terror into Fenian hearts. They came from Glencairn, Springmartin, the Shankill, Rathcoole, Monkstown, Braniel and Brownstown. We prided ourselves on our unconscious non-sectarianism. It became a badge of honour, another attribute that marked us out from the spides, the teenage thugs who marauded through the city centre on Saturday afternoons and evenings, usually inebriated, seeking out punks and Teddy boys to beat up. The majority of my Protestant punk friends knew nothing about my 'other' life, the one in which I sang songs about 'dirty Orange bastards' and threw stones at rival players and their supporters.

Only once was I 'caught', so-to-speak, on another bone-chilling afternoon at the Oval in early 1981. I had met Gowdy during the previous summer when Aidy McCartan and I were transforming our image from punk to skinhead. Gowdy shared a passion with us for early ska music, especially Prince Buster, the godfather of two-tone music. We became friends with this east Belfast rude boy and went to concerts and gigs together. When I returned to school, I saw less and less of Gowdy. By Christmas/New Year I hadn't seen him in about three months. Then he turned up on the other side of 'no man's land' at the Oval, right against the fence, screaming sectarian abuse and giving two-fingered salutes to the Reds at the City End of the ground. I was also pressed up against the security fence on our side of the stadium, and in an instant I froze. Gowdy did so as well. We recognised each other for a second and then he turned away and melted into the Glentoran crowd. It was the last time I ever saw him.

In the first half of Stanley Kubrick's masterpiece *Full Metal Jacket*, the character played by Matthew Bodine gains the nickname 'Joker' because of his mimicking of John Wayne and his general clowning around the base. The man who labelled Bodine 'Joker' is the sadistic training sergeant who ultimately drives another soldier to murder and suicide. In one hilarious incident later in Vietnam, a colonel confronts Joker, asking him to explain why he has a CND-style peace symbol on his helmet alongside the slogan 'Born to Kill'. Joker replies that he wears them to 'show the duality of man, sir'.

In 1979, I joined the Red Army and experienced Joker's 'duality of man'. On match days, I wore badges pinned to my black torn blazer with blatant sectarian messages like 'I hate the Glens' and 'Linfield shit', the latter a homemade construction, copyright the man who first brought me to Solitude, Michael Crawford. While with the punks or at home with my parents, I replaced these with red stars, hammer and sickles and CND peace symbols. The 'duality of man' for many growing up in a divided society like mine is the tussle between the individual and the tribal, the struggle of the rational against the visceral call of the wild. Nearly 20 years later, whenever I stood on the hill at Drumcree or the grass verges on the Garvaghy Road watching riots, violent demonstrations, vicious clashes between protestors and heavily armoured Robocops, some of the combatants barely out of primary school, wearing the new uniform of the post-ceasefire sectarian street battle, Celtic and Rangers shirts, I saw in flashback an earlier self from two decades before, as eager to get at the 'other' as the new foot soldiers of territorial struggle in Northern Ireland are today. The seductive quality of sectarian identity, the sense of belonging determined as much by the enemy without as the things that mark you inside as Prod or Taig, is as powerful as ever, arguably more so in the absence of outright terrorist war.

Most of the cadres of the old Red Army, meanwhile, are already into middle age. Many have long since shorn their truculent past and have become the new establishment at Solitude. They are the men who overthrew the old regime at the club in 2003 and turned the board into one of the youngest in the British Isles. They pick up the litter and patrol the pitch on match days to prevent trouble. They have established good relations between their Big Two rivals in the city and set out an example of people power in an era of Russian oligarchs, race-horse-owning managers and multi-millionaire shareholders to other supporters to follow. They, the vanguard of this people's revolution, have achieved something to be extremely proud of.

It is just over six years since I last visited Solitude, on the day Cliftonville won the Irish League in 1998, but I still see the shabby old stadium at the edge of the Waterworks every weekend. I drive past the park each Sunday en route to lunch at my mother-in-law's house in the Upper Cavehill Road. Despite a long absence from the terraces and the stands, despite many misgivings about the durability of sectarianism at Irish League soccer, I never forget to turn my head towards the home of the Reds and when Solitude comes into view my heart still skips a beat.

CHAPTER TWO

Alternative Ulsters

At the end of the hottest summer in living memory, the British government tried to force us to love our 'enemy'. A dozen of us, courtesy of the UK taxpayer, were taken away from our homes in the Markets and transplanted to a field in the English Lake District. Once there, we were expected to learn to like and understand a dozen other boys, most of them on the edge of puberty like ourselves, from the Protestant Suffolk estate, the last unionist area in Andersonstown, west Belfast.

In the 1970s, there was an exponential growth in cross-community holidays for the children of the Troubles. Kids at my primary school were scattered across the planet from Manchester to Minnesota, Brussels to Stockholm, West Berlin to Wisconsin, all in the cause of promoting trans-sectarian harmony. The Markets-on-tour August '76 was my first ever trip on this Northern Ireland cross-community world exodus. And, like most other projects designed to foster peace and understanding among the next generation, this two-week experiment in social engineering would fail.

Our team leaders on the holiday, Jube, a black Zimbabwean (then Rhodesia) reading medicine at Queen's University Belfast, and, Gerry, a retired British Army soldier from Suffolk, did their best to integrate the two sets of boys. On our first night, I was allocated a small tent to share with Protestant Andy Blain, who himself would later join the British forces. In the short-lived spirit of Prod/Taig cooperation, two days into our fortnight Andy and I received an award for having the cleanest, neatest tent in our camp. 'You could eat your dinner off that tent floor,' Gerry announced proudly to the rest of the camp gathered around the communal kitchen that morning.

Initially, the Prod kids were fascinated by my stories of life in the Markets, the tales of gun battles and my nightly recitation of the Hail Mary, a Catholic prayer they had never heard before; Andy and his chums asked me to say it every evening before we went to bed. But the early truce between the two sets of kids, both from areas of Belfast surrounded by larger 'enemy' strongholds, broke down. I think it fair and accurate to say that the Protestants started the trouble. A number of them, including one particularly aggressive boy in his early teens nicknamed 'Halfer', organised a 'black patrol' modelled on the UDA vigilantes that were guarding Protestant streets at night back home in Belfast. The black patrol of the Lake District would leave their tents once darkness fell, creep up on the tent where most of the Markets boys were sleeping, and kick and punch any bulge in the canvas that suggested a human presence. To this day, I can still hear the squeals of a number of Markets lads as boots and fists went into the tent walls.

Jube-the-Zimbabwean and Gerry-the-Brit did their utmost to work out a cessation of hostilities between the increasingly bitter and divided camp situated on land owned by a lady farmer who was also a member of the Liberal Party. They pointed to the example of 'Henry and Andy's tent' as a template for co-existence. Yet even that didn't last. After the Markets boys founded their own 'black patrol' and went on a revenge spree a few nights later, bombarding the main 'Protestant' tent with bricks and boulders, I felt under threat. Eventually, I left Andy's tent and ended up corralled in a larger green one with almost the entire Markets crew.

Only two things managed to bring us together over the next ten days: sex and shoplifting. The landowner had two blonde daughters, one about 14, the other a year younger. The Markets and Suffolk boys competed for the girls' attentions while helping them to feed the cows and poultry on the farm. They even tried to impress the daughters by displaying their manhood during a naked chase through the fields at eight o'clock one Saturday morning, which resulted in us all being banned from the farmhouse and thus missing the first *Match of the Day* of the 1976–77 soccer season, and me missing Everton's 4–0 away victory at Queen's Park Rangers.

Unity was restored again a few days later during a trip into Kendal, the historic market town in the Lake District. We got back together for a shoplifting spree, robbing everything from boxes of the town's world famous 'Kendal Mint Cake' to penknives and torches. We (the Markets boys) used the latter to amuse ourselves at Mass in the town the following Sunday, shining them all around the Catholic church, including at the priest's crotch.

When the holiday ended and we were transported back via coach to Stranraer, the bus was divided into two distinct zones. At the front, the Suffolk kids sang about 'The Battle of the Shankill' and 'Derry's Walls', while at the back we broke into renditions of 'The Boys of the Old Brigade' and 'The Soldier's Song'. By the time our parents picked us up at York Road railway station in north Belfast, we were exhausted from the journey and barely speaking to each other. The only person to come up and shake my hand, smile and wish me all the best for the future was Andy Blain. To this day, that handshake and his smile remains one of the most touching memories of my late childhood because, despite all that had happened in that quiet corner of the English countryside, some sense of friendship, some kind of personal warmth, had clearly survived.

A year after the holiday in the Lake District, I went back to England, this time with my family, and by sheer accident and the influence of an old friend, joined something that was to be infinitely more successful in bringing together Protestant and Catholic teenagers in Northern Ireland.

'Join' is probably an inappropriate word for the 'movement' that I signed up to at the end of 1977: punk rock. 'Movement' is also perhaps not the correct term to describe punk and its effect on our lives. 'Movement', as the Czech dissident writer Milan Kundera noted in his masterpiece on totalitarianism *The Book of Laughter and Forgetting*, reeks of the herd. In punk, especially in Northern Ireland, here was a revolt against the collective, a rebellion against tribalism. In this youth cult, a section of my generation found a way out of the sectarian pigeon-hole they had been placed in from birth. What the British government, the Peace People, the Christian community of Corrymeela on the north Antrim coast, the student movement, American philanthropists and English liberals determined to do something about the war on their doorstep had failed to achieve, we, the punks of 1977 to 1981, and arguably far beyond those years, succeeded in doing.

For me, it all began in Brighton during the 'Twelfth fortnight', when Belfast's Catholics attempt by any means available to escape the menace and tedium of the Orange marching season. My father had been promising for years to visit his lifelong friend Micky McCartan, who, along with his family, had fled their home in east Belfast at the start of the Troubles to build a new life for themselves in England, eventually settling in the Sussex seaside resort. And so, after several false starts over the years, we finally ended up in 45 Livingstone Road, Hove, in July 1977. On the night we arrived, their youngest son Adrian, Aidy, was sitting in the family living room watching *Top of the Pops*. Following the formal introductions, we sat down together in front of the television set. Up until then I had no interest in popular music, believing it to be the preserve of screaming girls (Bay City Rollers, Flintlock, etc.) and students. That was until a group of gnarling, offensive, cheesecloth-wearing young working-class men stormed onto the music scene. On our first evening in Brighton and Hove, the Sex Pistols appeared on screen and Johnny Rotten in his 'Destroy' T-Shirt, bright orange hair and permanent sneer sang 'Pretty Vacant'. In that instant, I knew all this was for me!

The next morning, Aidy, who already had his hair spiked and wore drainpipe trousers, brothel creepers and odd-coloured luminous socks, and I forayed into Hove seeking out the Sex Pistols' single. Our first port of call in Hove was a record shop run by a bearded man with a very effeminate bearing who announced that he 'didn't sell that rubbish'. Later, we found a large shop near the sea front in Brighton and while Adrian distracted the salesgirls with his charm and good looks, I swiped a copy of 'God Save the Queen' from a box full of recent singles near the door. Once outside, we ran back to Livingstone Road, went down to the basement of the house where Adrian slept, and leapt about the room to the chorus of 'No future, no future, no future for you'.

Walking around Brighton in those two glorious weeks in July, we kept bumping into gaggles of punks, including a group of young punkettes, one of whom had a kettle slung over her overcoat and another who blew kisses to Aidy and me as we passed them. For someone who had grown up in the monochrome streets of inner-city Belfast, where the merest hint of flamboyance or originality in your dress code could result in a hammering, these teenagers seemed like people from another planet, in equal part fascinating and fearsome.

Back home in Belfast a fortnight later, I pulled my wardrobe apart and singled out those clothes I could transform into DIY punk. Torn blazers, Dr. Marten boots and army trousers were in, along with granddad shirts and ripped black jumpers; out went parallel trousers and bell-bottom jeans, along with jet-wing-collar shirts and steel-capped Oxford brogues.

Two other things helped make the punk transformation complete: razor blades and *The John Peel Show* on Radio One. I used the blades to hack through my hair in order to create that messed-up spiky look I had seen first on Brighton's streets and later in downtown Belfast. From September I listened to Radio One at ten in the evening every weekday, more often than not with the play/record buttons pushed down, as part of my induction into punk and new wave. First Adrian and later some friends at St Malachy's College had advised me to tune in most nights to *The John Peel Show*, the DJ who had championed punk music even when its proponents were branded in the press as a threat to the entire British nation and civilisation.

At first, my parents were divided over my new allegiance. My mother referred to punks as 'dopey' and 'stupid looking'. She even invented scare stories to ward me off punk clothing like army trousers and PVC drainpipes. On the subject of army trousers, she told me that the British Army had issued a warning to kids in west Belfast to avoid the leg-wear, as their squaddies might mistake them for uniformed IRA men out on a mission! She offered a more mundane warning about the PVC drainpipes – they were highly flammable and could go on fire even if you were walking in the sun. Eventually, however, she accepted my calling and, being the loving mother she was and is, even designed my own bondage trousers made from stolen pieces of manhole tape and the buckles off old schoolbags.

My father's attitude to punk was more positive. He applauded its anti-establishment edge, especially the Sex Pistols raining on the Queen's Silver Jubilee parade that June. 'The punks are progressive people,' he announced one night after a drinking session with his comrades in Frank Donnelly's pub beside the British Army billet in the Markets.

In Belfast, there was another reason why he was right about labelling the punks 'progressive'. The movement, the social phenomenon, or whatever you care to call it, had by late 1977 pulled together scores of young Catholics and Protestants who, until then, had been consigned to their religious *and* (and this is overlooked in many accounts of Ulster punk) class ghettos, who were marked out from birth, who were burdened by the tribal placards placed around their necks since 1969.

One of the most important songs I heard during the period between 1977 and 1979 came to encapsulate everything Ulster punk was about and marked it out from its more nihilistic counterpart across the Irish Sea. Jake Burns, with a little help from the journalist Ian Ogilvie, penned the tune that also summed up the widespread disillusionment with the Troubles and the whole futile mess Northern Ireland had found itself in by the late '70s.

The opening lines and that gravelly voice conveying Burns' anger still resonate in the new century: 'I could be a soldier/Go out there and fight to save this land/Be a people's soldier/Paramilitary gun in hand/I won't be no soldier/I won't take no orders from no one/Stuff their fucking armies/Killing isn't my idea of fun.'

After more than 30 years of carnage, the lyrics of the Stiff Little Fingers anthem 'Wasted Life' might seem a little archaic, even a tad obvious today. But back in the 1970s, this open rejection of the paramilitary death cult was a truly revolutionary act. In the early half of that terrible decade, I, like thousands of other kids, looked up to and in many cases sought to emulate the 'fucking armies' that Burns and SLF excoriated on their brilliant and seminal debut album *Inflammable Material.* Before the arrival of punk, it was the height of chic and cool for working-class kids and teenagers to do what their older brothers and cousins were doing, to join the IRA (Official and Provisional), the INLA, UVF and UDA. Thousands of young men and women (some, like me, still at primary school) tried to join the paramilitary movement's junior wings on both sides of the divide. In the Markets, young boys and teenagers were divided into rival camps: the Provie and

Stickie Fiannas. Meanwhile, in Protestant areas, the UDA and the UVF's youth group, the Young Citizens Volunteers (YCV), competed for youngsters' loyalties.

For a large majority of the age group ranged between 10 and 18, rock 'n' roll – Gary Glitter, Mud, Slade, etc. – merely provided the soundtrack to the struggle for a United Ireland or the defence of the Union. Until punk, popular music was never an all-embracing lifestyle with its own dress code, social attitudes and outlook on life in general; pop was simply plastic manufactured escapism that occasionally produced a menacing backbeat to the sectarian and political clashes all around us. But after 1977 we had new role models to look up to.

That is why 'Wasted Life', arguably even more than SLF's more famous tune 'Alternative Ulster', was such a radically challenging social statement. The music on SLF's first album offered not only the teenage rebellion against the state, Church and family (a concept born in the 1960s) but also a loud, rude and courageous two-fingered rejection of the organisations that saw themselves as threatening the status quo. Whereas the Rolling Stones and their offshoots in the late 1960s eulogised the anti-establishment leftist revolutionaries with anthems like 'Street Fighting Man', Ulster punk, in particular SLF, recoiled from the myth of the guerrilla freedom fighters. In the latter's eyes, the men in the balaclavas armed with their AK-47s and their Che Guevaraesque sloganising were as oppressive and dangerous as the cops behind their helmets, visors and riot shields.

One incident from the golden era of Ulster punk still stands out as the epitome of what this social protest was all about. One bright sunny afternoon at the end of September '79, I was stopped and searched by several RUC officers, or, as it was then known, P-checked. I was part of a group of 25 young punks making our way to the mecca of Ulster punk, Terry Hooley's Good Vibrations record shop. We appeared on first sight to be a truculent band of young thugs, all piercings, chains, belts, studs, spiked hair, boots and even a Labrador dog called 'Brandy', whose top hair was dyed green for the day. Our procession had been halted while making our way along Belfast's Great Victoria Street facing the city's Europa Hotel, then the most frequently bombed establishment in Europe. The sergeant in charge of the RUC patrol started taking down names and addresses. He was startled by what he was hearing. There were kids from all over Belfast: the Shankill Road,

Divis Flats at the foot of the Falls Road, the Markets, Glencairn, Andersonstown and the Shore Road. These were areas where the majority of the violence was taking place and where no one from the 'other side' would dare visit. In a smaller way, this weekly walk from The Fountain in the city's Cornmarket to Good Vibrations was as revolutionary an act as the lyrics of 'Wasted Life'. Without adult supervision, the encouragement of do-gooders or the designs of the decent anti-sectarian left, we were tearing off the tribal placards and dumping the sectarian baggage. In the dark days of the 1970s, when at night Belfast turned into a ghost town of fear and destruction, this too was a two-fingered salute to the grim order of life in a divided society.

Impressed by the ecumenism of this bondage-and-leather-wearing group, the RUC sergeant released us from the P-check and let us proceed on to Hooley's temple of punk. I recall the old copper still shaking his head in amazement when I glanced back at his patrol.

Most of the crowd of punks I hung around with had first met in early 1978, either down by The Fountain – a popular haunt that attracted the glue-sniffers, the wine-drinkers, the lechers and the plain bored – or inside Hooley's shop. No one asked where anyone came from or what religion they were. There was nothing contrived or stage-managed about this show of solidarity every Saturday afternoon, when we would run the gauntlet of thugs who attacked punks – regardless of how young or small they were – in central Belfast or put up with the bigotry and stupidity of the public who looked down on us as dirty and depraved. We were making this up as we went along, without any idea where it would lead. It was the most natural social force to emerge in Northern Ireland in decades, and didn't need government grants or rich philanthropic aid. 'Cultural expression' – that empty phrase invented in the mid-1990s to legitimise sectarian tribalism and wean the paramilitaries off terrorism by flattery and financial largesse – was mercifully absent from the Ulster punk scene. It was another example of the DIY philosophy of early punk: organic, unstructured, unthinking, natural.

The group of punks I made friends with were in their early teens and had managed by subterfuge, make-up (both boys and girls), and brothel creepers that gave them an extra inch in height, to blag their way into that other temple of Ulster punk rock, the Harp Bar. In the first half of 1978, the Harp took on the mystique of a musical El

Dorado, a promised land of newly emerging bands, po-going, cheap and nasty lager, and freedom. Once past the grumpy barman Tony on Friday or Saturday nights, you entered another world from the colourless, aggressive and soul-destroying atmosphere of '70s Belfast. The DIY spirit that applied to the clothing and the image pertained to the music. Many of the bands were ad-hoc combos thrown together in a single night or had had a couple of weeks of practice in a garage, upstairs bedroom or youth club.

People under the age of 25 do not realise what a dank and depressing place Belfast was in the '70s after six in the evening. Inside the ring-of-steel – the fenced-off controlled zone at either end of Royal Avenue – virtually nothing moved at night. Pubs closed early, nightclubs were non-existent and no one dared walk the streets for fear of assassination or abduction. Up until 1977, there was hardly a music scene to talk about in the city centre, with the exception of the Pound Bar off Oxford Street, which was home to 'progressive rock' bands and later several punk acts. The Harp scene and the arrival of hundreds of teenagers from all over Belfast and beyond into Hill Street reclaimed the night and even the day. On Saturday afternoons, in between the striptease acts, young bands tuned up and rehearsed on the Harp's stage while hundreds of punks invaded the city centre. Their presence initially provoked a brief war between them and the Teddy boys who congregated around the Bailey Bar near Belfast's Docks. But the two teenage cults quickly abandoned their nihilistic hostility towards one another in the face of a common foe: the spides.

Short for Spiderman, this phrase described the teenage thugs still lost in the land that time should have forgot. Dressed in parallel trousers or bell-bottom Wranglers, with long hair and middle-shade partings, the obligatory moustache, Oxford brogues and Gilbert jumpers, they found the outrageous flamboyance of the punks and Teds equally offensive. There were several celebrated attacks on the Harp Bar itself between 1977 and '79 by the spides, who thought they could treat the punks the way gangs of queer-bashers used to terrorise gay men in the '70s. The unity between the punks and Teds was another unique aspect of the former sub-cult in Northern Ireland compared to anywhere else in the British Isles. While Teds and punks clashed along London's fashionable Kings Road or on the beaches of the English south coast on bank holidays (mimicking the mod–rocker wars of the 1960s), the two youth cults in Belfast fought alongside each other when attacked by gangs of spides.

The spides found punk either socially threatening or effeminate bordering on the gay. I remember, around 1980, being accosted along with my one of my oldest friends by a group of corner-boy spides in the Markets. They jibed that we looked like 'fruits' (street-speak for gay) and that we should listen to decent bands like the Village People . . . I am not making any of this up! Anto O'Kane and I were on our way to meet a group of punkettes in the city centre for a drink, all of whom were attractive and, unusually for those days, very sexually alluring in their leather miniskirts, fishnets and tartish Siouxsie-Sioux make-up. In a telepathic instant, we both looked at each other and burst out laughing at the sad smug absurdity of these spides. They didn't know what they were missing.

In the first few years, punks were demonised in the Northern Ireland media and society in general. As late as 1981 they were blamed (wrongly) for, among other things, a horrific knife attack on a young Catholic boy. The child's religion was marked out because of his First Holy Communion suit and badge. The assault took place inside one of Belfast city centre's public toilets and was actually carried out by a group of loyalist skinheads roaming around the commercial centre on a Saturday afternoon looking for Catholic prey. Word, however, got out and it seeped into the local press that a gang of punks had been responsible. As a result of this wildly inaccurate reporting and street hearsay, a number of punks were attacked in the days following the slashing of the young boy.

Belfast's punks, however, were not pacifists; they were not hippies-in-zips. They had fought the RUC after the police lost control of the crowd outside the Ulster Hall at the infamous 1977 Clash concert. They had beaten back a number of attempts by gangs of spides to enter the Harp over the next few years. They even teamed up with the Teds to take on the spides around Cornmarket. Protestant and Catholic, atheist, socialist and anarchist – they banded together to defend themselves when necessary. Ulster punk, contrary to the myth, wasn't always about peace, love and understanding.

Another of the bands that captured the mood of social ecumenism between '77 and '80 originated from one of the areas with the most ferocious reputation for sectarian violence, the Greater Shankill. Ruefrex formed while its members were still at school, and started to articulate the concerns of young working-class punks growing up in a world of terrorism, poverty and segregation. Unlike other bands on the scene at the time, Ruefrex were not afraid to play in community halls and clubs in working-class areas, inevitably in some cases the places where the paramilitaries exerted control. Despite this, Ruefrex were not put off denouncing terrorism and sectarianism. Paul Burgess, the band's drummer and now Dr T.P. Burgess of Cork University, summed up Ruefrex's philosophy thus: 'The idealism in our lyrics, about bringing the two communities together and rearing them as one. It's something we really believe in.'

These words alone were enough (and probably still are) to push four young men from the Shankill into the crosshairs of the local UVF and UDA. The band went further, though, and openly criticised the grip the loyalist organisations had on young working-class lives. Even as late as the mid-1980s, with the original spirit of punk a fading memory, Ruefrex's impact survived, with *NME* describing them as 'The most important band in Britain'. Nor were they shy about lashing out at the paramilitaries on the other side of the peacelines or their supporters both at home and abroad. Their most fertile period came in the mid-1980s when the band appeared on Channel 4's flagship music show *The Tube,* as well as touring North America. Ruefrex's 1985 single 'The Wild Colonial Boy' was a savage indictment of sentimental, ill-informed pig-ignorant Irish-Americans who donated their dollars to Noraid, which in turn helped fund the IRA's campaign of murder and terror. The original sleeve of the single featured an Armalite rifle (the favoured weapon Irish-American supporters smuggled in in their hundreds to Ireland for the Provos) but was deemed too controversial by their record company. The reissued single showed a little drummer boy standing in front of a green, white and orange-coloured Stars and Stripes flag. Because of its controversial subject matter, radio stations across Britain and Ireland were reluctant to play the song.

Long after punk had become a socially accepted part of UK 'heritage', with Yanks sending postcards of London teenagers with Mohawks and biker jackets to the folks back home, the unfashionably attired, unhip Ruefrex were still stirring the social pot. Due to their protest song about American support for the Provos, they were unfairly branded as 'Orange punks' and even the rock 'n' roll voice of Ulster loyalism. Elvis Costello at one stage, according to Burgess, thought the band were 'Orange bastards'.

As with anything in Northern Ireland, if you strike out against the sins of one side you are inevitably branded as belonging to the other. Ruefrex were consistently critical of the paramilitaries on both sides of the divide, but in the shorthand of media-land they were labelled as the 'Prod punks'. In reality, and unlike most of the bands to emerge from that era, Ruefrex put their money where their mouths were. At the height of their national and international fame, Ruefrex played a fundraising gig to raise money for Lagan College, the first integrated school for Catholic and Protestant children in Northern Ireland.

Even back in 1977–8, though, it would be wrong to assume that every punk and every band emerging from the scene was on some collective anti-sectarian mission. We were, and are, coloured by our roots and background. As already described, between '78 and '81 I lived out a double-life, with loyalties that straddled the Cornmarket punks and the faithful at Solitude, home of Cliftonville FC. Many of the west Belfast punks I became friendly with came from families with fathers, mothers, brothers and sisters in the Provisional IRA. A number of politically committed punks (always a minority) identified with the far-left allies of the PIRA and believed the Provos' 'armed struggle' was a legitimate form of so-called anti-imperialism. This latter group spent time hanging out in Just Books, an anarchist collective bookshop in Belfast's Winetavern Street. The bookshop contained posters praising the IRA's resistance to British rule and sold pro-republican papers and anti-H-Block material. The Clash's statements on Ireland encouraged those punks who bought this line around 1979. In an interview with the press, Joe Strummer, the late Clash singer, called for British troops to be pulled out of the North. He had also started wearing 'Smash H-Block' T-shirts at concerts, at least when he wasn't holding up clothing in praise of the nihilistic ultra-left terrorists of the Italian Red Brigades. For many punks in Northern Ireland, though, Strummer's statement and the adoption of republican causes like H-Block was a betrayal of the spirit demonstrated outside The Clash concert in '77, when Catholic and Protestant youth had been united. Several letters were sent to *NME* in 1979 to protest about The Clash's overt support for republicans. A 15-year-old correspondent described as a 'Siouxsie and the Banshees fan' accused Strummer of being a 'terrorist sympathiser', adding, 'He obviously supports the IRA, and he is opening up the gap between Protestant and Catholic kids that punk had closed.' Other punks saw it differently, of course, and by 1981 they were faced with new political challenges that would threaten to widen the split in this organic social movement.

The year 1981 is a crucial and arguably fatal one in the history of Ulster punk. Two events were to have a major effect on punk, diluting its ability to unite hundreds of Catholic and Protestant teenagers. The first involved the nucleus of a terrorist force that would eventually wreak havoc across Greater Belfast and beyond; the second concerned the fate of ten men who would starve themselves to death for a political ideal.

In January 1981, another concert took place at the Ulster Hall involving yet another band that preached the same peace and unity message the punks first espoused during the Troubles. The Specials' second gig in Belfast attracted an eclectic crowd of youth cults from punk and mods to rude boys and anti-fascist skinheads. It also provided a new gang with a platform to convey their message of sectarian and racial hatred – the Shankill Skinz. Comprising teenagers from the Greater Shankill as well as other parts of Protestant north Belfast, they wore the uniform of the skinhead revival: DM boots, bleached jeans, red-and-black Harrington jackets, Crombie overcoats, Fred Perry shirts, red braces and neatly pressed button-down Ben Sherman shirts. Unlike other skins who donned the same clothing, the Shankill gang was fired up by racialist and sectarian rage. They formed around a band that modelled itself on the new Oi! skin bands in Britain. Offensive Weapon contained two men who would later find fame and fortune not through their buzzsaw rock music and hate-filled lyrics but rather in crime and terrorism. Offensive Weapon's singer was one Jonathan Adair, later to become 'Mad Dog', the leader of the Ulster Defence Association's 'C Company' on the Shankill. The band's bass player and Adair's lifelong friend was Sam 'Scally' McCrory, a gay Shankill skinhead covered in tattoos from head to foot who would go on to command the UDA's prisoners in the Maze. The group sang songs denouncing blacks, republicans, Catholics and the government. They became the shock troops of the resurgent National Front, which staged several rallies in Belfast city centre in 1980–1. In those two years, the Shankill Skinz fought bitter street battles with rival Catholic skinhead gangs (including Cliftonville fans), punks and mods. By early 1981, the gang had gained a notorious reputation for street fighting across the city. Once the Specials concert was announced shortly after Christmas, Adair, McCrory and others such as Big Donald Hodgen were determined to make a name for themselves.

The Specials' 1981 concert turned out to be the second major riot at the Ulster Hall, but unlike the previous fracas at the Clash gig four years earlier there was to be no display of cross-sectarian unity in the face of state repression. If you argue that the Clash concert was the alpha of Ulster punk, then in a way the Specials gig four years later was its omega. The fighting that erupted along the lines outside the venue and later inside the hall took on a nasty sectarian turn, with the Shankill Skinz singling out knots of Catholic skinheads along with punks from either side of the religious divide – in fact, anyone who stood in their way that evening. Although hopelessly outnumbered, I remember a number of older teenagers I knew bravely fighting these thugs against the odds. They included Eamon O'Hara, an older brother of a classmate at St Malachy's College, who laid into a large group of the Shankill Skinz outside the Ulster Hall before we managed to escape up to the upper tier of the concert venue. By this time, the Ulster Hall had become segregated on broad religious grounds: the Catholic skins and their friends in the seats above; the Shankill Skinz dodging wave after wave of spit, urine, bottles and stones down below on the dance floor. In the punk era, the very idea that a concert venue could be divided into P and RC zones would have been unthinkable. The arrival of the Shankill Skinz, Oi!-chic and the racialist message of groups like Offensive Weapon and their 'heroes' in Skrewdriver had transformed the teenage cult scene in Northern Ireland. They had injected sectarianism back into youth culture and poisoned the atmosphere around the music scene in Northern Ireland.

The other, far more cataclysmic event of 1981 was the IRA and INLA hunger strike at the Maze prison, which claimed ten young men's lives by the end of that summer. The hunger strike forced people across Ireland and beyond to take sides and polarised politics like never before. The Irish left was convulsed with splits over how to approach the issue: establish a 'critical support' line (to use the Trotskyite parlance of the day) for the hunger strikers' demands; or the rejection of the campaign in the name of working-class unity and socialism. With few exceptions, my punk friends from west Belfast became radicalised from the time Bobby Sands won the Fermanagh/South Tyrone by-election. Sands was to be the first hunger striker to die. Many of them started attending rallies in favour of the hunger strikers. Even a few who had been beaten up by the IRA's junior wing in the west of the city, the Provisional Fianna (or 'Daft Lads', as we called them) were now turning up at Dunville Park and the Busy Bee rallying points to show their solidarity with the hunger strikers. My best friend and the man responsible for me becoming a punk in the first place, Adrian McCartan, got swept along with the H-Block tide. He started wearing Troops Out T-shirts both in England and on his trips back home to Belfast. On the other hand, I recoiled from the death cult associated with this phase of the H-Block struggle. I felt the issue was driving a further wedge between the working classes and forcing people back further into their tribal camps. In the febrile atmosphere of that spring and summer, many of my peers were abandoning the punk scene altogether and replacing their biker jackets with army coats, dumping their Sex Pistols badges for ones with the image of Bobby Sands, Francis Hughes, Patsy O'Hara, etc. on them. Because of the constant television replays of men in masks and military jackets firing over the coffins of the dead 'martyrs', that year paramilitary-style clothing came back into fashion. Not since the mid-1970s – pre-punk – did so many teenage wannabes dress like their older peers who actually belonged to the movement.

Paradoxically, the hunger strike saved me from myself; from the kid I was becoming in the early half of 1981. Disillusioned by the commercialisation of punk by 1980, those must-have Boy bondage trousers imported from Chelsea costing £50, I had rebelled again. This time, again following Adrian's example, I shaved my head to the bone and started wearing Fred Perry, bleached jeans, braces, Harringtons and Crombies, the uniform of the neo-skins. Unlike the Shankill Skinz, however, we listened to ska and reggae as well as the punk and new wave bands. But the crowd of skinheads I started hanging around with in the autumn/winter of 1980 included several Cliftonville hooligans and young Provo supporters from Turf Lodge in West Belfast. Gradually, I became sucked into a vortex of street and soccer violence, most of it with a nasty sectarian tinge.

The hunger strike and the hysteria surrounding it ironically brought me back to my senses and my socialist roots. In response to the Catholic sectarianism of the skins I knocked about with, itself an over-reaction to the blatant bigotry of Offensive Weapon and their following, I returned to punk, growing my hair until it was spiked up again, taking the biker jacket and the Dead Kennedys T-shirt out of the wardrobe and re-immersing myself in the fading new wave music scene in the city. By this time, however, my musical tastes (like so many others whose formative years belonged to the punk era) were evolving. The alternative music scene was taking on a more subtle, often darker edge, with bands like Joy Division, Cabaret Voltaire and Magazine. This was the age of individualism, the antithesis of the collective, the dawn of the self-obsessed 1980s. Is it really that fanciful to argue that punk – the revolution against communal taste, tribal loyalties, even class prejudice – had paved the way culturally for Thatcherism, with its emphasis on the individual, career-open-to-talent and the 'anarchy of the market'? Is it the ultimate sacrilege to suggest that Thatcher's most important mission statement, that there was 'no such thing as society only individuals and their families', was the natural progression of the anti-collective DIY entrepreneurial spirit of punk? Back during even Thatcherism's halcyon years, this would have been heresy to the vast majority of punk rockers, old and new, who hated the Tories and all they stood for. Yet, again with the hindsight gained from the distance of a quarter of a century, is it really that outlandish to argue that the death of the old post-war British consensus, coming as it did during the mid-1970s when punk reared its angry head, was pushed towards the grave of history by this iconoclastic, pan-class, ruthlessly individualist lifestyle? Certainly the anti-politics of the majority of punks (if you exclude the anarchist faction that followed bands like Crass and Poison Girls) suited the new times. Many of the teenagers who fought for personal freedom through punk entered adulthood in the 1980s mentally equipped to cope with the age of individual endeavour and innovation.

A few of us still flew the red-and-black flags in the face of the Thatcherite counter-revolution. The Anarchy Centre in North Street continued to provide a venue for new punk bands in the '80s, whilst also fostering an atmosphere of anti-sectarian and anti-establishment lifestyles. Groups such as Petesy Burns' Stalag 17 and its Warzone label continued to promote traditional punk bands from across Northern Ireland. Petesy and the crowd around Warzone have never received the praise or support they deserve for keeping the punk scene and its spirit of anarchy and anti-sectarianism alive through the selfish darker years of the 1980s.

The punk image in general had, however, become commercialised. One of the moments when this was confirmed to me took place in 1983 as I sat in front of my aunt's television set at her flat in north London. It depicted a line of men on a Tube train who had obviously not shaved that morning given the slashes of dried blood across their faces. At the end of the line was a Mohawk punk whose skull, where it was exposed, was scarred with razor marks. The punk image was now a saleable commodity used to advertise everything from Bic razors to electric cookers back in Northern Ireland.

I watched the Bic advertisement on the eve of another trip to Brighton and the McCartan family in Hove's Livingstone Road. By this time, Adrian, along with his older brother Peter, was dead, both the victims of suicide brought about by drug abuse. For me, punk had had it. Now it was time to move on.

All revolutions, as Danny in the '80s film classic *Withnail and I* points out, end in failure. 'They're selling fucking hippy wigs in Woolworths, man,' Danny laments to the two main characters, Withnail and Marwood, towards the end of Bruce Robinson's masterpiece. Bemoaning the death of the '60s ideal, Danny adds prophetically: 'The greatest decade in the history of mankind and, as my friend here so aptly puts it, "We have failed to paint it black".' When I first saw Robinson's wonderfully bittersweet comedy, those words of Danny's resonated. Crushed up in a narrow seat inside the Queen's Film Theatre in 1987, Danny's comments immediately struck me as highly relevant for these times: the end of the punk ideal, the Thatcherite '80s, the resurgence of violence in Northern Ireland, the re-assertion of tribal division.

Yet all revolutions still leave a lasting imprint on their society, a legacy left behind even when the caravan of history moves on. A year after *Withnail and I* came to cinemas there was the second Summer of Love and its accompanying soundtrack, Acid House. For another brief period lasting roughly between 1988 and 1990–91, that same spirit of

DIY defiance and indifference to sectarian labels that marked the punk era was resurrected. Those early illegal house parties in empty warehouses and fields on the edge of Belfast and other towns across the North attracted thousands of young people from every religious and class background of Northern society. It was only when the paramilitaries realised that the profits from Ecstasy, the 'love drug' associated with the House scene, could be so lucrative that they muscled in on the new teenage movement. The House scene moved quickly from the illegal gatherings at warehouses and fields, as well as Belfast's Art College, to paramilitary-controlled pubs and clubs in both urban and rural areas. And whilst the love drug helped dampen down the nihilistic passions of soccer hooliganism in Britain (witness Irvine Welsh's *Marabou Stork Nightmares* and the pacifying impact of 'E' on some of the Hibs casuals), in Northern Ireland Ecstasy eventually helped fill the war chests of terrorists like Billy 'King Rat' Wright and none other than our old adversary Johnny Adair and the new offensive weapons of 'C Company'. Both men's terror units were funded through Ecstasy dealing, and, in Adair's case at least, one of them was consuming as much Ecstasy as his comrades were selling. In the perverse moral universe of Northern Ireland, the love drug aided the loyalist war.

In Protestant working-class areas, it was the likes of Adair and Wright who became the new icons for loyalist youths. This deadly duo wore the same designer street gear adopted by a new generation of spides: the Nike trainers, shellsuits, tracksuits, baseball caps, chunky gold neck chains and earrings. Later, with the multi-nationalisation of soccer, came the legions of Rangers and Celtic shirts. The startling sartorial contrast between the youth of the 1990s and the early twenty-first century compared to the punk generation is the former's total uniformity. During the first two weeks of July every year between 1996 and 1999, I had to stand on either the hill at Drumcree, around the drab houses along Portadown's Garvaghy Road, or report from dangerous urban flashpoints such as Workman Avenue facing onto the republican Ardoyne in north Belfast. What always struck me about the knots of young men on either side of the police and army lines baying for each other's blood was how similarly dressed they were. They wore the same chains, the same sports gear, the same baseball caps and the same trainers. Even those with hair had the same crew-cut style, a spiky slash on top, the sides shaved to near-blue. The only item of clothing that marked them out as either P or RC were the Celtic and the Rangers tops.

The drive for uniformity, the imperative to wear the same designer sportswear and shoes, the dull conformity of their entire dress code, has created a vast army of spide lookalikes in working-class communities not only in Belfast or Derry but also across the British Isles. Although this is purely anecdotal, based on my own personal perceptions, individualism expressed either in dress or attitude in urban areas of Northern Ireland blighted by sectarianism is even rarer now than when the punks risked being beaten to a pulp in the murderous 1970s.

Academic research undertaken since the IRA and loyalist ceasefires demonstrates that most teenagers along the interfaces aspire to join the tribe rather than escape from it. The States of Fear project at the University of Ulster makes for depressing reading. Their surveys of young people from ten years of age have consistently shown that since 1994, the first year of relative peace, Protestant and Catholic youths have been moving further away from each other. Bigotry, according to one poll in 2000, was more virulent in the 16–25 age bracket than in any other age group interviewed by the UU researchers. This means that many teenagers in north and west Belfast who were still at primary school when the Provos, the UDA and UVF ended their dirty, squalid little wars detest the 'other side' far more than their parents and grandparents who actually lived through the worst days of the Troubles.

The drabness of Ulster youth and the tribalisation of those living in the poorest, most violent sectors of Northern society is a lethal combination, which one day could prove to be the undoing of the whole ten-year peace process project. There are many reasons why this has come about. There is the dearth of independent thought in music and popular culture; the rise of the boy-band phenomenon at the expense of the garage band; the hard-sell of the Celtic and Rangers product, which, whatever Celtic Park or Ibrox might protest, has become the new tribal identity-kit; the overall drive to dress identically to the next boy in the street instead of standing out in the crowd. To all this I would add another factor – the lack of an Alternative Ulster.

There are now two mutually exclusive tribal narratives in Northern

Ireland. Since the Good Friday Agreement we have been told we are unionist or nationalist, loyalist or republican. Depending on which 'story' you subscribe to, the Troubles was either a genocidal campaign conducted by the IRA to drive the Protestant people out of Ulster or a series of British-inspired atrocities against the nationalist people: Bombay Street, Internment, the Dublin/Monaghan bombs, the hunger strike, shoot-to-kill, Pat Finucane and Rosemary Nelson. Neither narrative is complex or morally multi-faceted. There is no room for the statistics of pain and death from the other side. In these parallel universes, educationally sub-normal and impressionable young men went out to bomb fish shops merely to defend their community, and bloodthirsty gangs sought out dozens of helpless victims to torture horribly because the perpetrators felt somehow 'under siege'. If you are raised with his kind of narrative, if that sense that you and only your own have been sinned against in this struggle is fed to you in your mother's milk, then it is hardly surprising that the new generation growing up in the most battle-hardened quarters of Northern Ireland are so eager to sign up to the tribe, to sink their individuality in a collective blur of tracksuit and trainers, to define themselves by the colours of the football top they are wearing. The tide of the spide therefore seems unstoppable.

Mercifully, however, there are still some young people in Northern Ireland who continue to swim against the spide-tide. The skateboarders, the goths and the neo-punks who gather around Belfast City Hall and other parts of the city centre after school and on Saturdays come from all sides of the community and every religious and class background. They have even found a new voice – a magazine called, what else, but *Alternative Ulster*. Copying the DIY philosophy of the original punks, even borrowing their magazine title from the name of the famous punk fanzine in the late 1970s, the founders of *Alternative Ulster* have invented a phrase that sums up the attitude of those teenagers who chose 'the third way', who, like our generation between 1977 and 1981, reject the tribal name tag attached to them. Shortly after its launch in 2003, the magazine's editors organised a concert with, among others, the Larne metal rockers Therapy?. Andy Cairns and co.'s most heartfelt performance on the night at Queen's University was a cover of SLF's 'Alternative Ulster'.

John Tierney, one of the editors of *Alternative Ulster,* defines this attitude as 'informed apathy'. Just prior to the November 2002 elections to the Stormont Assembly, I visited the *Alternative Ulster* office, which is located above a coffee shop in Wellington Place. I wanted to ask them if the 12,000 people aged between 16 and 25 who read their magazine cared at all about the electoral contest aimed at restoring power-sharing government to the Province.

'None of the people who read our magazine are interested in the elections because they don't like the idea of being labelled one thing or the other,' John admitted.

His co-editor Phil Crossey agreed that 'informed apathy' was the order of the day but still saw hope in the city's revived music scene.

'The scene in Belfast is probably the only place left where sectarianism is left outside the door. No one gives a damn about people's religion or politics.'

As for the election itself, Phil was candid: 'Almost all of our readers are more concerned about where the next big gig is.'

A couple of days later, those who did bother to vote elected an extremely polarised Assembly, with the extremes on either side, Sinn Féin and Ian Paisley's Democratic Unionist Party (DUP), supplanting the more moderate SDLP and Ulster Unionists as the leading forces in their respective camps. The outcome merely reflected the wider divisions opening up in Northern society. In that same autumn, for instance, the two largest political societies at Queen's University Belfast were also Sinn Féin and the DUP. Those unaffected by 'informed apathy', those driven by sectarian politics, went out and made it official: Northern Ireland is now more divided than when it was at war!

Who then can blame the followers of the new *Alternative Ulster* for their indifference? For their apathy is indeed informed. Apart from a few notable exceptions – Mark Langhammer in east Antrim, Davy Kettyles in Enniskillen or Eamon McCann in Derry to mention just three examples – there were no major socialist or radical alternatives for those belonging to the third way to cast their vote for. Moreover, the make-up of the Assembly itself, with no socialist parties represented and the sectarian voting blocs solidified, demonstrates little cause for hope in conventional politics.

The fact that *Alternative Ulster* has thrived since its creation in the summer of 2003 is one bright spot in an otherwise bleak cultural landscape. Although much more professionally produced than the original cut-and-paste punk fanzine from the '70s, the magazine's message is the same. Nor is it just a coincidence that the most important iconoclastic writer to emerge in Northern Ireland over the last five years is also a contributor and editorial board member of *Alternative Ulster*.

Newton Emerson burst onto the national and international media scene four years ago through his satirical website www.portadown news.com. A native of the north Armagh town that has become synonymous with the Drumcree dispute, the annual Orange marching season, violence and bigotry, Emerson relentlessly satirises Ulster's politicians, church leaders and opinion formers. Emerson unconsciously moves in the spirit of Ulster punk but, rather than spit and snarl, he deploys humour and cheek to kick against the pricks. He, too, is positive about the DIY spirit of this post-punk generation in Belfast.

'What impressed me about the magazine is it's not afraid to be intelligent. We haven't seen this kind of thing in a long time. They don't wait for government grants to be helped. They did it for themselves. It gives a voice to people the conventional media don't go looking for.'

If there is hope for an 'Alternative Ulster' it surely lies with this band of the youth population who, like us in the 1970s, refuse to be classified by accident of birth. The problem lies with mobilising this broad swathe of young people disgusted with the mainstream sectarian politics and the increasing tribalism of their society. They are essentially fiercely individualistic and autonomous. *Pace*, the far left, their very individualism makes it difficult, perhaps even impossible, to mobilise collectively. Therein lies the principal challenge for progressives in Northern Ireland. How to unite this disparate, anti-political, anarchic collection of potential voters behind some new coalition to challenge the sectarian power blocs of our society.

In the same month as the last Assembly elections, there took place another event that had much more relevance and meaning to the lives of thousands who survived the Troubles intact. On Thursday evening, 6 November 2003, Guy Trelford and Sean O'Neill (aka Seany Rotten) officially launched their written homage to Ulster punk *It Makes You Want To Spit*.

Inside the Belle Epoque-style grandeur of The Empire pub's upper dance floor in Belfast's university area, there were many reunions between former band members, old punks and even the odd Teddy boy. There were bear hugs and firm handshakes at the bar, meetings of old friends with the backdrop of John T. Davis's *Shellshock Rock* – the movie that captured Ulster punk's spirit in 1979 – playing on several large screens strategically placed around the theatre. There were also sequences from Davis's later film, when for Terry Hooley he documented the two Ulster punk festivals of 1979 and 1980 held at the Ulster Hall. Suddenly there was a picture of the New York punk band The Stimulators, and I was transported back 23 years to a hot, sweaty concert at The Pound, which ended with a then tender-aged teenager snogging Mercedes, the Stimulators' bass player who was then in her 30s and the aunt of the group's 13-year-old drummer Harley. Somewhere in a black binbag up in my mother's attic there is a postcard from the Big Apple dated Christmas 1980 with Mercedes signing off 'Love Ya' and a tiny red heart glued to the card at the bottom.

I was wrestled to the ground by Paul Burgess, whom I hadn't seen in nearly ten years, whilst Hooley ambushed his former customers at the door with a video camera. Hooley, a man to whom Belfast and Northern Ireland owe so much, asked the old greying and balding punks what the '77 to '81 experience meant to them.

Guy and Sean's seminal piece of social history was launched in the same month as a new book about Johnny Adair and his cohorts in 'C Company'. Although *Mad Dog* is a fine piece of journalistic investigation, it contains one jarring mistake, as the authors refer to Adair's Offensive Weapon as a punk band. So, when Hooley stuck the camera into my face I went off on a booze-fuelled tangent about Offensive Weapon.

'They weren't a punk band at all. They stood for everything the punks were against. They were racist and sectarian while we were anti-sectarian, anti-racist, radical,' I barked passionately into the lens.

And with that counterblast I was gone, off to a birthday celebration in downtown Belfast at the John Hewitt pub, a bar run by a workers' collective (another throwback to the spirit of punk?) from the Centre for the Unemployed. I slipped out of the gig at The Empire like a thief in the night, before the old bands like Outcasts and Ruefrex even got to the stage.

As the evening drew to a close, I stumbled on the tiled floor outside the toilets and fell painfully on my left arm. A night of punk nostalgia ended in the accident and emergency department of Belfast City Hospital. This stumble and the subsequent hours spent in casualty was perhaps some form of weird karma, payback time for not trusting my earlier instincts and staying the course of Guy and Sean's book launch. I should have stayed with 'my people', some of the best people to emerge from this still bitterly divided society, people who broke the sectarian taboos and refused to be classified as simply P or RC, who proved there was another life far beyond the narrow confines of orange and green.

CHAPTER THREE

The Last Walls of Europe

My aunt Peggy is living proof of the power of love and the possibility of reconciliation. On 8 March 1943, my grandfather Henry died after the merchant navy ship on which he was working sank in the Atlantic, another victim of Admiral Dönitz's grey wolves, the submariners in the U-boats who were seeking to starve Britain into submission during the Second World War. Peggy was only four, my father just three at the time of the tragedy. My father was left with only fleeting memories of his own father – as the man who sang 'Harbour Lights' the night before he set off on his final fated voyage and promised his son that he was only going on a 'wee boat' rather than a big one.

Just over 20 years later, Peggy emigrated to work in West Germany and soon met the love of her life, Fred Schmidt, a mild-mannered Rhinelander whose own family had suffered unbearable deprivations during the war. History, memory, personal loss, national differences all meant nothing to the couple who had fallen in love. Their story is an individual metaphor for the success of post-1945 Western Europe, of its ability to regenerate through forgiveness, of the necessity to move on, of the imperative to become unchained from the past.

In 1974, with the Troubles at their height, Peggy returned home for the first time since emigrating, going to stay at her mother's house in

Reilly's Place, a cul-de-sac backing onto Belfast's gasworks, a time capsule of the city's Victorian past with its gas lamps and cobblestones. On the day she arrived, Peggy distributed presents among her many nephews and nieces. My sister Cathy and our cousin Jennifer each received cute little clockwork German dancing dolls with blonde pleats and traditional Bavarian dresses. The boys got toy guns and packets of German sweets. I was disappointed, however. Although I adored weapons, plastic tanks, model aeroplanes and soldiers, there was one thing I wanted her to bring me from Germany above all else: a picture of the Berlin Wall.

Ever since I had seen my first spy film (the black-and-white version of John Le Carré's *The Spy Who Came in From the Cold* starring Richard Burton) I was fascinated with the Wall. The desire to see it chimed with an obsession for marking out territory on a geo-political basis.

It had all started in my house, with battles arranged around imaginary occupied and disputed land. The Soviets were holed up in a wooden chest in our living room – Stalingrad; the Germans defending the mantelpiece from fireplace to the candlesticks – the Reichstag; British commandos laid out along the stairs, strategically positioned on each step – which in my imagination became the mountains of Crete. Borders and territory even led to the creation of two imaginary states: Starta and Chinchilla, one communist, the other capitalist. They were the inventions of Liam Murray and myself in the winter of 1975, when we decided to stage a war in his grandmother's living room in Joy Street. And as every war needs two competing states, thus we created Starta and Chinchilla, and spent a rainy afternoon invading, conquering or ceding territory to each other using Airfix planes and tanks, and legions of inch-high troops. Exhausted after the plastic slaughter, and having reached stalemate, we ended the day with a peace treaty, which Liam drew up on a school exercise book and included the red star of Starta and the crossed swords of Chinchilla.

Maps also mattered to me. They evoked dreams of faraway exotic places like the rainforests of Brazil, where I retreated in my imagination during a pilgrimage with my mother and sister to Lourdes in June '75. Inside our chalet in the Cité de Secours at the foot of the Pyrenees, I escaped into my imagination once again, picturing myself as an explorer mapping out unknown corners of the Amazon. Maps also taught me about the divisions in my own prosaic, grey city. The crudely drawn outlines of Belfast, with their Orange and Green zones, and the letters 'P' and 'RC' in books and newspaper articles covering the early Troubles, also became an obsession. Boundaries and interfaces filled me with morbid fascination. I can still remember being intrigued when hearing about places like Hooker Street and Manor Street, where Catholics were outnumbered and surrounded on the sectarian front line. In the Markets, we were insulated from these divides; our only border being the upper end of Cromac Street with the Donegall Pass lurking just behind a row of pubs, shops and the city's commercial gas store. The sharp end of sectarianism was elsewhere.

Peggy never sent the picture of that Berlin Wall I had asked her for. Yet seven years after her trip back to Belfast I got to see the Wall for myself. It first emerged as the green East German train snaked its way through West Berlin towards the Reichstag and on to the internal border cutting the city into two geo-ideological halves. I pulled down the top end of the window of our carriage and gazed out across the lawn of the pre-war parliament illuminated in the night with orange lights, the red, gold and black flag of the Federal Republic hanging limply from the pole on the Reichstag roof. After we passed through the Tiergarten, in a matter of minutes we were at the Wall itself, with its watchtowers, spotlights, border guards, barbed wire and then not one but two barriers: the first a smaller construct, the graffiti-covered western Wall; and then, beyond a track of no man's land known the world over as 'the death strip', stood the taller, more imposing eastern Wall – the 'anti-fascist' barrier as the official propaganda of the state called it in this the year of its 20th anniversary.

Our passage through the Wall was uneventful and ended at the Friedrichstrasse border station, where our delegation of 12 idealistic young Marxists, a mixture of students and former Fianna boys and girls, were greeted by a smiling, thin-faced and bearded apparatchik from the Free German Youth or FDJ, the junior wing of the Socialist Unity Party of Germany (SED). For boys like me, surrounded back at home by the tomes of Marxist-Leninism and the iconography of communism, even this dark, sinister station with its armed guards rifling through the luggage of the other visitors to the 'capital of the GDR' felt oddly like home. Enormous red banners were draped from the station's roof along with the East German flag, the same red, gold and black horizontal band of colours as the Federal Republic, but with a coat of arms showing a hammer and compass in a ring of rye, symbolising the working class, intelligentsia and farmers.

It had been a long, taxing and at times precarious journey, starting from Dublin the previous day then progressing through Britain, across the North Sea to Hoek van Holland and on to Berlin. On the way, we encountered drunken British squaddies on the voyage from Harwich, some of whom, such as a party of Welsh cadets, were friendly, while others were menacing and threatening, muttering darkly about 'murdering Paddy bastards'. It was lucky for us that their officers saved the day. But for the latter's intervention during a bad-tempered poker game in the ship's bar, several of the older members of our delegation could have been beaten to a pulp.

The atmosphere on this bizarre trip got even weirder when we boarded our train at the Dutch port. Into my carriage stepped a diminutive British soldier returning from home leave in Liverpool. I suspect he joined our little group when he saw us cracking open a bottle of Paddy Whiskey that we had originally planned to give our East German hosts. The only other 'outsider' to enter the carriage on the 12-hour ride east was a West German mathematics teacher whose dark features and wild unkempt beard made him appear more like an Orthodox Jew than a member of the Teutonic race.

Necking down our whiskey, the squaddie regaled us with tales of his tours of duty in Belfast. He had been billeted in the North Howard Street army base, a disused mill on the 'border' between the Falls and Shankill roads. Like us, he too knew all about dangerous frontiers and violent interfaces. The soldier told us he had driven Saracens and jeeps along the Falls during some of the worst of the riots in the early Troubles. Compared to service with the British Army of the Rhine (BAOR), Belfast for him was a thrill. He admitted that he had learnt his rioting skills engaging with young republicans in west Belfast. As the Paddy bottle emptied, he even confessed (or was it just boasting?) that he had taken part in the Toxteth riots during his home leave.

On our train journey eastwards, our token German in the carriage awarded the army driver hero-status. The mathematics teacher thanked the soldier in clipped English for protecting West Germany from communism, a jibe no doubt directed at us. He then went to the bar on the train and bought the squaddie a beer and a box of malted biscuits. For most of trip he then sat in silence playing with a Rubik's Cube. Near the end, the Scouser cheekily asked the German if he would buy him another drink. When his benefactor left for the bar, the squaddie winked at us, poured a glass of water we had used to thin out the whiskey over the Rubik's Cube and then started to peel off the colours. When the cube was bare black, the soldier stuck each face with a single colour code before the mathematician returned to our compartment. The second he came in, the German was astonished as the soldier held the cube aloft in triumph. 'I think you are a genius,' the mathematician gasped.

When they both left the train at Hanover, we were relieved to be rid of them but also slightly puzzled. For all the soldier knew, we could have been a unit of IRA activists posing as a student peace group on our way to carry out a campaign of murder and sabotage directed at the BAOR. Some of my companions, the Belfast ones anyway, certainly had experience in the early to mid-1970s of attacking the British Army with abuse, bottles and stones. After all, we belonged to the Irish Democratic Youth Movement (IDYM), the junior wing of Sinn Féin, the Workers Party, the old Official Republican Movement that had eschewed armed struggle and nationalism for democratic politics and Marxism.

Back at home, it was the summer of bumfluffed wannabe-martyrs. Many of my peers in the Markets donned army jackets and sprouted tufts of hair from their chins; they were growing up fast amid the chaos of nightly riots and daily demonstrations. Che Guevara also made a comeback, his iconic image stencilled onto jeans and Wrangler jackets along with badges of Bobby Sands in that famous black-and-white photograph complete with the legend: 'His name will live forever'. Early on in the hunger strike, I decided to rebel from this death-cult chic. I recoiled from the black flags and the armbands and the nightly rosaries and the cross-eyed Jesus-like character clutching a pair of prayer beads while the Virgin Mary beamed golden rays into the prisoners' cells from one of the earliest murals of west Belfast on the Falls Road.

In response, I joined the IDYM while still at St Malachy's College, having been impressed that at least one of Ireland's legion of left-wing parties was actually standing against the H-Block tide. A friend in

Dublin had also sent me up a copy of *The Irish Industrial Revolution*, though I only understood bits of it fully at that time. This seminal revisionist document, which laid the blame for tragedies such as the Potato Famine as much at the door of the Irish Catholic bourgeoisie as the British, shattered any remaining nationalist illusions that I still harboured. The ground-breaking arguments in *The Irish Industrial Revolution* coincided with the 'new' history being taught in relation to Ireland, a subject I was passionate about at school. This fresh, non-dogmatic and unemotional approach to the Irish question was later adopted by my A level history teacher Gerry McKeown, who championed it in the sixth form. Then there was the Newry trade unionist Tom Moore standing alone in the middle for the Workers Party/Republican Clubs in the Fermanagh/South Tyrone by-election, ranged against none other than Bobby Sands – in my mind the unpopular, but still the right, place to be. Within a matter of weeks of signing up I was informed that I had been chosen as part of the student delegation to Germany, although at this stage I didn't know that they actually meant the 'other Germany', the one beyond the Iron Curtain and the Wall.

Life for us behind the 'anti-fascist barrier' was conducted in a carefully controlled but not unpleasant bubble. We were insulated from ordinary East Germans, given that we were staying in an international youth camp near Kopenick in Berlin's eastern suburbs. Our daily regime involved getting up at 6 a.m., being collected in East German army trucks and taken to the Moscow to Berlin railway line, where, every day for four weeks, we dug up old kilometre stones and replaced them with brand-new ones. Each night on our return, we held parties in the 'Irish' tent, where crates of cheap beer were guzzled down and songs were sung well into the early hours, often accompanied by the dawn chorus.

The camp was under the supervision of the FDJ (and no doubt the Stasi's eyes and ears) and quickly became a hive of hedonism and bed-hopping. It felt like an international Olympic Village. Directly in front of our tent was a smaller one containing two Vietnamese soldiers who would play badminton against one another every morning before the work brigades departed. Two tents across from the Irish HQ were the Spaniards, who were divided into a myriad of squabbling leftist factions from the hard-line Stalinists of Catalonia to the

Eurocommunists from Madrid. There were also Russians, Bulgarians, Czechs and Mongolians. The Polish delegation, however, went home early after going on strike in solidarity with Solidarity. Then, of course, there were the East Germans themselves, including our minders, the nervous, bumbling but sweet and genial Jurgen from Erfurt and the fat comedian Winny, the latter of whom I am now convinced was a Stasi watcher.

We were as far away from the Wall as our minders could send us. Only once, when I slipped the leash from the official discos and after-gig piss-ups on camp, did I confront an ordinary East German about the armed frontier penning them into the 'first workers' and peasants' state on German soil'. I had fallen for a girl on our camp from Leipzig called Nelli. She had Asiatic features, with high cheekbones and slightly slanted eyes that were the colour of black cherries. Nelli offered to take me for a night out in Berlin, to the Palace of the Republic, a GDR Disneyland which staged discos and gymnastic displays as well as housing the state parliament. The Palace was packed with young Berliners dancing to Smokie records, a band that were still very popular in the GDR that year judging by the number of their T-shirts that were being worn. As I wanted to be alone with her, I suggested we head instead for dinner in the restaurant up in the globe of the giant television tower that still dominates the East Berlin skyline. Over dessert, I remember noticing Nelli staring out through the glass dome to the Brandenburg Gate, to the golden angel on top of the victory column in the Tiergarten and behind it, the three-pointed symbol of Mercedes Benz, the ultimate icon of West German capitalism. I asked her if she wondered what life was like on the western side of that border. She turned her head away from the window and looked at me, wondering if I was setting a test for her, whether I would inform the 'comrades' back on camp if she happened to say the wrong thing. Nelli never answered my question. Only after the Wall came down and the whole edifice of 'actual existing socialism' collapsed in ignominy did I begin to understand her silence and her diffidence.

James Joyce called them epiphanies, spots of time in which a single incident reveals a wider truth about your overall life and the world around you. I experienced one such moment on my return to Berlin six years later, alone now, a freelance traveller riding the rails of Europe on a monthly student pass. While visiting friends in the West German border town of Saarbrucken, I got the urge to take a diversion from plans to tour around southern Europe and first revisit Berlin, that city where many rites of teenage passage had taken place in the summer of 1981.

I took the train to Hannover and joined the same East German locomotive with its familiar green carriages and that distinctive smell – a noxious mixture of leather and glue – making its way from the Dutch coast to the divided city. My companions this time around were a party of sullen German teenage heavy-metal fans who filled the carriage with hashish smoke throughout the entire journey; thanks to passive smoking, I got high for free.

After passing through the Iron Curtain at the Helmstedt/Marienborn crossing point, we were joined by a file of poker-faced GDR border guards, one of whom wrenched open our carriage door and immediately demanded five West German Deutschmarks from each of the passengers, claiming our transit visas were somehow not intact. He looked over this rabble of biker jackets and long unkempt hair then sniffed the air before holding out his hand in expectation of the hard currency. As he walked out of the carriage, I noticed that he had put the coins, totalling 20 Deutschmarks, into his back trouser pocket rather than the suitcase in which he was carrying official documents and the stamp that left the familiar GDR insignia on our passports. The real moment of revelation, however, the realisation that the game of communism was definitely up, occurred just as we coasted into Potsdam. To the right of watchtowers and armed guards on the railway station, and behind a fence with barbed wire running across its summit, were two volleyball teams. Our train was now crawling forward at a slow pace, so it was possible to stare out at the young men fisting and slapping the ball over the net. A number of them also stopped playing and stared while I waved. They waved back and then watched as our train disappeared eastwards, traversing the frontier again and on into the outer edge of West Berlin towards Wannsee and the prosperous suburbs of capitalist Charlottenburg. In that instant, I felt a frisson of guilt and shame. Three years earlier, I had come to the volleyball players' country for a 'cheap holiday in other people's misery', as the Sex Pistols' song 'Holidays in the Sun' had put it, oblivious to the fact that we were in fact visiting a vast prison camp, a paranoid state, a society run by a self-serving and hypocritical elite who thought they knew what was best for the workers and peasants. Now here I was making a brief sentimental journey, a two-day nostalgia-fest, to a country from which at any time I was free to escape. The volleyball teams behind the wire were not so fortunate. For them that summer there would be no tour of Italy, no island-hopping around the Aegean, no weekend pounding the pavements of Paris and London en route back to Northern Ireland.

Following three raucous drunken days in West Berlin, which ended with me staggering along the Ku'damm at one o'clock in the morning past a café near a sex shop, I was propositioned by what must surely have been a hooker, who asked in American English if I 'want to make love' (I didn't oblige!). I felt depressed that my return had ended so unsatisfactorily. The illusion of the justness of the communist cause and the necessity despite all the defects to support the Soviet bloc against 'Anglo-American imperialism', a peculiar form of what George Orwell had identified 40 years earlier as 'transferred nationalism', lay in ruins.

Yet there was something more here than just the realisation that the dream of socialism had turned into a nightmare for my contemporaries living behind the Wall. For the first time, I admitted to myself that I had been transfixed about the city of the Wall because I too came from a city of walls. It dawned on me while travelling by taxi from a guesthouse in Charlottenburg to the Zoo station, where I would catch a train back to Saarbrucken and ultimately south to Rome. The rotund bald-headed driver asked me in German where I came from and I replied, 'Belfast.' When he halted the car at traffic lights near the blackened stump of the Kaiser Wilhelm memorial, the elderly taxi man, incongruous in a blue Hawaiian-style shirt, searched for something in his glove department and, after rummaging around for a few seconds, pulled out a gun, a snub-nose .38 revolver. He waved the weapon about and I genuinely thought he was going to shoot me. But all he kept saying was, 'Belfast, Belfast, boom boom', as he drove through an unseasonably grey and wet July morning in Berlin.

Since those epiphanic three days in the mid-1980s, I have made many more visits back to Berlin. I was there just a few months after the Wall came down and the Cold War effectively ended. Just over a year later, I returned again as the first Gulf War broke out. On a freezing Saturday afternoon in February 1991, I sneaked away from yet another official delegation, this time a West German government junket for journalists to look around the reunified city. From my hotel close to the Tiergarten I had planned to walk through the Brandenburg Gate towards Unter Der Linden in the east and ultimately Alexanderplatz, where a mass demonstration was being held against the American-led war to eject Saddam Hussein's forces from Kuwait. Although I had wanted to link up with the procession from the east, I stopped myself around the victory column because I could go no further. Across the former East–West barrier the chants of the demonstrators were audible in the chilling winter air, the denunciations of American imperialism exactly the same as the mantras we once repeated ad infinitum with clenched fists raised to the sky in our camp near Kopenick ten years earlier, now punctuated in both German and English with cries of 'No blood for oil'. But I was no longer part of this grand march and I have been moving steadily away from it ever since.

On 10 September 1969, just under a month after the loyalist assault on Catholic homes along the invisible line between the Shankill and the Falls Road, the new General Officer Commanding of the British Army in Northern Ireland made a foolhardy prediction. Lieutenant-General Sir Ian Freeland's troops had been on the streets of Belfast since 14 August, after the torching of Catholic homes in Bombay Street, and had just completed the construction of a series of so-called 'peace lines', closing off routes between the Falls and Shankill, as well as a number of other streets in north Belfast where Catholic and Protestant areas intersected. 'The peace line will be a very, very temporary affair,' the GOC assured the world's media. 'We will not have a Berlin Wall or anything like that in this city.'

I first arrived in Berlin in 1981, just as the East German regime was organising a show of military and ideological strength to mark the Wall's 20th birthday; their barrier only lasted another eight years. The temporary peace line, as Sir Ian called it back at the genesis of the modern Ulster Troubles, has now outlasted the Berlin Wall by seven years. Our wall, or to be more accurate walls, are likely to reach their half-century and perhaps endure even beyond that depressing birthday.

There are obvious differences between the 26 mini Berlin Walls that separate people into sectarian cantons in Belfast and that ultimate symbol of the Cold War. The Berlin Wall was universally loathed on either side of it. The first chance the people got to tear it down, especially those living in the eastern section, they did so with a gleeful rapidity. With few exceptions, the walls of Belfast are regarded as a necessary evil, a last barrier of defence to protect mutually suspicious communities from one another. So there are no border guards permanently patrolling a death strip of no man's land between any of Belfast's barriers. There are no dogs, no tanks, no watchtowers, no mines and no booby traps. The one recent addition to the Belfast peace lines that in part perhaps resembles the Big Brother state apparatus around the Berlin Wall are the spy cameras contained inside impenetrable black glass, which are located at certain interfaces and can beam back pictures to police stations alerting them to trouble erupting on the line. But, again, these hi-tech added extras to Belfast's sectarian borders have been placed there because of popular demand rather than the orders of a paranoid, undemocratic clique. Finally, the walls of Belfast do not physically cut the city into two neat sectors the way Berlin was carved up from August 1961 to November 1989. The majority, bar two, are to be found on the northern side of the River Lagan, and are scattered only across north and west Belfast. On maps of the city, they appear as a series of disconnected thick black lines that come to abrupt ends at various locations, like some sign denoting elevation on an Ordnance Survey map. To those who don't live near them, especially the population in affluent south Belfast, the walls are somebody else's problem. It is possible to live in Belfast and never see the interface barriers that scar the poorer parts of the city.

The most abnormal thing of all, however, about the walls of Belfast is that virtually no one thinks of them as abnormal anymore. While Berlin became defined by its Wall for 28 years, the peace lines have attracted far less international attention or debate. Nor have they become the defining symbols of Belfast for the last 35 years. The fact that only one book – Frankie Quinn's stark but remarkable photo-essay from 1994 – has been published about our walls is evidence of this. Quinn's *Interface Images*, originally published in the year of the IRA's first ceasefire, opens with a black-and-white panoramic shot of Belfast. The opening wide shot captures the 'peace wall' made from one million bricks that separates Catholic Springfield Park in west Belfast from Protestant Springmartin. Laid out below the barrier is the skyline of Belfast, with its familiar twin yellow cranes, a couple of skyscrapers and the spiky spires of Protestant and Catholic churches poking through the gloom.

Some of Quinn's black-and-white portraits contain that same sense of claustrophobia conveyed in the images of communities in West Berlin that were once contiguous with their Wall – of normal lives being lived literally at the edge of a world. There is a particularly poignant picture of teachers and children outside St Gall's Primary School, which lies right up against the Cupar Street barrier, one of the walls that most resembles its defunct equivalent in Berlin. The Catholic boys are leaving school, laughing and smiling, seemingly oblivious to the huge barrier behind them. Quinn illuminates further the paranoid atmosphere of life along the walls through images of homes covered with protective wiring and grilles, which even create a 'roof' over their back yards – all permanent shields to prevent homes right beside the Cupar Street wall from bricks, bottles and petrol bombs being hurled from the other side.

Children are the main subjects of Quinn's project, with several shots of kids playing around the interfaces, including one of a young boy crouched in a pool of fetid water right up against the Cupar Street wall, obviously on the Catholic side given the faded outline of 'IRA' daubed on the peace line. There is also a touching wide shot capturing a line of pubescent boys pressed up against the wall in Alliance Avenue, a street separating the Catholic Ardoyne from the loyalist Glenbryn area. They stand in hope rather than expectation. Quinn explains that their ball had just been kicked over into the Protestant side. The boys wait in vain for someone across the line to throw it back over; the ball, of course, is never returned. Another image shows a young boy wearing adult-sized sunglasses, a jumper pulled over his face to make him look like a masked man and holding a piece of rifle-shaped wood in his hands. Behind him lies one of the walls.

The one weakness of this otherwise important piece of photojournalism is the tendentious foreword by the writer and former republican prisoner Ronan Bennett. In his introduction, Bennett blames the existence of the walls solely on the British, saying, 'The peace lines are, in every sense, a British creation. The presence of one is inextricably linked to the presence of the other.'

His implication seems to be that if and when the Brits leave Northern Ireland, then somehow the walls of Belfast will crumble and those on the loyalist side will abandon their 'false consciousness' (to borrow an old Marxist phrase) and become true Irishmen and women. This observation at the very least is naive and at worst deliberately misleading. For does anyone really believe that if power was transferred to a Dublin administration tomorrow, that the walls could start to come down? Anyone who has spent time tracking the growth of the peace lines over the last three decades knows that in that scenario there would be almost immediate and violent pressure, initially at least from the Protestant side, for even more barriers to be constructed as part of a rapid grab for ethnically pure territory.

Frankie Quinn's largely neglected but historically significant work was photographed before the IRA and loyalist cessations, when there were 16 walls cutting through the patchwork of sectarian borders in the city. His last image points depressingly to a future of further division: the laying of foundations for a new peace wall on the Springfield Road, which was finally completed in exactly the same week as the IRA announced its ceasefire. There are now 10 more peace walls of different shape, size and material. Meanwhile, the other original 16 have been fortified and extended, turning them into near-permanent structures.

The most haunting image of all in Quinn's collection is of a solitary bare tree standing in front of a metallic barrier along Duncairn Gardens. This 'dead street' between the nationalist New Lodge and the loyalist Tigers Bay areas reminds me, particularly at night, of those old ghost streets of East Berlin, those Strasses and Allees that simply ran out at the Wall, which the GDR authorities had left deliberately empty to create enough space in order to prevent their citizens from gazing across into the affluent West. Duncairn Gardens – Belfast's very own ghost street – is an appropriate place to begin a tour of the 26 peace lines.

9 March 2000: a cold and grey mid-morning on the cusp of spring. My travelling companion is my mother's youngest brother, who has not visited north Belfast for more than 20 years. Nor has Uncle John seen any peace line since the Troubles started. He can remember the first barriers being erected in the streets linking his native Lower Falls to the Shankill in 1969; the hastily built corrugated iron barricades and the reams of barbed wire stretched across the routes between the two most infamous roads in Northern Ireland. Nothing in his memory, however, can prepare him for what he is about to see.

John cannot recall if he has ever been to Duncairn Gardens, which, after dark, is one of the most dangerous streets in the city. There are seven separate walls/barriers cutting off the nationalist New Lodge from loyalist Tigers Bay in this one thoroughfare. They vary in shape, size and form. Some are decorative red-brick walls, others are constructed from steel, the same colour as the protective fencing built around military bases across the Province.

A two-minute drive up Duncairn Gardens and we turn right along the Antrim Road and then veer right again away from the local police station on the other side to the entrance to Alexandra Park. Uncle John has vivid memories of day trips to the park as a boy, when the Antrim Road was home to the prosperous and the well heeled. When we stroll on to raised ground, the quarter-of-a-mile-long security fence separating the park into Catholic and Protestant green spaces comes into view. John is visibly taken back by the vista. He stands gawping at the reinforced 30-foot barricade cutting through the park from a street adjacent to the now defunct Dunmore dog track and stretching out towards Mount Collyer Street and yet another invisible border on Limestone Road.

The peace-line-in-the-park is a permanent structure strengthened with steel sheeting welded into thick beams laid in the ground. On the Catholic side, the graffiti belongs to the republican dissidents: 'CIRA', 'Brits Out' and 'The Provos are sell-outs'. On that section of the wall, close to a local bowling club, there is a fringe of barbed wire to stop youths from either side clambering over the barrier. The park is empty today and the only noises are the metallic twittering of a huge magpie pecking the ground near a charred tree set on fire in a wanton act of vandalism and the hammering of workmen building a cluster of new houses just across in the loyalist zone.

Uncle John seems overwhelmed by what I have brought him to see. He shakes his head as we walk the entire length of the barrier. 'Imagine if kids come into this park and see that monstrosity. It will be burned on their wee brains forever. They'll be asking their mothers and fathers about that wall all the time,' he says.

We leave Alexandra Park and head north up along the Antrim Road until we reach the outer perimeter of Belfast Zoo before turning right down the Serpentine Road, a narrow route that winds all the way down from the slopes of Cavehill Mountain to the shoreline of Belfast Lough.

Midway along the road from mountain to lough lies one of the newest of the peace walls in the city. The barrier erected at the end of 1999 keeps apart the communities of the loyalist White City estate from mainly Catholic Whitewell. The wall here is the most unusual of all the 26 barriers across Belfast. All the other mini-borders, with the exception of Alexandra Park, are located in the poorest parts of the city, whereas the wall at the White City/Whitewell interface is based in a typically lower- to middle-class area of private semi-detached housing. What was once seen as a desirable part of north Belfast for the aspirant working class to relocate to is now a private version of a 'sink estate'. Six out of the eight semis closest to the White City/Whitewell barrier display 'For Sale' signs in their front gardens. Directly across the road, three shops and three houses are boarded up, all their windows covered with brown-coloured metal grilles. In any other British or Irish city, houses like these would fetch between £100,000 to £200,000 on the property market. But the owners of these homes beside this latest sectarian borderline have been unable to sell and move on. They are trapped, as much prisoners of history as those living along the traditional flashpoints between the Falls and Shankill.

From the youngest of the walls we head back towards the city centre and on ultimately to some of the oldest frontline barriers. We pass from north to west Belfast via Manor Street in the Lower Oldpark area. In the 1970s, Manor Street was the focal point of fear. It was the location of apocryphal stories of sectarian savagery such as the tale about a Catholic teenager caught by a Protestant gang while walking along Manor Street late at night. The legend goes that the loyalists leapt on their victim, held him down and then used a nutcracker to squash his testicles. Maybe the story is true, maybe not, but the net effect was to create an atmosphere of threat and danger around this half-empty ghost street.

Out of Manor Street, Uncle John drives us through the Shankill, crossing the peace line back onto the Falls at Northumberland Street, a no man's land of business parks, small factories and warehouses where his late sister Margaret used to work back in the early 1970s. This borderland is the reason why I have taken John with me on this day-long tour of the city's 26 walls. Before the Troubles erupted in August 1969, the McManus family thought nothing of traversing the line between the Falls and Shankill every week. My maternal grandmother,

Florence Stewart, was a Shankill Road woman who married Geordie McManus, a radio and television engineer from the Catholic Lower Falls. As John and I double-back along the Falls and cross into the Shankill through North Howard Street (the place where our Scouser soldier was billeted in the '70s), my uncle recalls his own grandmother, Mary Stewart, who stayed on the Shankill side even after her daughter 'defected' to the Falls. When our car halts at the Cupar Street wall, the highest barrier in the city and the one that resembles more than any other the Berlin Wall, John gazes towards a group of houses in the Middle Shankill.

'See that place over there?' he points. 'That's where your great-granny used to live. I can remember walking from the Falls every week before the Troubles to her house in the Shankill. It was a normal thing to do, you never thought twice about doing it.' The wind is now howling up the road running parallel to the wall. Is it the biting cold or the memories of an arcadian childhood that have caused John's eyes to water?

To follow my uncle's footsteps today would be regarded as foolhardy, possibly suicidal. There are children and teenagers growing up on either side of this barrier who never have and probably never will cross this particular frontier. Uncle John belongs to the last generation that once thought it perfectly normal to move through the streets from the Falls to the Shankill, routes that are now almost all permanently sealed off.

The Cupar Street wall has become a tourist trap for curious foreigners on their history tours around the divided city. Mimicking the graffiti artists of pre-1989 West Berlin, they have left their mark along the steel and concrete 'curtain' that cuts off the Lower Falls from the Shankill. The statements they have made are touching and naive.

'You are the children of tomorrow, don't hang on your yesterdays' (Germany); 'Jesus loves you regardless of which side of the wall you're on' (written in both English and Welsh); 'Live in peaceful unity' (Berlin). And my personal favourite of all from Houston, Texas: 'Pray until something happens'.

Driving north on the road running parallel to the wall, we eventually come out onto Lanark Way, a favourite escape route for the killers of Johnny 'Mad Dog' Adair's 'C Company' from the Lower Shankill after they had committed murder and mayhem along the Falls and

Springfield roads. As we turn away from the wall and back into republican west Belfast, there are other more truculent messages directly to our left. One at the junction of Lanark Way and the Springfield Road, written large for the benefit of Rangers fans on the Protestant side, reads: 'Celts 2 – Scum 0'.

Our journey takes us past the other peace walls constructed at the time of the 1994 IRA ceasefire, running alongside Workman Avenue, a barrier through which the Protestants only emerge once a year for the annual Orange Order march along the Springfield Road. We pass by the gargantuan, heavily fortified police station that also acts as a buffer zone between Catholic Springfield Park and loyalist Springmartin, and then on to the wall of one million bricks dividing the two areas.

Finally, we cross Belfast again via Blacks Road through the Suffolk estate, the last Protestant bastion in republican Andersonstown, on to the M1 motorway, into the city centre and eventually across the River Lagan and into east Belfast towards the latest wall to be built. It is tucked away from one of the main routes into the eastern end of the city, in a cul-de-sac off the Albertbridge Road. Cluan Place is an L-shaped street that runs into the Catholic Short Strand, itself a besieged enclave in predominantly loyalist east Belfast.

Cluan Place has become a siege-within-a-siege ever since sectarian rioting broke out in the summer of 2001. Republicans in the Short Strand blamed UVF-aligned youths for the trouble, claiming they had started the conflict which was to rage on for several months. Loyalists, on the other hand, claimed the violence was republican-inspired and designed to draw local nationalists into street battles with the newly formed Police Service of Northern Ireland (PSNI), which in turn would cause embarrassment and electoral damage to Sinn Féin's rivals, the SDLP, the latter party having just taken up their seats on the North's Policing Board.

Regardless of the genesis of this localised conflict, the result has been the creation of another giant wall, in this case towering over homes on either side of Cluan Place. When John and I arrive in the area, our presence is immediately noted. The curtains in a number of houses twitch and eventually a middle-aged man comes to the door to ask us if anything is wrong. When we tell him we are here to see the wall, he seems to understand and replies: 'You are very welcome.' The residents are clearly used to the sight of tourists in Cluan Place. People here have left out old beds, cookers and washing machines from homes that have been abandoned because of repeated attacks with bricks, bottles, stones, petrol bombs and even bullets coming from the other side. Uncle John asks the man at the door if there has been any trouble today. The Cluan Place resident checks his watch and answers: 'No, not yet, it's too early.'

Cluan Place's peace wall is now as permanent as the one in Alexandra Park. But it is the latter, of all the 26 barriers, which is the most potent symbol of sectarian separation in Belfast, where even green spaces, trees, a stream, the swings, the slides and the roundabouts cannot be shared. Moreover, its birthdate is loaded with historical resonance. The foundations for the fence that cuts Alexandra Park in two were laid down on 1 September 1994, just 24 hours into the IRA's first ceasefire. I came here on that same day, while the world's media was descending on Belfast to record the fledgling peace and with it all the hope that a lasting settlement could be found in this small troubled corner of the planet. The major national and international news organisations gathered on the Falls and Andersonstown roads to film Gerry Adams addressing republican supporters while Sinn Féin activists drove around in triumphalist cavalcades, waving Irish Tricolours around in celebration, thus forging an early myth that the IRA had actually won something by ending their violent campaign. A smaller number of reporters crossed the peace lines to the Shankill, in order to capture the fears and suspicions of unionists, who, initially at least, believed that the IRA must have secured some sort of clandestine deal with the British government behind the Protestants' backs, otherwise why would the IRA give up? None of the press corps and news networks bothered to notice what was going on at Alexandra Park and the long-term importance of what the new barrier would represent, none that is except this writer. BBC *Breakfast News* had commissioned a short report from me about the park on 1 September, but on a day when even the most hardened journalists were caught up in the euphoria over the ceasefire, virtually no one wanted to hear about the one core problem that would endanger the peace process and throw an eventual historic compromise between unionism and nationalism into near-terminal crisis – sectarian division.

The peace-line-in-the-park is now ten years old, the exact same age as the Provos' cessation. While there appears to be little chance of the

IRA going back to a full-blown armed campaign, there is even less likelihood that the barrier through Alexandra Park or any of the other 25 peace lines will come down in the foreseeable future. They have all become permanent fixtures of life for those who reside on the sharp edge of Belfast's divided quarters.

Between June and July 2003, my oldest daughter experienced what life is like for those unfortunate enough to live next to the interfaces. Up until then she had been insulated from the realities of bigotry and division in her native city. Lauren, then aged six, was chosen to act out the character of Aoife in the BBC drama *Holy Cross*, a fictional but close-to-life account of the violent stand-off outside a north Belfast Catholic girls' school in 2001. Following clashes at the end of term outside the school involving loyalists from the Protestant Glenbryn area and Catholics from Ardoyne, protests and pickets were held along the road leading to Holy Cross. The loyalists, sensing a chance to cut off their area from what they saw as republican encroachment from Ardoyne, staged demonstrations outside the school both at the end of term and then from the beginning of the new school year in September. The disgraceful scenes outside Holy Cross, with grown men hurling abuse and eventually bombs at young children, were beamed around the world; it was the biggest story from Northern Ireland since the Good Friday Agreement was signed in 1998.

Holy Cross captured those disturbing events by focusing on two families from either side of the line. Lauren's story came into sharper focus when she started her first day at school, which also happened to be one of the worst days of the actual loyalist protest, when hardcore pornographic magazines were waved in the children's faces and balloons of piss were lobbed at mothers walking their kids to the school. All of this actually happened. I should know because I was there reporting on the real-life events on the Ardoyne Road in the autumn of 2001. Never could I have imagined that within two years my own child would be acting out these scenes for a television drama. Nor was I to know that this would be Lauren's first introduction to Ulster's sectarian divide.

When the film was first screened back in the autumn of 2003 for a selected audience of cast and crew, I noticed that there were tears in my wife's eyes as we sat in the cinema watching our child on screen. The young actresses beside us, however, were oblivious to the depressing theme that the screenwriter Tony Caffula had explored: namely that the bigots are always with us. The girls, including Lauren, sat around giggling, slurping Coke and flicking popcorn at each other during the film. Only when we were driving back home along Belfast's Ormeau Road were we made aware of the film's impact on Lauren. From out of the darkness at the back of our people-carrier a weary and weak little voice cried out: 'Daddy, what's a Fenian?'

Both in the film and in real life, the hidden agenda of the loyalists eventually comes to the surface. At a public meeting of Glenbryn residents in the movie, the mantra goes up: 'What we need is a wall.' In order to secure their territory, to prevent the Catholics from taking over, the Protestant residents call for another peace line to be constructed. It is a demand that still echoes across the interfaces of north and west Belfast.

In real life, the Catholic parents and the board of governors opposed the creation of a peace wall because it would imprison Holy Cross Primary inside sealed-off, loyalist-controlled territory, bringing about the school's closure. Yet it would be a mistake to assume that all of the walls have gone up solely in response to Protestant agitation. In a majority of cases, the walls are there by mutual consent, making Belfast unique among cities and states where rival ethnic and religious groups are physically kept apart.

The huge security wall the Israelis are constructing along the West Bank has majority support among the Jewish population on one side but is universally loathed by the Palestinians on the other, and in July 2004 was declared illegal by the International Court of Justice in The Hague. The Turkish Cypriots in Nicosia find themselves, like the Israelis, largely in favour of the wall cutting through their city, while for the Greek Cypriots it is a universal symbol of the illegal partition of their island by the Turks in 1974. Even the former shell-shattered city of Beirut, with its infamous Green Line separating Muslim west from Christian east, has undergone a reunification of sorts. Only in Belfast are the walls an accepted fact of life on both sides.

In March 1999, the *Irish News* ran an excellent series of articles charting the 30-year history of the walls. One headline summed up succinctly the ambiguity communities share towards the barriers. 'Relief and sorrow as the walls went up,' it read. Relief and sorrow – the only appropriate words to convey the ambivalent attitude towards these necessary evils. Furthermore, no politician from the unionist or nationalist mainstream on either side of the sectarian borders of north and west Belfast would dare campaign for the barriers to be knocked down. To do so would be to commit electoral hara-kiri and risk being doomed to political oblivion – as has happened to some of my former comrades who have refused to play the sectarian card, including some who travelled with me to East Berlin in 1981.

Beyond Belfast, the sectarian divide is less obvious and at times more subtle. Nonetheless the 'line' of division is there. The River Bann, which runs from Coleraine in the North towards Portadown and on southward on to the border, is effectively a watery curtain. West of the Bann, the population is majority Catholic, while the area east of the Bann has evolved into a Protestant stronghold. The picture is, of course, complicated further by enclaves and mixed towns on either side of the river. In frontier towns like Enniskillen, the scene of an IRA massacre on Poppy Day 1987 when a bomb killed 11 Protestant civilians, even the dead must rest apart. At the beginning of 2004, Fermanagh District Council issued plans to build a second cemetery on the northern edge of Enniskillen. The council's plans had to be abandoned, however, after protests that there was no sectarian zoning, no separate Protestant and Catholic sections of the graveyard. An alliance that included Sinn Féin and Ian Paisley's Democratic Unionist Party forced council officials to think again. Eventually it was decided that a pathway which bisects the graveyard at Cross village will become the de facto border between Protestant and Catholic burial places. In a town that survived the Poppy Day bomb and likes to think of itself as a model of reconciliation, Protestants and Catholics quite literally won't be seen dead with each other.

The sole voice on the council to speak in favour of an integrated graveyard is one of only two Independent Socialist councillors elected in Northern Ireland. Davy Kettyles has served on Fermanagh District Council for the last 15 years. Unlike the representatives of the mainstream parties, Kettyles supported the concept of an integrated cemetery. 'If this was Alabama and there was a black section of the graveyard separated from the white section, the whole world would stand up and take notice. But, in Northern Ireland, it's the accepted norm. It is very sad that some people have exploited this issue and made a sectarian dog fight out of how we bury the dead. What we now will have is two tribal burial grounds partitioned off from each other.'

Ironically, I first met Davy in 1981, on the night before the IDYM delegation set off from Dublin on our two-day boat and train journey to East Berlin. My abiding memory of him from that summer, however, was when we reached Dublin on our return from the GDR six weeks later. I remember him throwing a few clothes into a suitcase and jumping on the first train north in order to join Tom Moore's campaign team for the second Fermanagh/South Tyrone by-election to fill the seat left vacant after the death of Bobby Sands. His dedication to a decent but doomed cause was and is extremely touching. Twenty-three years later, Davy still swims against the sectarian tide. Following the council's decision to segregate the graveyard at Cross, he even started agitating for a 'neutral third' of the cemetery for those who don't mind whom they are buried next to.

About a week after I wrote the story about Cross cemetery, I found myself being berated in a south Belfast bar by an acquaintance with a similar left-wing past. His gripe was that the report contained nothing new, that in most cases the dead are buried separately along sectarian lines. He simply couldn't grasp the import of the Enniskillen grave row. Or rather he, like so many in Northern Ireland, not just hardline unionists and nationalists but also some of those who consider themselves to be on the left of centre in politics, preferred to downplay the fact that since the peace process began, the religious 'apartheid' across Ulster has become more entrenched. Those who point to the sectarian elephant in the living room certainly get no thanks. Rather, in both academia and the media they are traduced as spoilers, wreckers and even enemies of the peace process.

One of the few voices to warn that sectarianism was intensifying along the interfaces is Dr Peter Shirlow. His research, taking as its base the 1994 ceasefires, has consistently shown that segregation has actually got worse, with attitudes in the enclaves and interfaces hardening. 'The people who were supportive and interested were the Northern Ireland Unionist Party (NIUP), sections of the DUP and the anti-Good Friday Agreement faction inside the Ulster Unionist Party. What shocked me was that these people were the ones who did want to make assertions about what was actually going on in these areas. It was as if they [the other political parties] were in denial.

'Those who purported to be pluralistic and supportive of the peace process stated that this work was foolish, malign, unaccountable, irrelevant, biased and even one person said it was irredentist. What was fascinating about these allegations was that they were made behind my back. None of them would say it to my face. They would label me "Anti-Agreement". The odd person at community relations conferences would denounce what I had done openly from the floor. Overall, their line was essentially we should not be telling the truth, the peace process is more important than the truth!'

For a brief time, Shirlow felt like the skull at the banquet for the peace process. When he completed his study of Ardoyne, the year before the Holy Cross dispute, there was no response from any politicians, community organisations or policy makers. Shirlow believes they simply didn't want to hear or know about the durability of sectarianism.

'What shocked me more than anything else was when we returned to working-class communities and presented them with our research data, they too went into denial. When you showed either loyalist or republican areas the findings from the other side, they would say "That's not true. They are welcome here. They're telling lies." Truth was binary. They could not see the others' complaints.'

In January 2002, Shirlow presented a paper in Belfast to the Royal Geographical Society and Institute of British Geographers. The University of Ulster academic based his report on a survey carried out among 4,800 households in a dozen areas along the peace lines. One of the most disturbing conclusions of Shirlow's research was that among young people aged 18–25 there was even less religious integration compared to older age groups. In the former age bracket, Shirlow found that 68 per cent had never had a meaningful conversation with anyone from the other community. In all age groups, six out of ten said they had been the victims of sectarian abuse, both physical and verbal, since the 1994 ceasefires; the same number said they believed community relations had actually worsened during the same period. Some of the other findings in this report (later backed up by material from the 2001 census for Northern Ireland) are equally disconcerting.

- 72 per cent of all age groups refuse to use health centres located in communities dominated by the other religion
- Only 22 per cent will shop in areas dominated by the other religion
- 58 per cent will travel twice as far as they have to in order to get to shopping, health and leisure facilities where they feel safe
- 62 per cent of unemployed people refuse to sign on in their local social security office because it is in an area dominated by the other religion

Shirlow does not believe that this mutual suspicion and fear is solely due to the legacy of history. He adds in a wholly new factor that took hold shortly after the ceasefires and was nurtured following the Good Friday Agreement: the way history is told. The fatal design fault in the agreement was that it institutionalised sectarianism and elevated the separate narratives each community imagined was the true version of history. Instead of accepting their respective responsibility for three decades of carnage and waste, both sides blamed the other.

'Everyone sees themselves as a victim in Northern Ireland. There is a complete denial of the other side's victimhood; people cannot see themselves as perpetrators of violence and intimidation, only as victims of the opposite camps,' Shirlow says.

The upshot of this is that the IRA has managed to rewrite history and present it to a new generation (some of whom were still at primary school at the time of the first ceasefires) not as an aggressive campaign to forcibly achieve a United Ireland. Instead, the 'armed struggle' is recast as both a defensive reaction to loyalist violence and, more perversely still, an extension of the peaceful civil rights campaigns. Without the Armalite, reforms within the Northern state – job equality, one man-one vote, human rights – would apparently not have been implemented. Conversely, and equally perversely, the loyalist paramilitaries and their allied parties reshape their violence in propaganda terms, portraying it as merely defensive and reactive, with the UVF and UDA the sole defenders of beleaguered Protestant communities. As if, in the case of the Shankill Butchers gang for example, abducting lone Catholic men at night, torturing them for hours and then slitting their throats is somehow an act of communal defence!

Back in October 1982, Margaret Thatcher flew to West Berlin following talks with her German counterpart Helmut Kohl in Bonn. In her memoirs, *The Downing Street Years*, she recalls getting her first glimpse of the Berlin Wall and the 'grey, bleak and devastated land beyond it in which dogs prowled under the gaze of armed Russian guards'. (Actually they were East German guards.) Thatcher recollected her speech that Friday afternoon on 29 October during which she prophesied the fall of the Wall: 'But the day comes when the anger and frustration of the people is so great that force cannot contain it. Then the edifice cracks: the mortar crumbles . . . one day, liberty will dawn on the other side of the wall.'

In an aside for the world's television cameras on the same day during a visit to the Potsdamer Platz, where Westerners could peer from a raised platform into the East, Thatcher echoed the sentiments of her speech. 'One day they will be free. One day they will be free,' she kept repeating.

Watching her climb the wooden viewing area on the wasteground by the Wall in time for the BBC's *Six O'Clock News*, I scoffed at what appeared then to be simply the rantings of an unreconstructed Cold Warrior. Even in the early 1980s, the idea that the Wall and the system behind it would simply crumble in the face of capitalist threat without a proper fight seemed unthinkable. But realising the unthinkable often begins by first thinking unthinkable thoughts and not being afraid to express them aloud. And as Thatcher later admitted in her autobiography, even she was taken back at how relatively quickly in historical terms her prediction had come true.

Twenty years after Thatcher's prophecy by the Wall, another Tory came to Europe's last divided city and made a similar call. The honourable member for Grantham and Stamford – the constituency where Thatcher grew up – Quentin Davies toured around the interfaces of north and west Belfast in the last week of November 2002. After sharing beef curry and rice with a Protestant couple living on the Glenbryn estate, Violet and Billy Coleman, Davies came out of their home and demanded that the peace wall that dominates the back of their house be pulled down. This wall and others, Davies argued, 'should not be tolerated in any civilised city in the twenty-first century'. He added: 'These walls are not a solution, they are a way of avoiding a solution, by institutionalising and crystallising division.'

Davies, like his hero and mentor, was thinking the unthinkable. Tear down the walls, pull up the barriers and let the people unite. They were laudable humanitarian sentiments that any liberal or leftist can sympathise with. But Belfast, like much of the rest of Northern Ireland, is still 'another country', trapped like a fly caught in the amber of history, penned inside a prison that the people have constructed for themselves.

CHAPTER FOUR

Loving the Alien

I was lost and tired. It had been a long day on the camp and I had just driven my landing craft across the Channel towards Normandy's beaches on D-Day. There were dead Germans everywhere, at least the ones I had managed to gun down. And now I was fighting my way across France towards the Rhine. No wonder I had become disorientated, for it was just another day at Butlins in Mosney.

My mother, sister, cousins Anne-Marie and Carol, along with Aunt Margaret and myself, had only arrived at Mosney a few days earlier. Completely surrounded by women, I had retreated into my imagination, daydreaming in the children's play-pool behind the wheel of a toy motorboat about Second World War heroics. After several hours playing soldiers in the centre of Mosney, I was sent to bed in the chalets while Mum and Margaret went out for a walk. The children were meant to have been monitored by Redcoats, but it seemed this was not done vigilantly enough, as one young desperado woke up, climbed out of bed and then, still half-asleep, went walkabout around the camp.

Eventually, I was picked up by a couple of Redcoats out on a late-night date, who shook me from my semi-slumber and then marched me to the camp's radio station. Once inside, the DJ broadcast an appeal

over the PA system for the parents of Henry McDonald, aged seven, to pick their child up. In the meantime, the man with the headphones on asked me if I wanted to sing a song. My choice reflected the events that had shaped our lives over the previous 12 months and I belted it out at the top of my little lungs.

> Armoured cars and tanks and guns came to take away our sons
> But every man shall stand behind the men behind the wire.

I sang that chorus line over and over again until the door was flung open and I was snatched outside by a red-faced, deeply embarrassed and angry mother.

We were the children, the brothers, the sisters, the cousins and the friends of 'The Men Behind The Wire' – the prisoners interned without trial in Long Kesh. We were also the 'nordies', 'yer men and women' from the Six Counties, the embarrassing reminders to our fellow holidaymakers from the South of the conflict raging north of the border.

All of the children, the McManuses and the McDonalds, had witnessed the war at first hand. The older girls, Anne-Marie and Carol, were caught up in the Falls curfew of 1970, when the Official IRA took on the British Army in a ferocious gun battle that lasted for hours. I can still recall the two of them, along with their younger sister Lisa, being evacuated to our house in the Markets, their tiny eyes streaming with water after their street was wreathed in choking tear gas fired by the British troops. Cathy and I had also been temporarily evacuated up to our grandmother's house in Reilly's Place at the very edge of the Markets on Internment Day 1971. We had fled after the British Army Saracen troop carrier crashed into the front door of our house and Joe McCann and his men started firing from the middle of Eliza Street to slow down the army incursions that early summer morning into the Markets.

We were refugees once more now in the holiday camp by the sea between Drogheda and the northern outskirts of Dublin. The kids spent their time paddling in the swimming pools or else riding on the Puffing Billy train-on-wheels that coursed around the complex. We finally felt safe. We were on 'home' territory, because here was where the Tricolour flew, where the shamrock sat atop dancing poles and where even the little wedges of butter at the breakfast table had the harp insignia on their front label.

Such a trip to Butlins also provided some respite for our mothers – a chance to escape from the boiling sectarian warfare of 1972, which by the end of the year would have claimed 496 lives, making it the bloodiest 12 months of the Troubles.

At the beginning of 2004, I took time out to inspect a photography exhibition that paid homage to the Butlins holiday camps located all around the British Isles. John Hinde's pictures are shot in the same wide angles complete with the familiar garish colours (on both humans and walls) of the late 1960s and early 1970s. On display at the Irish Photographic Gallery in Dublin's Temple Bar were portraits of holidaymakers enjoying themselves at Mosney in the early '70s. My two favourites were the images of the restaurant underneath the swimming pool, where diners were able to eat while watching through the reinforced glass as their fellow campers glided and paddled below the water. All of the pictures in the exhibition were weirdly elegiac. Their subjects were the British and Irish working classes at play. The British ones are particularly touching. The middle-aged men and OAPs all seem to wear those same black- and pointy-framed Mick McGahey-style spectacles; the women bulging out of tight-fitting short dresses while supping Babycham. For the older generation in the photographs, this was their reward. They had fought in the war, voted out Churchill, ushered in the Welfare State, enjoyed the never-had-it-so-good society and had in their twilight years experienced the first wave of mass consumption. They had earned their two weeks in Butlins at Bognor, Clacton and Ayr, and their nights of *Come Dancing*, Double Diamond, bingo and glamorous granny contests. Before the opening up of the Costas, the Algarve and the Greek Islands, the Butlins experience was their holiday-in-the-sun, their escape from the humdrum. Hinde's work at Butlins is, whether he intended it or not, a requiem on film for a class that has been weakened and atomised through the years of the Winter of Discontent, Thatcherism, globalisation and the inexorable march of individualism.

As late as the 1980s, Mosney was still a tourist trap for Northern holidaymakers, almost exclusively from the poorer sections of the Catholic community in Belfast. Twenty years ago, Northern Ireland's young nationalists still looked upon Mosney as a safe haven from the Twelfth and the threat of July's Orange marching season. But not any longer, because if you visit those familiar chalets by the Irish Sea – if you can get beyond the security guards and the wire fence – you will find an entirely new population of refugees in Mosney today.

There are now several hundred people from all over the planet who are temporarily housed in the former holiday camp while seeking asylum in Ireland. Some have opted to stay at Mosney; others were located there by the authorities when they first entered the Republic. The former group preferred the surreal atmosphere of life on a former Butlins resort to the depressing misery of B&Bs or hostels in inner-city Dublin. Both groups have been there now for four years and almost all of them are families. Not that this stopped hysterical reporting in the Irish press about alleged brothels on camp or the site being used as a base for foreign drug dealers. Despite the fact that the Gardai in early 2004 dismissed these lurid tales as nonsense, the negative reportage continues, which merely exposes the level of hostility the new aliens have to endure on entering Ireland. The men, women and children behind the wire at Mosney have become easy prey for the tabloid press and therefore, for many of their readers, a new enemy-within to target, fresh quarry for the prejudices of the press and society in general.

A week after the Hinde exhibition, Dublin threw a party for the Chinese. On 22 January – the Chinese New Year – the City Council organised a three-day festival to celebrate the social and cultural contribution of its newest citizens. The New Year celebrations focused on Smithfield, the second oldest human settlement in Dublin. In this small area north of the Liffey, close to Dublin's Four Courts, live 4,000 legal Chinese workers.

The festival was launched in Smithfield Square to the sound of dreamy, soothing, harp-like music played by four young Chinese women flown in from the People's Republic the day before. Chinese state television, along with all of the main Irish broadcasters, recorded the launch complete with Chinese dragons, giant red and yellow flags with huge Mandarin legends on them and dancers in traditional costume. Among those attending the festival was Li Dan, a 23-year-old teacher who has been in Dublin for over four years. She has studied at the city's Centre for English Studies and is now teaching art at George's Hill Primary School in the nearby Markets area of Dublin. Her brief now includes teaching local inner-city kids how to write Chinese script.

'I found it very friendly here. I love art and it's great to get a job teaching art to local kids. Most people I've met here are fine; I've had no problems, especially living in Smithfield. The people that have given me trouble, who've said "Go back to your own country", have been alcoholics.'

She had just returned from an interview on RTE television for the children's programme *The Den*, where she was interrogated by one of Ireland's most respected and feared interviewers, the puppet Dustin the Turkey.

Like Li Dan, her friend Xuan also comes from Shen Yang, the fourth-biggest city in the People's Republic, located in the north-east of the country. Xuan, whom the locals have nicknamed Kevin, has also spent almost four years in Dublin and plans to stay there for another decade. 'I prefer Dublin to anywhere else I've been in Ireland. The people here make you feel very welcome,' he said in between drinking his pint inside the Cobblestone Pub, a traditional inner-city bar that has become a favoured haunt of the Smithfield Chinese.

Beyond Smithfield, the entire centre of Dublin appeared to be taking part in the festivities. In Moore Street, where market traders have been selling fruit, veg and fish for more than a hundred years, there has been a remarkable transition. Almost every shop on the right-hand side of the street facing the ILAC shopping centre caters solely for Chinese and African immigrants. The amount of Chinese and Arabic script is bewildering; there are cramped little cafés with no English on their menus, international call centres offering cheap rates to ring Shanghai, Shen Yang, Abuja and Cape Town, and the odd shop selling hair extensions and wigs, principally for Nigerian women. Around the corner, in the windows of Penneys department store, black-skinned mannequins stand alongside white ones. While back in Moore Street, even one of the famous butchers on Dublin's north side has adapted to the new Chinese influence in the inner city. F.X. Buckley's, renowned since the early twentieth century as a meat purveyor, wished their Chinese customers a Happy New Year. The food labels in the front window were bilingual, with Chinese script written on white cards beside pigs' heads, cows' ears and bull's tongue, along with traditional fare.

One of the female traders, guarding her wooden stall that displayed huge white slabs of monkfish, piles of mackerel and buckets of crabs, initially seemed welcoming of the new immigrants. She pointed down to the assorted fish for sale and said that her main customers are the Chinese. The woman bemoaned the fact that eventually Moore Street will be utterly transformed due to plans to replace the sad cramped squalor of the knockdown price shops adjacent to the ILAC centre with a giant shopping mall. She will lose her Chinese custom. She hoped the Chinese could stay. 'They'll move somewhere else in the city. I like them 'cos they work hard and keep to themselves.'

Then I asked her if she was sad that Nigerians clustered around their little cafés and call centres are being displaced as well. She replied bluntly: 'The only place they should go is home, back to Africa. They're not like the Chinese, them niggers!'

Racism in Ireland exists in a series of gradations, with the Chinese seemingly the most 'acceptable' of the recent immigrants, followed by the Eastern Europeans and then, at the bottom of the pile, the Africans. (Although there is one stratum of Irish society looked upon by the settled community with even more hostility – the Irish Travellers.) As far back as 1997, when the first unprecedented wave of new immigrants arrived in the Republic, there was polling evidence to suggest the Irish were not immune to racist attitudes. A European Commission survey for that year found that 55 per cent of Irish people regarded themselves as racist. The same poll revealed that 25 per cent admitted they were 'quite' or 'very' racist, while a third said they were a 'little' racist (*Irish Times,* 20 December 1997). Within three years, the numbers of those immigrants who said they had experienced racist abuse had shot up. In a 2000 survey of 121 people from Ireland's ethnic minorities, 64 per cent had suffered outright racist insults. This figure rose sharply to 87 per cent for black Africans. Referring to the findings, the African-American academic Joy White compared the lack of national outrage over this report to the widespread outcry about the remarks of *Sunday Independent* columnist Mary Ellen Synon, who wrote that some of the disabled athletes at Sydney were 'perverse and grotesque'. As a result of her comments, Ms Ellen Synon lost her job at Ireland's bestselling Sunday broadsheet. Ms White draws a parallel with the Ellen Synon case and the vast volume of immigrant scare stories in both the national and regional Irish press from the late 1990s onwards, noting that no such editorial sanctions were imposed on the writers and journalists responsible for this hysteria.

Racism sometimes boils over into outright violence but more often than not it involves casual remarks on the street, insults at the bus stop, and in one infamous instance a Dublin bus driver was fined for making racist remarks towards an African passenger. It also exists at every level of society. On the same day as the Chinese New Year festival, I had lunch with two senior members of the Gardai in the city. When I informed them that I had spent the morning roaming around the immigrant areas of the north inner city, one of the officers interjected: 'Here is the latest score from the African Nations Cup – after 90 minutes and a no-score draw and no goals in extra time, Gardiner Street beat Parnell Street 3–1 on penalties.' (The two streets, one of which is mentioned in James Joyce's *Dubliners*, are now home to hundreds of African immigrants.)

The stereotype of the Eastern European immigrants, first copyrighted in Wexford town in 1999 during a wave of hysteria stoked up by the local newspaper, is of feckless dole scroungers with five o'clock shadows, men leering at the fresh-faced, virginal (allegedly) Irish colleens at the school gates, or else Romany gypsies with the obligatory child under their arms begging in the main street of every big- to medium-sized Irish town. The couple I met a week after Chinese New Year in one of north Dublin's Georgian houses in Belvedere Place were the complete opposite of this nasty and racially loaded caricature. Anca Lupu, from the Moldovan province of Romania, risked everything to find a better life in Ireland. She paid human traffickers thousands of euros and spent three days locked in the dark inside a lorry container before arriving in Ireland four years ago. Anca left for love: her husband Paul had fled the province a few months earlier after receiving death threats for exposing a prostitution scandal. Both were desperate to work legally in the Republic and even expressed a hardline stance towards fellow immigrants who refuse to take up employment.

Anca, who spoke flawless English and is a qualified primary school teacher, was adamant that if immigrants are allowed to work they should do so. 'First of all, any immigrant coming to Ireland should learn to speak English, and, after that, you should be prepared to work if you are allowed. All I would ask the Irish government is to give us a chance for, say, six months. After six months, if there are immigrants who refuse to find work, then they should be sent back.'

The Lupus, whose child was born in Dublin, have spent the last four years 'living in a cage', to use their own words. Paul, who bears a slight resemblance to Chelsea's Romanian star Adrian Mutu, has a degree in computer programming, but since the rules on employing foreigners were changed in the autumn of 1999, the couple have been unable to work legally, earn money or pay taxes. He said he felt deeply frustrated at not being able to work.

'All I want to do is earn money, pay my taxes and contribute to the Irish economy. I really don't want to be living on welfare. I have a diploma in computer programming but I can't use the skills I have to contribute to the Irish economy. For the last few years, all I have been able to do is voluntary work.'

He then stressed: 'We are not for an open-door policy. I think that immigrants should be offered the chance to work and if you don't bother taking a job within six months then you should be deported. I accept there is abuse of the system in Ireland. Some women do come here already pregnant just to get their kids an Irish passport and then the right to stay in Ireland.'

Anca interjected: 'Everyone who comes here should become integrated with Irish society. They should not retreat into a ghetto.'

Like the Lupus, Ovidiu Matiut left Romania because of his political beliefs. The 40-year-old mining engineer campaigned for regional autonomy for the province of his native Transylvania. He fled the region at the start of 2000 after being warned that lackeys from the central government in Bucharest had taken an interest in his activities. As we sat down to coffee, Ovidiu pulled out his papers from a drawer – official documents that prove he is now an Irish citizen. In the second week of January 2004, inside Court 40 at the Small Claims Court in Dolphins Barn, he became 'officially' Irish. The whole ceremony, he said, was a total anti-climax. 'All the officials did was hold up a piece of paper, I swore allegiance to the Irish constitution and that was that. Of course, I'm delighted that I'm an Irish citizen but the ceremony didn't make me feel like this was an important moment in my life.'

The story of the last four years of his life in Ireland is familiar: 'I was working in the black economy. I've been a porter, a waiter, a shop assistant and a labourer on several building sites.' Unlike, say, most of the Africans you speak to, Ovidiu said he has experienced very little racist abuse and the one incident in which he did turned out to be more farcical than threatening.

'A girl who was very drunk came into a shop I was working in one night and started being abusive at the counter. She told me to go back to my own country. To go back to "bleedin' Italy". She thought I was an Italian because of my accent.'

Thousands like Ovidiu, and, hopefully, the Lupus, are planning to stay in Ireland for the foreseeable future. They will, if the Irish government allows them, start families, pay tax, take out mortgages, vote in elections, put down roots and by their presence change the nature of Ireland and what it means to be Irish.

After our mid-morning chat, I walked through bedsit-land between Belvedere Place and Dorset Street, where the streets were full of black and yellow faces, shops which now cater for ethnic and exotic cuisine, fly-posters advertising cheap calls to Nigeria, China, Brazil, South Africa, Latvia and Romania. I hailed a cab near the North Circular Road and asked the driver to take me across town to the Shelbourne Hotel. En route we got talking about the way Dublin has been radically transformed and the new people on its streets. At first, the driver was full of praise for the Chinese. 'It if wasn't for the Chinese, the early-morning taxi business would be dead,' he remarked. Why? He explained that the Chinese start work at 6 a.m. in dead-end jobs in the catering and service industries, jobs which the Irish no longer wish to do. De-regulation of the taxi business has led to more cabs competing for a shrinking market, he complained. 'It's the Chinese workers who mainly take taxis now in the mornings,' he went on, 'and once the LUAS [Dublin's light rail/tram service] gets going, it will just be the Chinese using these taxis.'

But, again, the gradations of racism are evident. When I asked if he got any Nigerian custom, the taxi man looked at me slyly and answered: 'I deliberately drive by them in the street. They're too much trouble in the car. I won't take them if I can avoid it.'

One of the few Irish academics to chart this change and expose racist attitudes in the South believes the Republic could become more like a normal secular European republic through immigration. Bryan Fanning, a lecturer in the Department of Social Policy at University College Dublin, has even suggested that Ireland adopt the American model of citizenship.

'We need to move to an American model of hyphenated identity, where one day we will have African-Irish, Bosnian-Irish, Romanian-Irish, etc., as in the States where you have people referring to themselves as African-Americans, Irish-Americans and so on.'

There are now more than 100,000 foreign immigrants living and working in the Republic of Ireland, Fanning noted. Since the enlargement of the EU, he pointed out, 65 per cent of immigrants in Ireland will be legal. By 2031, the Republic's Central Statistical Office has predicted that there will be 205,000 foreign immigrants residing in Dublin alone. A further 48,000 immigrants will move to the west of Ireland.

They will also exercise new political muscle in the state, Fanning added. 'They could play a pivotal role in elections down here. Even in Bertie Ahern's Dublin Central constituency, a couple of thousand immigrant votes could swing an election, lose or secure Fianna Fail a seat. Or take Clare, where there have been some racist incidents, 1,000 asylum seekers were allowed to vote in the June [2004] local government elections. These people are here to stay and so the question remains: what are we going to do with them? I think the answer is that there needs to be formal naturalisation, a ceremony where they can swear allegiance to flag and constitution.'

The concept of Ireland as a monolithic Catholic state is also under assault due to the influx of immigrants with different religions and cultures. Their arrival has led to a mini-renaissance of Protestant churchgoing in the Republic. For the first time since the foundation of the state, all the main Protestant churches have reported a surge in membership thanks to those immigrants from Africa and Eastern Europe who happen to be evangelical Christians. The Methodist, Baptist and Unitarian churches have all reported swollen congregations.

Among those Protestant churches 'rescued' from closure is the Clontarf Methodist Church overlooking Dublin Bay. Built in 1857, its congregation had dwindled to just five in the mid-1990s and it was set for closure. Foreign immigrants, mainly Methodist Africans from the Congo, have since boosted the church's membership to 50. And to cope with their multi-cultural, multi-lingual congregation, Clontarf Methodist Church's hymnbooks are now printed in English, French,

Lingala and Swahili. The surge in the number of Romanian immigrants, meanwhile, has increased the Baptist and Pentecostal communions as well as leading to the opening of two Romanian Orthodox churches in Belvedere College and Arbour Hill.

A wholly new and growing Protestant population in the Republic will undermine unionist charges that Home Rule is still Rome Rule. However, the presence by 2031 of nearly a third of a million non-Catholic immigrants will radically transform the nature of Southern society. Their presence in the Republic begs a number of fascinating questions. Will a more secular Republic become increasingly attractive to Northern unionists alienated from Blair's Britain? Or will the prospect of an additional influx of one million unionist/Protestant voters be too frightening a scenario for a Southern political establishment already trying to cope with almost 300,000 'new Irish'?

Bryan Fanning has concluded that the immigrants will radically transform the Republic of Ireland, whether that establishment likes it or not.

'With the presence of so many non-Catholic people, a new challenge is being thrown up to mono-cultural Catholic Ireland. This new scenario calls into question what the Republic should mean in the twenty-first century. We are faced with a choice: do we adopt the fully secular republican values of say France, which leads to Muslim girls being forced to take off their hijabs in schools? Or do we take on the USA-style model of hyphenated reality?'

The hypocrisy of the Irish government and elites regarding the immigrant community is breathtaking. In the 1980s, Fianna Fail in particular actively encouraged young Irish men and women to emigrate to Britain, North America and the Continent at a time when there were more than 300,000 people officially unemployed. Irish politicians practically begged the Americans to allow thousands of Irish people to work legally in the United States and eventually got their wish through the Morrison Visa system. Nor does their newfound hysteria over the numbers of immigrants supposedly 'swamping' Ireland equate to the figures for Irish migrants escaping the '80s recession at home and settling in cities across Western Europe and North America. Aine Ni Chonnaill's rantings during the last general election about 4,000 foreigners flooding into Cork, for instance, should be seen in the context of, say, the 6,000 Irish immigrants who lived and worked in Munich during the 1980s or up to 10,000 young Irish in Madrid in the same period.

Not only is the Irish government suffering from selective amnesia over its current attitudes to immigrants but it is also guilty of incredible double standards. Nationalist Ireland, and most vehemently of all Bertie Ahern and Fianna Fail, continually chide unionists that there will be no re-negotiation of the 1998 Good Friday Agreement, despite the fact that Northern Protestants clearly rejected the peace accord in the November 2003 Assembly elections. The present Dublin administration's attitude to another aspect of the agreement goes to show that there is still one law for the people of the South and another for the people in the North.

Michael McDowell, the Minister for Justice, Equality and Law Reform, in fact, successfully sought a renegotiation of the agreement – specifically that part which guaranteed an Irish passport to any child born on either side of the border from Easter 1998. In June 2004, the Irish people were asked to amend that section of the agreement that allowed the children of immigrants born in the Republic full-blown Irish citizenship. Even the hallowed agreement is not safe from tinkering if it means stopping African and Eastern European parents from gaining legal status in Ireland once their children are delivered in the Rotunda and Holles Street maternity hospitals. Nor did this doublethink appear to upset the indigenous Irish electorate. On Palm Sunday 2004, the *Sunday Independent* reported that two-thirds of voters in the Republic backed the removal of citizenship to 'foreign' children born on the island of Ireland. The poll also demonstrates a latent danger in the country. At present, the influx of foreign workers has been largely tolerated simply because they are needed to do the jobs the Irish no longer want to carry out. If and when, however, the Irish economy takes a sharp downturn and unemployment starts to climb again, there is undoubtedly the potential for the 'native' Irish to turn on these new guests of the nation.

The government's amendment was clearly a populist ruse, a move to placate the media-driven fears about more black babies than white being born in the Rotunda, claims that actually do not stand up to forensic and empirical scrutiny. While a handful of racist micro-groups have attempted to exploit these fears, they remain irrelevant and marginalised forces. Only the far left has talked up the presence of groups like the Celtic Wolves or an Irish version of the BNP. Ultra leftists, of course, have a perverse interest in exaggerating the influence and size of these neo-fascist groups. The presence of these racist buffoons somehow justifies the 24-hour activism and hyperbole of the extreme left.

The reality is that, in the Republic, racism exists in a subtle and populist form within the Irish political mainstream. Individual TDs from the two main parties take up racist causes, whether they are directed at immigrants or more usually the Travellers, for opportunistic reasons, and those politicians who exploit the presence of the alien can harvest huge support in their constituency. In contrast, openly racist campaigners like Aine Ni Chonnaill and her Immigration Control Platform can only garner a few hundred votes. The recent career of the Cork North Central Fianna Fail TD is a case in point. In the 1997 Irish general election, Noel O'Flynn barely scraped into the Dail on the last count; four years later, having denounced asylum seekers in the city as 'scroungers', he topped the poll in the same constituency. Almost every commentator agreed that O'Flynn's stunning comeback was in large part due to his focus on the asylum issue in Cork. (It is worth noting, however, that the two main beneficiaries of the Immigration Control Platform's transfers under Ireland's system of proportional representation have been Sinn Féin and Fianna Fail. In the 1997 election, 24 per cent of Ni Chonnaill's 926 votes were distributed to Sinn Féin, while Fianna Fail received 21 per cent of her transfers.)

Racist populism is not, however, a new phenomenon in post-1921 Ireland; it has been a bacillus lying dormant in the Irish body politic since the state was conceived. The virus was at its most virulent during the 1930s and '40s, and survived right into the following decade. It took on the form of anti-Semitism both at official and unofficial levels. Jewish refugees fleeing Nazi persecution from 1933 were repeatedly denied entry into Southern Ireland under the Aliens Act. Moreover, Irish refugee policy reflected the bio-racist 'logic' of the Nuremberg Laws, as even Jews who had 'converted' to Christianity were still classified in official-speak as 'non-Aryan' and therefore barred entry into Eire. During the period from Hitler's accession to power and the outbreak of the Second World War, Ireland was represented in Berlin by Charles Bewley, an unapologetic anti-Semite. Bewley became an enthusiastic supporter of the Nazis and their genocidal war on the Jews. Yet, incredibly, it was Bewley who also had the power to grant visas to Jews seeking refuge in Ireland.

Official anti-Jewish policies survived the Second World War and Holocaust. Whilst Eamon de Valera remains untainted by charges of anti-Semitism, it is undeniable that his government continued to refuse entrance to Jewish refugees from the death camps even after the war was over. The Department of Justice actually opposed refugee status to 100 Jewish orphans who had survived the horrors of Belsen concentration camp. To his credit, it was de Valera who overruled the department and granted the children temporary shelter in Ireland. Almost 1,000 war orphans from Europe were allowed to settle in Ireland after the war, but the 100 orphans from Belsen were the only Jewish children granted refugee status – and only once it was assured that they would eventually be shipped out to other countries.

Even oppositional republican politics have been coloured by vicious anti-Semitism. One of the most notorious Jew haters was the legendary IRA figure Sean South, who died during a botched raid on Brookeborough RUC station in 1956. South was a devoted follower of Fr Dennis Fahy, a founder of Maria Duce, the right-wing anti-Semitic Catholic pressure group. Much of this group's deeply anti-Jewish ideology was rooted in pre-Vatican II ideology and its emphasis on the collective guilt of Jews for Christ's crucifixion. It festers on to this day, despite Vatican II and successive popes' denunciations of Jew-hatred.

There is a monument to Irish republicanism's flirtation with Nazism still standing in a corner of north Dublin. It is a statue situated in Fairview Park overlooking Dublin Bay, to which the present generation of republicans still flock every September. The man they come to pay homage to is Sean Russell, the IRA's chief-of-staff during the Second World War, who died on board a Nazi U-Boat during an aborted operation to destabilise Britain's war effort on the island of Ireland. Russell's IRA had been responsible for hundreds of deaths in Britain during the Blitz and had been in open collusion with Hitler's regime. The IRA was undoubtedly willing to be used as a tool of the Nazis in a future invasion of Ireland. No doubt they would have played their part in rounding up the 7,000 Jews living on the island who had been earmarked for extermination along with millions of others at the Wannsee conference in 1942.

Remarkably, modern day Sinn Féin still honours a man who would have handed over Ireland to the Nazis if Hitler had won the war. Even the new squeaky-clean Shinners like Dublin Euro-candidate Mary Lou McDonald have spoken at commemorations to Russell in Fairview Park. Think about it. If a prospective MEP in, for example, France, Belgium or Holland delivered a speech at a statue commemorating a man who had been allied to the Nazis, there would be widespread condemnation and outrage all over democratic Europe. Yet virtually no one in Ireland either on the left or in the liberal media cared to remark upon, let alone speak out about, this unseemly gathering at the Russell statue. Nor did they accuse Ms McDonald of blatant hypocrisy. In any other part of the European Union, a candidate portraying herself as a radical, even a socialist, yet who was willing to speak at a commemoration for a Nazi ally in the Second World War would be held up to ridicule and excoriation. Not so in Ireland, where in academia, the leftist salons of Dublin, RTE and the *Irish Times* there is an unofficial policy of not being at all beastly to the Provos. Indeed, the mere fact that the existence of the Russell statue almost six decades after the Shoah is not and never has been an issue in Dublin is proof positive of this intellectual and moral surrender.

At the beginning of this century, the Republic's Department of Justice estimated that 70 per cent of those claiming asylum had come via Northern Ireland. The Police Service of Northern Ireland confirms that the trafficking of people through the Province is a 'very lucrative business'. The PSNI and the Gardai still have two Northern taxi firms under surveillance who the two police forces believe pick up would-be asylum seekers at Belfast International Airport and the ferry port of Larne and drive them south across the border. For the minority who choose to stay in the North, life can be even grimmer and the hostility they encounter more trenchant than in the Republic.

Thousands of immigrants, legal and illegal, the majority of them Chinese, have settled in Belfast over the last five years. They tend to end up in poorer, depopulated parts of inner-city Belfast such as the loyalist Village area in south Belfast. The Chinese have also found themselves in rented accommodation along the sectarian interfaces of north Belfast. A large group of Chinese families are currently living in one of the city's most dangerous flashpoints, Manor Street. Their house is one of the last still standing before the dead-ground of no man's land between the Catholic Lower Cliftonville and the loyalist Lower Oldpark. No one else wants to live there. Ironically, the young Chinese workers' home is around the corner from another house with a blue plaque on its front denoting that someone famous once lived there – in this case the ex-President of Israel, Chaim Herzog.

Since Christmas 2003, the UK and Irish media have become fixated on the upsurge of racist assaults on foreigners in Belfast. The Village has been a focal point of racist intimidation and violence, most of it carried out by local members of the Ulster Volunteer Force. The increase in racist incidents in the Village is down to two main factors: greed and paranoia. Up until last Christmas, the UVF in south Belfast had been operating a lucrative protection racket aimed at the Chinese and African communities. Local UVF activists referred to their extortion scam as a 'nigger tax'. When a Chinese businessman refused to pay the terror group, its membership launched a series of assaults. The roots of the upswing in racism are also down partly to the perception (however unfounded) in places like the Village and nearby Donegall Pass that unscrupulous landlords are prepared to displace the indigenous Protestant population with houses filled by immigrants. Although the UVF's leadership acted to halt the attacks and discipline its own membership, resentment and mistrust remain.

While loyalists have been responsible for the overwhelming majority of racist beatings and intimidation, nationalist areas are not immune to racism. Twenty-four hours after St Patrick's Day 2004, a Chinese man was subjected to a terrifying and prolonged assault along the Falls Road in west Belfast.

Overall, according to figures released by the Province's Policing Board, there was a 60 per cent rise in racist attacks in Northern Ireland in 2003–4. There have also been some ugly examples of politicians playing the race card in their own backyards. Even allies of the Nobel peace prizewinner David Trimble have been prepared to risk stoking up racist passions. When the growing Muslim community in Craigavon sought to build a mosque in a rural part of north Armagh, unionists on the local council strongly objected. One of the councillors leading the campaign to stop the mosque at Bleary was Fred Crowe, a long-time friend and confidant of Trimble in his Upper Bann constituency.

The colour and religious make-up of Ulster is changing much more slowly than that of the Republic. Nonetheless, the presence of foreign immigrants is starting to alter the social and political landscape north of the border. Already, some sectors of society are adapting to these new citizens. The local paper in Dungannon, for instance, now publishes a special section every week written in Portuguese for the thousands of workers from Portugal shoring up the food processing and packaging industries in counties Armagh and Antrim. Portuguese workers now make up one-tenth of Dungannon's population.

Some politicians, just like their counterparts in the South, are waking up to the fact that legal immigrants now have the right to vote in European and local elections. In Upper Bann, for instance, the foreign workers could contribute as many as 5,000 extra voters onto the electoral register, which is the equivalent of a seat in the Northern Ireland Assembly. A similar figure pertains to that other area recently plagued by racism, south Belfast.

Violent loyalism has been traditionally associated during the Troubles with far-right groups in Britain. As far back as the National Front's surge in the mid-1970s, there have been links between the UDA and UVF and British neo-fascists. Certain loyalist leaders, flattered with the pin-up boy adulation they have received from the British Nazis, have forged links across the Irish Sea. Johnny 'Mad Dog' Adair, for example, cultivated connections with Combat 18 and invited them over to his 'Day of Loyalist Culture' on 19 August 2000, which ended in a shooting war between his 'C Company' of the UDA and the UVF on Belfast's Shankill Road.

It would be a mistake, however, to assume that all Ulster loyalists are driven by the same racist ideology as groups like Combat 18. Most loyalist terrorist leaders deeply mistrust the British far right and suspect that many of them are fronts for MI5 and other branches of the security services. In Ballymena, Ian Paisley's hometown, the UVF's political wing, the Progressive Unionist Party (PUP), ran a successful anti-racist campaign to drive neo-Nazis out of the town. Led by the former loyalist prisoner Billy McCaughey, the PUP helped ostracise the White National Party, which was conducting a hate-drive against

Filipino nurses (mostly, of course, defenceless women) living in the north Antrim town. So while in south Belfast UVF/PUP members were terrifying the Chinese, in Ballymena their comrades were defending Filipinos! All of which has caused profound embarrassment to the socialists and old labourites such as the PUP leader David Ervine.

In some British newspapers, Belfast had suddenly become 'the racist capital of Europe', a gross piece of hyperbole if ever there was one. There are undoubtedly nasty, racist thugs in the Northern capital, almost exclusively operating on the fringes of Ulster loyalism. Yet to suggest that Belfast is more racially intolerant than, say, Antwerp is blatantly absurd. A quarter of the Belgian port's electorate vote for the neo-Nazi, overtly racist Vlams Blok, whereas the last time the National Front stood for an election in Belfast its candidate received a paltry 26 votes. Just like in the Republic, racism rather slips into and eventually poisons the political mainstream in Northern Ireland rather than producing a surge in support for marginal far-right parties.

In the early to mid-1970s, the only black people I ever encountered patrolled in the street wearing camouflage flak jackets while carrying SLR rifles and walkie-talkies. Black soldiers billeted in areas like the Markets faced double opprobrium. First, they were taunted and bullied by their fellow white troops. The Brits often sprayed racist graffiti on the street walls about the 'Kunta' and 'Nig Nog' in their company, slogans that went alongside snide references to local IRA men, including one whom the army described as a 'puff' (*sic*). Second, black soldiers often endured racist chants and catcalls from young republicans all the way from five to fifty. A former colleague of mine who owned a pub in the Lower Falls during the early '70s recalls the reaction of his customers when the first black soldier came into the bar as part of a raiding party of troops. Many of his clientele were Official IRA volunteers who spouted Marxist slogans about the workers of the world or compared their 'struggle' to the plight of blacks in apartheid South Africa. The publican-turned-photographer (who still wants to remain anonymous) remembers that the OIRA men left their proletarian internationalism outside when the 'black Brits' came through the door. Almost all of them, he says, called the soldiers 'black bastards' or 'monkey men'.

The only other arena where my friends and I saw black people was on the football field playing for teams like Glenavon. With a sense of real shame I remember joining in taunts of 'Kunta Kunta' every time Tim Gracey, a very talented black Glenavon player, touched the ball at Solitude in 1979. When Linfield signed two black players at the end of the 1980s, there were idiots in many clubs who were still bellowing out racist insults. This kind of behaviour has abated since the 1990s, although the sectarian slogans and songs are very much still the norm at many Irish League games, including those between almost exclusively Protestant-supported clubs, where the main preoccupation among the fans is to see which set can sing 'The Sash' the loudest!

Sport has become a foil against racism North and South. Sport Against Racism in Ireland (SARI) has its own multi-ethnic football team, with nine different nationalities represented in the side. It also has a Romanian physio and a Chinese medical expert who employs alternative healing techniques on players' injuries. Aer Lingus sponsors the team, which competes against other amateur soccer sides around Dublin. The brainchild behind SARI and the side was one of my oldest friends in Dublin, the veteran community activist Ken McCue. He and those around him have done far more to combat the ignorance and fear that lie at the root of racism than the protest posturing of the far left's anti-racist crusade. Born and bred in Ireland's other Markets, an inner city working-class area between Dublin's Four Courts and Constitution Hill, McCue is attuned to the attitudes of indigenous Dubliners, particularly their views on the new citizens. McCue agrees that there is a 'grading system' of racism in Ireland, with locals having the highest regard for the Chinese, followed by Eastern Europeans and the black Africans at the bottom. There is, of course, one social group, he agrees, that is hated even more than the Nigerians.

'I hear comments in the pubs around where I'm from and throughout the inner city like "I like the Chinese, I don't even mind the blacks but I hate the fucking knackers [Travellers]". It's as brutal and blunt as that.'

So far in the Republic, anti-asylum racist politics has been the dog that has yet to bark. In contrast, drumming up populist resentment towards Travellers has reaped electoral dividends. Nor does the use of inflammatory language against Travellers land politicians in trouble with the law. In March 1999, a Mayo county councillor John Flannery was acquitted of inciting hatred at Galway District Court. He had described Travellers as 'dogs' and suggested that they be tagged to allow the authorities to track their movements. Although prosecuted under the 1989 Prohibition of Incitement to Hatred Act, which makes it an offence to incite hatred against any group on grounds of their 'race, colour, nationality, religion, ethnic or national origins, or membership of the Travelling Community', Councillor Flannery beat the rap. Since then there has only been one successful prosecution under the Act, when a Dublin bus driver was found guilty of racially abusing a black man at a city-centre bus stop.

Powerful interest groups can also get around the supposedly tough anti-racist laws in the Republic. Bryan Fanning points out that the Licensed Vintners Association (LVA – the body representing rural publicans) successfully campaigned for Irish equality laws to be changed so that their members could still reserve the right to refuse Travellers entry into their pubs. The key point about the LVA's victory is the capitulation of the Irish government. The Fianna Fail–Progressive Democrat coalition was prepared to take on and beat the LVA over the 2004 smoking ban on public places. However, the government buckled under pressure from the LVA over the ban on Travellers in bars. What this shows is that anti-Traveller racism is the least 'sexy' issue surrounding all ethnic minority groups in Ireland.

While an unofficial Chinatown of sorts exists in Dublin, unionist councillors in Belfast are now toying with the idea of building an official Chinatown in the city. It remains to be seen whether their intentions are to shunt off the Chinese into a dragon-and-lantern-covered ghetto or rather to create a space where Belfast's newest community can thrive and demonstrate to the rest of the city the positive contributions they are making to Northern life. In the area of Belfast where I was born, the Chinese community has just completed the construction of an old people's home for their elderly population. It is situated on the site of Geordie Stone's legendary scrapyard on land between the back of what was once Inglis Bakery and Belfast's old gasworks. I am proud to say that the people of the Markets have welcomed the arrival of the Chinese OAPs; to the locals' credit, there has not been a single voice raised in protest over the centre.

Ireland's absorption of hundreds of thousands of immigrants, particularly in the Republic, is another milestone in the incredible success story of the Celtic Tiger economy. The old saw about Ireland's best export being its people no longer applies. Other nations, mostly in the Third World, are exporting their people to Ireland, which is seen around the planet as one of the best countries on earth in which to live and work. Butlins at Mosney, however, stands as a symbol for the inability of the Irish state to cope with this new twenty-first-century reality. Where once we were welcome refugees enjoying a brief respite from the horror of the Troubles, there now reside in the former holiday camp 600 families caught in limbo, uncertain about their future, unable to earn money legally, segregated off from the rest of Irish society until such time as governments can work out what to do about the unstoppable flight of desperate people to our shores.

And yet Mosney, or rather recent events inside the camp, also points to the way Ireland often handles social challenges, i.e. through the politics of opportunism and pragmatism. Just prior to the Republic's 2004 local government elections, the ruling party in the state, Fianna Fail, announced that it was setting up a branch inside Butlins. North County Dublin Fianna Fail claimed it had recruited hundreds of new members from the families living in the holiday camp chalets where we once took temporary refuge. Fianna Fail in north County Dublin scented votes once it realised that legal asylum seekers and immigrants (mainly those from Eastern Europe) had the right to vote in local Irish elections. Some of our new citizens are now signing up to the same party as Noel O'Flynn, into arguably the most successful and enduring political force in Western Europe. Now that is a 'privilege' that has long since been denied to the 'Men behind the wire' and their children in the North, despite it being the self-declared Republican Party.

Back in Dublin, little Andi Lupu received his Irish passport at the start of 2004, but unless there is a change of heart Andi will not have it for much longer.

The Lupus were lighting candles under a grotto dedicated to the Blessed Virgin inside Our Lady of Lourdes Church in Dublin's Sean McDermott Street a couple of days after they learned from the Department of Justice they face deportation at any time. Anca Lupu was filled with dread over the prospect of returning to her native Romania.

The Lupus' local TD and Irish Justice Minister Michael McDowell is determined to drastically cut the numbers of foreign workers that have flocked in their tens of thousands to the Republic over the last five years. The young couple who fled to Ireland in the late 1990s are the collateral damage in the Minister's war to drive down the immigration figures now that thousands of legal workers from the east will be able to seek work in the Republic.

'I don't even want to think about it,' Anca said, clutching her child, 'I've been here so long now I can't imagine life outside of Ireland. It's four years now and, for me, Dublin is my home, my life, my future.'

The Republic's Department of Justice says it refuses to discuss individual cases, but the Lupus' plight is typical of the 20,000 Romanian asylum seekers and illegal immigrants living in the Republic.

Their friend Ovidiu, now, as he says, 'an official Paddy', has been criss-crossing Dublin every day, gathering hundreds of signatures from friends, welfare workers, priests and even local politicians for a petition urging the authorities to let the Lupus stay in Ireland.

'Ireland was not prepared for the influx of so many people but the country should remember that other nations once welcomed the Irish by the tens of thousands when times were bad here and unemployment was high. Families like the Lupus are not spongers; they want to work, to contribute to Irish society,' Ovidiu added.

In this election year, the Fianna Fail–Progressive Democrat coalition went to extraordinary lengths to speed up the deportation process. The Dublin government chartered two jets from holiday companies to transport deportees back to Romania and Nigeria. The Irish effectively run a 'deportation taxi service' around the EU: the jets not only fly Romanians and Nigerians out of Ireland but the two planes also pick up other deportees in European cities like Amsterdam, Brussels and Paris before travelling on to their final destination. On board the deportation flights each week will be police officers from several EU states that, like the Gardai, have to accompany their 'illegals' out of Western Europe. In Romania, the Irish Embassy in Bucharest has hired law firms to check up on the social and political backgrounds of asylum seekers currently residing in Ireland. The average cost of these check-ups is estimated to be around €3,000.

Back in the Our Lady of Lourdes Church – one of the support centres for Dublin's 1,000 Romanian Catholics – Anca Lupu pulled out what appeared at first to be an ID card given to her by the Irish authorities. It includes a colour photograph of an attractive 27-year-old woman and on the other side the harp insignia of the Department of Justice. Beneath, written in red, is a warning: 'This is not an identity card.'

'The card says it all,' Anca sighs, as her young son plays with his Bob the Builder toy in the church pews. 'We have no status, we can't work, I can't even use this card to vote, we are in limbo. But I pray to God every night that we can stay.'

At the time of writing, the Lupu family still wait in limbo uncertain whether or not little Andi will grow up an Irish citizen. Ireland has now effectively shut the door to other families like them after 12 June 2004, when an overwhelming majority, 80 per cent, endorsed plans to strip citizenship from children born on the island of Ireland to foreign parents.

Just 24 hours before the vote, on 11 June, I was killing time before a meeting, sauntering down O'Connell Street enjoying the brilliant sunshine. At the junction of O'Connell and Middle Abbey Street I noticed a poster attached to a streetlight. It contained a hard-hitting message and a reminder about the situation Irish people used to find themselves in, alone and alienated in economic exile in cities like London, Birmingham and Manchester. The words came from the signs outside B&Bs in English cities designed to drive away black and Irish custom.

'No blacks, No dogs, No Irish – Remember this? Vote No.'

But, instead, the sons and daughters, the grandsons and granddaughters of those desperate Irish immigrants subjected to such humiliations in the past chose to ignore the parallels between their plight and that of equally desperate people in the twenty-first century. Ireland-of-the-welcomes has just shut the door to the alien.

CHAPTER FIVE

Devil Lodge

Every time the subject of sex was raised in my puberty days, the devil always seemed to make an appearance. In my last year at primary school, Satan materialised in the guise of a raven-haired beauty riding on a horse; six months later at St Malachy's College, the Prince of Darkness was found dressed up as an Irish tart in Soho.

At St Colman's Primary, in the same street where I lived in the Markets, there was a makeshift way of coping with a teacher's absence. Whenever one of the staff went on the sick, his or her pupils would be divided into six groups and dispatched to all the other classes in the school. Towards the end of my final term at St Colman's, our Primary Seven teacher fell ill and our class was split up and sent to the other classrooms for the day. I went to the Primary Six class.

As it was the end of the year, the P6 teacher was implored by his boys to tell the P7s his ghost story, the one he often recounted to his classes towards the close of the school day. 'Tell us the story of Egdol Lived,' the P6 boys chirped in unison. The master, a tall, imposing man with slicked back hair, tweed jacket and the uncanny bearing of Padraig Pearse, stood up, cracked his fingers and then began to tell his chilling tale.

Egdol Lived is the story of a traveller who gets lost on a lonely road late at night. While walking, he meets a dishevelled old bearded man who asks the traveller if he is lost. The old man offers to guide the man on his way but the traveller mistrusts the tramp-like figure and dismisses his help. After a while, the traveller then hears the beating of a horse's hooves behind him. Eventually, the horse and rider pass him and then pull up in front of the traveller. In the saddle is a beautiful woman with flowing black hair, ruby-red lips and stunning ice-blue eyes. The woman asks the man if he is lost and when he tells her he cannot find his way home in the dark, she too offers to help him. The rider tells him that he can stay at her homestead, 'Egdol Lived', until the following morning. But, just as the traveller climbs up on the horse behind the female rider, the old tramp appears again. He again offers to show the man the way, this time pleading with the traveller to come with him instead. The woman turns around and advises the traveller to brush off the old man's aid. Angry about this old boy's persistence, the traveller tells him to go away. The woman kicks the horse with her boots and she and the traveller take off along the road to 'Egdol Lived'. As they are riding, the traveller looks back and sees the old man still standing on the same spot where he countered the rider and her horse. The shabbily dressed tramp is crying. Then, as the traveller faces the front again, the atmosphere turns darker and the horse goes faster, reaching breakneck pace. The traveller asks the woman her name and she turns around, her face transformed into a scarred and leprous mass of damaged skin, the eyes more animal-like than human and her voice turning male and sinister. 'You know who I am and you will be with me forever,' the rider says as the duo are transported to 'Egdol Lived' – Devil Lodge.

Six months after our blood was chilled by that morality tale, the 'Father of All Lies' turned up again during a sex education lecture at St Malachy's. The priest began to tell us what we already knew by writing all the slang words for intercourse on the blackboard. 'Bang', 'Screw', 'Ride' and 'Buck' were among the street nomenclature for sex. At the end of the class, Junior 1A were offered the floor, to ask questions, even to debate what the priest had just said. No one wanted to talk about fucking. Instead, one boy put his hand up and asked the priest if he had ever come across the Devil or his demons. This was the time when *The Exorcist* was first widely available on video and several of my classmates had seen the horror classic that summer. But our celibate sex

128

The morning after the gun battle in the Markets –
local men are arrested and interned without trial.

Joe McCann's funeral –
even his pet Irish
wolfhound is there to
pay homage.

Normal life during wartime –
horses taken for a stroll through the Markets.

Normal life during wartime – the author rides out
close to the spot two years later where Joe McCann
took on the British Army.

Cliftonville and the Red Army celebrate victory in the 1979 Cup final. Somewhere in the throng the author is going mad.

Hatred on display – soccer sectarianism.

The RUC riot squad go in hard at the Waterworks end at Solitude during disturbances.

The author's post-punk band but the
anti-sectarian message stayed the same.

One of the most infamous walls of Belfast
cutting through Alexandra Park.

Titty Von Trump struts her stuff in Belfast's The Kremlin.

Inset: In desperation, another Dublin addict shoots heroin into his foot.

Hardened heroin addict in Dublin – the dark side of the Celtic Tiger.

The new Dubliners – Chinese immigrants in Smithfield Square,
the Irish capital's new Chinatown. (© Kim Haughton)

The new Dubliners – the Lupu family take time out from
their troubles wondering if little Andi (left) will be
allowed to build a future in Ireland. (© Kim Haughton)

The new Dublin – twenty-first-century trams whoosh by the city's eighteenth-century Georgian houses. (© Kim Haughton)

The Spire – symbol of postmodern Ireland (© Kim Haughton)

The author on the Saudi–Kuwait border after the routing of Saddam Hussein's forces in 1991.

Darkness at noon in the Kuwaiti desert. The author amid the oil fires detonated by Saddam's retreating army which blotted out the sun.

educationalist had nothing demonic or genuinely frightening to offer us. Instead, he said he first came across the presence of evil-in-the-flesh while on a trip to London when he was still a student priest. The priest passed through Soho one day wearing his dog collar. Out of a dark corner near a sex shop came a thin voice with an Irish accent: 'All right there, Father?' the teenage hooker from Dublin called out. That incident, that voice, that temptation, the priest assured us, proved for him the existence of evil.

I experienced almost total recall of these sex-in-the-Satan tales from the '70s following a trip to the cinema to see Mel Gibson's gospel of gore *The Passion* shortly after Easter 2004. It was the presence of Satan in the Garden of Gethsemane, the androgynous figure who at one later point in the film suckles a hideously deformed baby, that triggered the memory of Egdol Lived and the demonic figure in fishnets in Soho. Is it really an accident that Old Nick is portrayed as a woman or half-woman in Gibson's movie? For throughout the history of Catholicism misogyny, sin, sex and shame have been intertwined. And what better way to discourage good Irish Catholic boys from the allure of sex, either DIY or with others, than to associate all its works and pomp with Satan. (Not that this had any lasting impact on altar boys like myself. One of the reasons I took up the offer to serve on St Malachy's altar in the mid-1970s was because the vantage point at the top of the Belfast city-centre church gave you an excellent view of the 'talent' on display in the pews. I spent every Sunday of 1975 lusting from the marble steps underneath the tabernacle at a certain 'Lorraine' from the Malone Road who turned up for Mass every week with her parents.)

One very good Catholic boy who understood long ago the linkage of martyrdom between Catholicism and nationalism was Padraig Pearse – the sartorial and cultural template for our P6 teacher. When Pearse stepped out of the GPO in O'Connell Street on Easter Monday 1916 to proclaim the Irish Republic, he knew that his actions and those of his comrades inside could end in their deaths. But from blood sacrifice, Pearse concluded, free nations could be born, and thus began the destruction of the old world of parliamentary Home Rule nationalism and its replacement by a more violent, uncompromising and separatist ideology.

Pearse's undoubtedly brave, if myopic, utopian single-mindedness turned the GPO into a sacred place for generations of Irish people. Even for those of us born on the 'wrong' side of the Irish border, trapped in the state cut adrift from the rest of Ireland in the Partition of 1921, the GPO remained a Holy of Holies, a Mecca to those in the North who regarded the dead of '16 as untainted by the later compromises the survivors and their successors had to make.

Any visit down South, whether to the Dundalk races on 12 July or school study trips to Dublin, was welcome respite for young Northern Catholics in the 1970s. Outside your ghetto, it was extremely dangerous to wear any badge of Irish identity in Belfast back then. I remember one St Patrick's Day in the early '70s when the sprigs of shamrock and gold paper badges cut into the shape of Irish harps were taken off my green jersey and the green cardigan my sister was wearing when we went to visit our cousins, the Bell family. They lived in the Upper Ormeau Road, which was then being terrorised by gangs of loyalist thugs known as the Tartans. Any open display of Irishness, even on the national day, would have put us at risk, marking us out as 'Taigs' in the Tartans' eyes. So a day out in the Republic, where you could buy cheap little plastic Tricolours or break a tooth gnawing at thick green, white and gold sticky rock, was a small liberation. A pilgrimage, however, to the hallowed portals of the GPO, to see where the men whose portraits hung on the walls of relatives in the Lower Falls and other parts of republican west Belfast, was more than just a treat; it was an honour.

On my first ever journey to the place of the 1916 Fallen during a school trip, I sought out the bullet holes still scarring the exterior of Dublin's main post office, placing my finger into the cavities where the rounds had struck, wondering if it was this shot that wounded the Irish Labour hero and my personal favourite of the rebels, James Connolly. While ordinary Dubliners milled about the interior of the GPO buying stamps, sending parcels, wrapping up presents for loved ones who have taken the boat and plane out of the state, our class wandered around awestruck in the place where 'it' all began.

Many years later when I lived in Dublin, first as a student and then later as a journalist for the de Valera family's Irish Press Group, the historical significance of the building had faded. At times you were reminded of its centrality to the republican narrative when activists from the various IRA factions and their off-shoots would sell their newspapers, or, at Easter, the green, white and gold lilies (the symbol of the Rising), outside the GPO's doors between the giant exterior columns looking onto O'Connell Street. But it is only recently that I have paid more attention to the GPO, not so much for what it represents from 1916 but for how much the Irish Republic has moved on from that vision of Ireland imagined by Pearse way back then.

If Patrick Pearse's ghost returned to the very spot where he laid down the Proclamation, the unilateral declaration of independence that draws, in its own words, legitimacy from 'God and all the dead generations', then this spectre would be truly horrified. For directly across O'Connell Street from that very historic point is a shop that represents all that Pearse once abhorred: materialism, hedonism and, worst of all, Britishness. In the Ireland of the twenty-first century, Pearse would be looking over towards an Ann Summers shop!

This particular Ann Summers store symbolises on the one hand the sexual revolution Ireland has experienced over the last decade or more, yet on the other still exposes the double standards of official Ireland when it comes to matters of sex and sexuality.

Up until 2004, it was the only Ann Summers store anywhere not to have the company's title and the little heart-shaped logo above its front window. Ann Summers of O'Connell Street became the latest casualty of the age-old Irish-solution-to-an-Irish-problem: the authorities in Dublin simply pretended it wasn't there. Before the start of 2004, every time you would pass by the shop it would be packed with customers, mostly female as well as a few embarrassed, sheepish males. Dubliners knew the shop was there but their local council played out a farce that allowed the shop to trade while ensuring that the famous Ann Summers title/logo was kept safely away from Irish eyes.

On the other side of O'Connell Street, after passing the hideously grey gigantic hypodermic spike of Dublin piercing the skyline on a late April day, there are just two tourists inside that part of the GPO where you can buy postcards commemorating the Rising or stamps with the names and faces of the Proclamation of 1916 on them. In the main post office, a series of portraits commemorating the Rising are placed on either side of the interior. Stylistically, the paintings are J.M.W. Turner meets socialist realism. Only a group of giggling American tourists takes any notice of the pictures, the obscuring swirl of dark paint over the heroic, homoerotic figures in the centre. Following the

Yanks around the mini-tour of the Rising pictures, I am suddenly reminded of those days leading up to all the Easters of my childhood when on Good Friday we would be taken around the edge of St Malachy's Chapel, retracing the footsteps of Christ to Golgotha. Strolling around the inside of the GPO, it suddenly strikes me that these portraits of sacrifice and death are secular versions of the stations of the Cross.

Traversing Ireland's main street again, I can count about 25 people, mostly women, although there are a few men but none in dirty raincoats, inside the Ann Summers shop, scanning the shelves for Rampant Rabbit vibrators, leopardskin-lined handcuffs, butt plugs and glow-in-the-dark dildos. Remote-control love toys are laid out alongside the racks of PVC bras, frilly knickers, sex manuals, soft-porn videos, French maid costumes, tubes of KY jelly, stimulant creams and condoms. At the counter, a girl barely out of her teens, who has several parts of her body pierced and an exposed midriff that reveals a Celtic-style tattoo on the small of her back, is wiggling her hips to the beat of loud garage music. In order to counter any suspicion that I'm just a dirty old browser flicking through the panty rails, I take a packet of champagne-flavoured condoms and a copy of an Ann Summers sex guide to the pay point. As the gyrating girl gift-wraps the presents, she notices that I'm watching her body movements.

'I'm tryin' ta liven the bleddin' place up,' she explains in a gloriously unapologetic thick Dublin accent.

Retracing my steps from the GPO, I then saunter down a packed Henry Street on what is now a beautiful spring afternoon. I pass by a news-stand beside an arcade that has copies of *Playboy* and *Men Only* displayed openly on its kiosk – magazines that just over a decade earlier had been banned in Ireland. Through the throng of shoppers outside Arnotts, I move on towards my final destination, to a street that is turning into Ireland's Soho.

In the 1980s, Capel Street was one of the drearier routes from the north inner city down to the River Liffey. It was a place where you bought carpets, paint, army surplus clothing and musical instruments. There was and still is a seedy downbeat feel to the area, a perfect location, therefore, for the invasion of sex shops that began shortly after 1993. There are at present four such establishments in Capel Street, each catering for every legal sexual taste in the Irish capital. They include the international adult sex shop and pornographic chain, Private. Judging by the traffic at the doors of Private, Utopia and the other shops, business is booming.

To anyone outside Ireland, the presence of these shops in a busy commercial city-centre street would be unremarkable. But in the Ireland of pre-1993, their existence would have been unthinkable. There are parallels here with other Catholic countries of the EU who have evolved from authoritarian, traditionalist societies into the post-modern, multi-cultural, individualist era. When my cousin, Tony Matthews, first visited Spain in the 1970s, he later reported back that it was still a society locked in the grip of Catholic authoritarianism. After Franco died, the lid was lifted not only politically but also socially. I remember Tony coming back from Madrid at the start of the 1980s and telling me that the Spanish capital had changed almost overnight. One of the indicators of this new freedom was the explosion of sex cinemas and adult shops around the city – hedonistic and very public pleasures that had been repressed under Franco. Ireland, of course, remained a democracy through slumps, world wars and the Cold War, while most of Europe had succumbed to dictatorship, occupation or both. Yet Irish society up until the personal revolutions of the early 1990s remained culturally repressed and socially retarded. The conspicuous consumption in the twenty-first century of every new pleasure, including those of the flesh, is in part a reaction to that legacy.

Vintage Irish double standards were on display during the summer of 2003 when the tabloids (both British and locally owned) became obsessed about a couple in a farmhouse on the edge of Wexford town. Nuala Moran and her Belgian husband Paul were turned into national celebrities overnight after they were exposed for running swinging parties at their rural home. For several months, photographers with telephoto lenses camped out in fields around their house while reporters posed as farmhands, council officials and tourists as they tried to extract any salacious detail about the sex parties taking place there. The Tony O'Reilly-owned *Sunday World* even snapped a picture of the couple outside their farmhouse along with their pet Labrador dog Salem. The animal also became a star during this summer of swinging at the 'Lover's Leap' farm, and Salem's fame was to result in absurd farce.

Nuala and Paul were at first perplexed and then later deeply distressed over the massive and disproportionate attention they received. I met them in September 2003 inside the Marine Hotel overlooking Dun Laoghaire harbour. Nuala was first to breeze into the bar of the hotel, which for some inexplicable reason was packed with OAPs from Northern Ireland. She wore a plain, black, long-sleeved T-shirt with a New Age crystal bouncing between her breasts. Her husband followed, also dressed totally in black, with trendy polo-neck jumper and razor-thin designer glasses.

When they sat down to afternoon tea, Nuala recounted a hilarious incident in the weeks following their exposure in the Irish press.

'After the photo of Salem appeared, a man came around to our house from the Irish Society for the Prevention of Cruelty to Animals. The ISPCA man was very apologetic, almost embarrassed, to call on us. But he told us that someone anonymous had rung the ISPCA to express concern about Salem's welfare given all the awful stuff that was going on at our farmhouse.'

The mind boggles over what the caller might have thought was being done to Salem during the swinging parties the couple had been holding at their farmhouse every weekend prior to the media intrusion.

Paul was more amused than angry over the hysterical coverage of them and their friends' sex lives.

'In Belgium, or next door in Holland, going to swingers' clubs isn't an issue, it isn't the kind of thing the newspapers would ever want to write about,' he told me in a perplexed tone.

The couple met in Belgium and spent many weekends travelling to the legion of swingers' clubs in the Low Countries and north-western Germany. When Nuala returned to Ireland in the late 1990s, she and her husband decided the time was right to bring the swinging experience to the Irish.

At the height of 'Lover's Leap's' popularity, they were receiving a minimum of ten calls per day from other couples or single women and men wanting to meet other couples for sex parties. Nuala said she estimated that over two to three years there were between four to five thousand regular hardened swingers in the Republic. Others in the 'lifestyle', as swingers call it, estimate that this figure is much higher, possibly up to thirty thousand.

It is hard to believe that this 36-year-old freckled-face strawberry blonde with a west of Ireland accent would become a crusader for sexual freedom in Ireland. But in the aftermath of the media storm that broke over them, Nuala and her husband founded an association to defend the human rights of swingers. Their Irish Lifestyle Association was set up to support local swingers and dispel myths about their activities.

'We set up the Irish Lifestyle Association to fight all this nonsense printed about us in the rags. The Association gives an accurate picture of the swinging scene, which shows that it is women who are in control at our parties, that no one is coerced into the lifestyle, that there are absolutely no drugs and no drunks at our get-togethers,' Nuala protested in between the Earl Grey and buns overlooking the lawn of the Royal Marine.

What kind of people attended their parties? Paul reeled off a number of professions, including businessmen, shopkeepers, doctors, nurses and even members of the Garda Siochana. Most surprising of all, Paul said that the majority were from rural areas as opposed to the liberal and affluent suburbs of South County Dublin.

In the autumn of 2003, Nuala and Paul maintained a defiant stance on the Internet and in the press over their defence of swinging. They developed a website (www.Irishlifestyleassociation.com) that included advice for couples thinking of joining the swinging scene.

'One of the things we advise is that people are sure of themselves sexually before joining the lifestyle. That's why it's better if they are mature, rounded couples who know what they want,' Paul, the IT web-designer for the site, pointed out.

At the time, Nuala and Paul portrayed themselves as crusaders for freedom and defenders of the last of Ireland's sexual minorities to come out of the closet into the public glare. Nuala even compared their campaign to the gay pride struggles of the '70s and '80s in the Republic. However, within six months the website had disappeared from cyberspace, with Nuala and Paul retreating back into private obscurity. The demented and often skewed coverage of this adventurous and refreshingly open couple's private life had placed unbearable pressure on them.

The targeting of the couple by newspapers who not only thrive on a diet of sex and tales of kiss-and-tell but also print scores of advertisements selling everything from phone sex lines to adult dating agencies encapsulates the immature and hypocritical attitude of Ireland towards sexual liberty. Disapproval goes hand in hand with salacious attention to detail, moralising is accompanied by the soundtrack of schoolboyish sniggering. The Republic may have indeed undergone a remarkable sexual revolution over the last 15 years but sections of Irish society have not yet grown up when it comes to the new freedom people enjoy in the bedroom since the shackles of sin and shame were lifted in the early 1990s.

With his tongue barely in his cheek, the author and social psychology lecturer at University College Dublin, Michael O'Connell, contends that sex in Ireland started in 1993. In his tour through postmodern Ireland called *Changed Utterly*, O'Connell borrows that infamous phrase from the English poet and weird misanthrope Philip Larkin, who wrote that 'sexual intercourse began in nineteen-sixty-three'. Why then 1993? Because by then a number of important milestones on the road to individual freedom in the bedroom had been passed. Homosexuality had only been decriminalised in 1990, condoms only became legally and widely available two years later, and in 1992, through the case of a 14-year-old rape victim who the state initially tried to intern in Ireland to prevent her from having an abortion in Britain, the rights to freedom of information on termination and to travel out of the Republic to have the procedure performed were established. Although abortion-on-demand remains strictly illegal, the escape valve that Catholic fundamentalists tried to close remained open. Moreover, in that same seminal year, the Irish people voted in a referendum to allow couples suffering marital breakdown to divorce – only ten years after a previous referendum in which the population of the Republic had rejected Garret FitzGerald's proposals for divorce.

The X case (the issue of the 14-year-old victim pregnant through rape) became the defining moment in the struggle between liberalism and fundamentalism in the South. One cartoon summed up the cruelty and absurdity of the state's role in seeking to detain the child against her will to prevent her from having a termination. Martin Turner of the *Irish Times* drew a map of Ireland with the 26 counties of the Republic sectioned off from the north-east by barbed wire, and in the middle of the island there was a child with pigtails clutching a teddy bear. Above the cartoon ran the headline: 'The re-introduction of internment – for 14-year-old girls.'

The very morning I picked up my *Irish Times* and spotted Turner's brilliantly succinct image over the op-ed page, I knew that the X case would rebound on the government and the fundamentalists pushing for the child to be stopped from travelling to Britain; that the people would vote for freedom of information and travel even if they, by a large majority, abhorred abortion.

It is hard to convey to non-Irish people, especially those in the rest of the EU or North America, how sexually repressed Irish society was even up until the 1980s. As late as the end of the '80s, I was still carrying boxes of condoms in my holdall for friends while returning to Dublin from Belfast on the Enterprise train. When I then worked on the de Valera-owned *Evening Press* in Dublin, I sought out some files from the library for a story I was writing on condoms at the time of liberalisation. I couldn't find them under 'Contraception' or 'Sex' and eventually ended up asking the serially unhelpful librarian where to find condoms in the catalogue. He reluctantly shuffled out of his seat on the top floor of his soporific office overlooking the River Liffey and grumpily flicked through the file-index until he found all the cuttings on condoms: they had been classified under crime. And that was in 1992!

As with the X case, it took a titanic battle in the Irish courts to give people the right to have access to condoms in public places like bars, clubs and cafés. The struggle began in the sixteenth-century splendour of Trinity College Dublin and at the centre of it stood a young woman who almost went to jail to promote this freedom.

Ivana Bacik personifies the social revolution in Ireland over the last decade and a half. At the start of the 1990s, she was on her way to prison for printing abortion information in Trinity and distributing condoms to students, which was still illegal then under Irish law.

Bacik and her colleagues were saved from the prospect of several nights in the overcrowded, Aids-ridden Mountjoy jail only through the intervention of their lawyer, Mary Robinson, who argued that the students had the right to print the abortion clinics' details under the European law defending freedom of information. Several months later, Robinson, the Labour Party's candidate, was elected as President of Ireland.

I remember sitting in the cramped and crowded press bench inside the Four Courts reporting on the fate of Bacik and her students' union colleagues who were taking on the might of the Church and state. It never struck me at the time that this was a key turning point in the liberalisation of Southern Ireland, that Bacik and her friends were the vanguard of this revolution.

We meet again 14 years later, once more inside Trinity College. Ivana is dressed in funeral black from head to toe, flicking through her legal tomes inside her rooms at Trinity. Outside, as a howling wind prowls around the cobblestoned streets of the 400-year-old college, the death toll from the Madrid bomb massacre continues to rise on the news wires she checks on her computer. She is preparing for the forthcoming 2004 European elections campaign. Now a law lecturer, social commentator and latterly one of the Irish Labour Party's candidates for Dublin, Bacik admits that she is still staggered over how much has changed in the Republic.

'Sometimes I pinch myself and remark that it's all been amazing,' she says. 'What is most amazing of all is that it is not that long ago that you could be prosecuted for simply publishing the numbers and addresses of abortion clinics in Britain, or that it was illegal to distribute condoms to students on campus.

'From the court case to Mary Robinson's election, and then the X case and the referenda liberalising information, divorce and so on, the country underwent rapid change. It was great to play a part in that revolution.'

The Catholic right try occasionally to turn the clock back but Ivana says she was encouraged by the outcome of the last referendum in March 2002 when the female urban vote played a decisive role in defeating the traditional right's move to roll back freedom of abortion information.

Because of her outspoken stance on contraception, abortion and gay rights, Ivana has been subjected to a torrent of abuse from the Catholic right for the last 14 years.

'Back in 1989–90, during our court case, I kept getting hate mail and loads of rosary beads and prayers from a group of extreme right-wing people. The messages went from lines like "You are going to be shot" to "We are praying for you". There was some pretty nasty stuff back then.'

Bacik's candidacy is again attracting the fire of the right. But she comes from a family well used to threats and abuse from zealots. Her grandfather was a Czech resistance fighter under the Nazis and fled to Ireland in 1946 after the communists seized power in a Soviet-backed putsch. Despite growing up in Cork and later Dublin, Bacik's Czech antecedents, along with her liberal radicalism, has sparked a new wave of abuse.

'Ever since I became a Labour candidate, the rosary beads are back, as well as one racist note that stated: "Go back to Romania."'

The death toll from Madrid reaches 100 on the wires as we talk about the bad old days when condoms were filed under 'crime', threats were made to ban British newspapers like *The Guardian* for printing abortion information and women like Ivana could be sent to one of the most dangerous jails in Western Europe for handing out contraceptives to students in order to protect them from rising Aids levels in the Irish capital. As the wind outside pulverises a bare tree at her front window in the college, we laugh together about the quaintness of the Ireland we have left behind, the one where Irish politicians on television used to warn the people against the evils of condoms on supermarket shelves just like 'heathen England'. Condoms are now widely available on the shelves of Tesco and Sainsbury's stores throughout the Republic. As Michael O'Connell reminds us, there has been 'no audible outcry' over that scenario. When I leave Ivana and make my way through the storm that is battering the college's historic walls, I feel a shudder of horror running along my spine, not so much from the bone-penetrating cold but rather the memory of those dark days pre-1993 when the bishops and cardinals and their allies in the Dail exercised an iron grip on the private lives of every Irish citizen. Our laughter in the tutorial room about 'quaint old Ireland' just a few moments before was uncoloured by any dewy-eyed sentimentality over our youth because far too many lives have been blighted through decades of repression and oppression and the corrosive terror of morality tales like 'Egdol Lived'.

In *Changed Utterly*, Michael O'Connell stretches the Philip Larkin analogy further by quoting the poet's infamous and now hackneyed line: 'they fuck you up, your mum and dad'. O'Connell adopts this for Ireland arguing: 'they fuck you up, those priests and nuns'. By the end of the twentieth century, a litany of court cases, national political scandals and public inquiries revealed the extent to which 'those priests and nuns' were at times quite literally 'fucking up' generations of Irish children.

In the summer of 1994, Albert Reynolds was enjoying national and international acclaim over his efforts to secure the IRA ceasefire on 31 August of that year. Along with John Hume, the then Taoiseach had been responsible for weaning the Provos off their violent campaign and into the democratic, constitutional fold. Yet, by the end of that historic year, Reynolds was out of office and cast into political oblivion. So much so that when he indicated he might run for Fianna Fail as President of Ireland three years later, the man who undoubtedly helped bring about the IRA ceasefire was dumped for Mary McAleese.

Reynolds' downfall began with the Fr Brendan Smyth affair – the Catholic priest wanted in Northern Ireland for the repeated abuse of children in care and whom the Catholic authorities moved on from parish to parish instead of revealing the extent of his paedophile activities to the police. Worse still, when Smyth's crimes against children became public thanks to the efforts of investigative reporter Chris Moore, the Irish state delayed the priest's extradition to Northern Ireland to face the accusations of the children he tormented. Three months after the IRA cessation, Reynolds sought to appoint Harry Whelehan as President of the High Court in Dublin. However, Whelehan had been blamed during his time as Irish Attorney General for delaying Fr Smyth's extradition to the North. Reynolds' junior partners in the coalition, the Labour Party, then pulled out of government and the administration collapsed.

The deluge of dirt that had engulfed the Catholic Church since it was revealed two years earlier that the Bishop of Galway, Eamon Casey, had fathered a child and was dipping into diocesan funds to pay for his son's upkeep in the United States, as well as to buy the silence of his former lover, was now turning into an unstoppable landslide. After the Smyth affair led to Reynolds' exit from government, hundreds of victims of clerical sexual abuse came forward to tell their story. The courts became clogged up North and South with cases involving priests who sexually molested and abused their young charges. By the beginning of 1995, a joke was doing the rounds across Ireland that summed up the low standing of the Catholic Church.

Q: What does Priest stand for?
A: Paedophile Residing In Every Single Town.

Relations between Church and flock reached their nadir during a live interview on RTE's *Late Late Show* conducted by the king of talk shows Gay Byrne with the then leader of Ireland's Catholics Cardinal Cathal Daly, when the latter was shouted down by members of the audience angry over the hierarchy's dismissive, arrogant attitude to the scandals of sex and lies erupting all around them. Daly, like other bishops and cardinals at the time, appeared like a rabbit caught in the headlights.

When David McCullough (now RTE's political correspondent) and I confronted the Bishop of Ferns, Brendan Comiskey, in 1993 to ask if he had known about Eamon Casey's affair with Annie Murphy and the son the lovers had produced, he seemed like a broken man. Jet-lagged after a flight from the Far East, all too aware of the futility of further cover-ups and obfuscations, Comiskey openly admitted to two startled young reporters from the *Evening Press* that not only had he known about Bishop Casey's son for years but also the way the Diocese of Galway had been used as Casey's private bank to cover up the affair. For a boy like me growing up in a world where priests were feared and respected, where to speak out against the clergy was tantamount to national betrayal, especially for those of us surrounded by the Prods in the North, these almost daily revelations of sexual abuse, secret lovers and corruption were earth-shaking moments. And yet there was even worse to come when it became clear that among the most vulnerable children growing up in the Republic after the Second World War there was systematic and industrial-scale abuse (sexual and physical) going on.

In early March 1998, through one of my closest Dublin friends, a man approached me to talk about his life inside one of the most famous orphanages in the Irish state: Artane Industrial School in north Dublin. Thomas 'Anto' Clarke had been a 'pupil' there between 1968 and 1972, and was later transferred to another Industrial School in Letterfrack. Because he continually tried to escape from the institutions, the priests, including a perverted duo known to Artane boys as 'Batman and Robin', beat and starved Anto. Clarke describes his time at Artane and Letterfrack as 'life in a gulag'. Not only were many of the boys used as sexual playthings for some priests and subjected to ritualistic beatings and humiliations, 'pupils' were turned into squads of free labour for the Brothers and businesses and farms connected to the industrial schools. 'Pupil' is an entirely inappropriate word to describe the status of children like Clarke in these institutions; 'inmate' is a more apposite term. The children sent to Artane and similar places in the years following the war and up to the eventual closure of the schools in the early 1970s were processed like criminals, sent through the courts, often taken away from their parents against a mother or father's will and treated as if prisoners in institutions where they were forced to work as slave labour.

After Clarke's testimony of abuse and exploitation went public, dozens of other men and women who had been similarly incarcerated, either on the word of their parents but more often the Gardai or 'concerned citizens', came forward to tell their stories. A couple of days after Anto's story appeared in *The Observer*, a former member of the Artane Boys Band, now a businessman in London, contacted me. Patrick Walsh had a similar tale to tell and recognised many of the figures Anto identified as the chief abusers and exploiters at Artane, such as the infamous 'Batman and Robin'. An articulate, organised and highly determined man, Walsh set about establishing an organisation to represent men like him, the Irish Survivors of Child Abuse (SOCA).

Walsh was incarcerated in Artane along with his brother John in 1963, and stayed there until 1969. Throughout that period, he played in the world-famous Artane Boys Band, which entertained millions around the world, including the crowds at the All-Ireland Hurling and Gaelic Football finals every September. Walsh reminds us that, behind the idealised image of Ireland's pure sons dressed up to look like Thunderbird puppets, marching around in military fashion while playing patriotic tunes, there was a hidden world of sexual abuse and violence.

'Violence was a constant companion at Artane; most came from the Christian Brothers, who appeared to get perverse satisfaction from inflicting pain on the children. Sexual abuse by its nature was usually secretive, though around 1968 a former Christian Brother took to calling up to Artane to take children out for the day. He had a minibus and was on good terms with the Christian Brothers in charge. This guy had the run of the place even at night but he had a creepy feel about him and had caught me in a corridor one day. It was lucky for me a group of lads came along and he let me go. Others, as I found out, were not so lucky,' Walsh recalls.

The impact of Irish SOCA and other aligned organisations working on behalf of the victims obviously had an effect on the Irish state. In a secret paper from 1999, which I obtained and later published in *The Observer*, Irish civil servants briefed ministers about sex abuse in orphanages and industrial schools. The document labelled the victims of these crimes as dysfunctional potential paedophiles who were a danger to their own and other people's children. The memo revealed the true attitude of the Irish establishment and its intertwined relationship with the Catholic hierarchy. Its authors regarded those who suffered clerical abuse not as victims but rather possible perpetrators of future crimes. This nasty smear, drawn up long after it had been proved beyond reasonable doubt that there had been systematic and widespread abuse of children in these Church-run, state-funded schools, demonstrated that victims who spoke out were somehow 'enemies within'. This attitude prevailed right up to the dissolution of the 1997–2002 Fianna Fail/Progressive Democrat coalition. Indeed, the very last piece of legislation the outgoing government introduced before the country went to the polls in June 2002 exonerated the Catholic Church from having to pay compensation to thousands of men and women who claimed they were abused in the industrial schools and orphanages. Education Minister Dr Michael Woods' last act as a minister was to shift the cost burden of a new commission/compensation scheme for victims from the land-owning, asset-holding, multinational Catholic Church to the hard-pressed Irish taxpayer. The latter would have to pay the full costs of the Catholic Church's crimes against children. This sordid episode at the fag-end of Bertie Ahern's first government proved that, despite the scandals and exposures involving bed-hopping bishops and paedophile priests, the hierarchy continues to exercise considerable political influence in the Republic despite the protestations of Irish ministers and their special advisers that the state is becoming increasingly secular.

Socially, the Republic has undoubtedly evolved from a mono-Catholic, culturally homogenous, deferential society into a modern European state. The Irish Republic is still very much a Catholic country, religiously and culturally. In the last census of 2002, it was found that Roman Catholicism commands the allegiance of 90.2 per cent of the population, albeit this shows a drop of 3.6 per cent compared to 1991.

But Irish Catholics, particularly along the eastern seaboard where most people live, take an à la carte approach to their religion and morality. They still go to Mass in comparatively higher numbers than the population of any other EU state. They send their children, in the main, to Catholic-run schools and their offspring still go through the early spiritual rituals of Confession, First Communion and Confirmation. They get married in and bury their dead from Catholic churches. The overwhelming majority of them hold onto a belief in God.

These same people, however, use condoms regularly when they have sex, even if the Church teaches, to borrow a quip from a Monty Python film, that 'every sperm is sacred'. (The film in question – *The Meaning of Life* – was actually banned in Ireland in the 1980s.) Fewer Catholic couples are getting married. The Irish birth rate is slowing down. Births outside marriage – once the subject of social stigma and public scorn – leapt between 1988 and 1998 by a staggering 150 per cent and the trend continues to rise sharply. In conjunction with this tendency towards à la carte Catholicism among the laity, the number of men and women entering the Holy Orders has declined dramatically. Between 1990 and 1998, for instance, the number of priests leaving Holy Orders was five times higher than those being ordained.

There have been numerous attempts by the traditional Catholic right to roll back the frontiers of liberalism. Traditionalists, initially at least, were encouraged by the election of a conservative Catholic president in 1997, the Northern Ireland-born academic Mary McAleese. During the presidential election campaign, McAleese became embroiled in a surreal row over her alleged sympathies for Sinn Féin. This was based on two Irish government briefing papers, one of which took advice from the SDLP's Brid Rogers that the future president had been supposedly 'soft' on the republican movement. Regardless of the veracity of these claims, the issue, which would dominate the campaign and generate sympathy for McAleese, crowded out a far more important question regarding her traditional Catholicism. Fergal Bowers, the editor of the *Irish Medical Times*, and myself uncovered a letter McAleese had written during the 1992 X-case controversy. In the letter, McAleese supported those who would have preferred to keep the 14-year-old rape victim in Ireland, against her will, rather than exercise her right under European law to travel and have her pregnancy terminated. McAleese's stance on the X case, however, was lost in the furore over the Irish government memos about her alleged political sympathies. Mary Holland, the veteran and deeply respected commentator for *The Observer* and the *Irish Times*, later told me that she battled in vain inside the latter's D'Olier Street head office to persuade the news desk that the 1992 McAleese letter on the X-case was a far more significant issue to focus on than the tittle-tattle of secret government briefing papers. Regrettably, Mary Holland lost that particular editorial battle.

It was no accident that this perceived champion of Catholic traditionalism came from the Northern nationalist community. Although she would later uphold the neutrality of her office, reach out to the loyalist community in the North and antagonise the bishops by taking Communion in a Protestant church, McAleese undoubtedly represented that segment of Ireland's four million Catholics who were less enthusiastic about the sexual and personal revolution taking place in the Republic from 1993 onwards. In Northern Ireland, the nationalist press devoted far less coverage to the Brendan Smyth, Eamon Casey and other clerical scandals undermining the Southern public's confidence in their hierarchy. Northern Catholics were more inclined to blame the 'self-loathing liberals of Dublin 4' (whoever they are) for allegedly hyping up and exaggerating the depth of hypocrisy and the extent of abuse committed by the religious orders. During two unhappy years I spent as security correspondent at BBC Northern Ireland, other reporters, not only myself, met with stiff resistance from news managers when trying to cover the clerical abuse scandals. Although we were fobbed off with excuses, such as these stories not being 'picture-rich', I was later told privately that a number of prominent lay Catholics in senior positions and on broadcasting watchdogs did everything in their power to protest about what they saw as 'disproportionate' coverage of clerical abuse stories.

Although the urban Catholic working class in the North had long ignored some of the most important moral imperatives laid down by their bishops – that, for instance, it was 'sinful', to use Cathal Daly's term, to vote for any party linked to the IRA's murder campaign – the middle classes in Northern Ireland remain among the most conservative and reactionary anywhere in Western Europe. As far back as 1981, they formed up as the infantry in the Catholic Church's war to prevent the merger of third-level teaching colleges into one secular institution. They collected petitions, wrote letters and agitated their politicians to ensure the Chilver Report into the future of teacher training colleges was discarded and the system would remain demarcated along sectarian lines.

The anti-Chilver campaign boiled over into hysteria. One elegantly dressed, pristinely made-up woman with dyed-ginger neatly coiffured hair called at our door to gather our family's signatures in opposition to the Chilver Report. When I informed this lady, who had come around to the house in the Markets before to canvass for the SDLP, that I supported the merger of the colleges, she became indignant. Thus began a fusillade of warnings about what the 'Prods' would do to the Catholic people. 'They [the Prods] would turn the air off on us if they could,' she assured me, as if the bonehead loyalists had any influence or interest over the future of teacher training in Northern Ireland! The Catholic Church's subsequent victory ensured that teachers, never mind children, would continue to be trained apart in separate Catholic and state colleges.

But social attitudes and bedroom activities are changing even amongst this conservative section of Ireland's Catholic middle class. Growing prosperity for Northern Catholics – brought about through equality reforms to ensure no more unionist-based discrimination, the peace dividend of the ceasefires and the expansion mainly through the public sector and the legal profession of the nationalist middle classes – has led to unforeseen consequences. In the run-up to the publication of the 2002 Census report in Northern Ireland, republicans crowed about the growth of the Catholic population at the expense of Ulster Protestants. Sinn Féin's Mitchell McLaughlin, for instance, predicted that, for the first time in the history of the Northern state, the Protestant population would fall below 50 per cent. However, republican projections – their assumption that their constituency was out-breeding the Prods, their crude bio-sectarian head-counting – proved to be entirely unfounded. The Protestant population remained over 50 per cent and the Catholic birth rate was starting to fall. The principal reason for this slowdown in the Northern Catholic birth rate was rising prosperity. Following the trends in the rest of the EU, including the Catholic countries of the Mediterranean, Northern Irish

Catholics were having fewer children as their income levels rose. Which in turn meant that, despite what their bishops and priests laid down from the pulpits, their flock in their thousands were taking the pill or using condoms on a regular basis, even in the conservative redoubts of rural, middle-class Catholic Ulster.

Just a few weeks after returning from honeymoon, on a second holiday in San Remo on the Italian Riviera in 1996, I was forced to go to Sunday Mass in the beautiful Madonna della Costa situated on a hill overlooking the famous Ligurian resort. During the homily, the parish priest thumped the lectern several times in what was obviously an impassioned plea to his parishioners. My wife's aunt later translated: like other priests across the Italian republic that Sunday morning, he was imploring couples to have more children. Italy's birth rate was then and still remains lower than Ireland's.

The 1993 sex revolution meant more to one sexual minority than any other section of the Irish adult population: the gay community. The contrast between the Republic pre-'93 and today is glaring for gay men like Brian Finnegan. His journey back to Ireland personifies the progress gays and lesbians have made in the South over the last 11 years. He left Dublin in 1987 for London, where the gay scene was just emerging out of the underground; it would take the Irish gay scene more than a decade to do the same.

Finnegan is the current editor of *Gay Community News*, once a dull news-sheet modelled on the lines of a solemn left-wing agit-prop paper but now a slickly produced, glossy colour magazine, which is more style bible than activist propaganda organ. We sip at steaming coffee, Evian water and pure orange juice upstairs in a café located around the corner from *GCN*'s new offices inside the trendy Temple Bar 2 quarter at the back of Dublin's Wood Quay. He agrees that 1993 was the critical year for gay liberation in the Irish Republic.

'When *GCN* was distributed around Dublin before 1993, it had to be sent out wrapped in brown paper bags like a dirty book or something. There were only two or three bars that were openly gay, whereas in England the Soho scene was thriving and Manchester's gay village had just opened. It was the dark ages back in Ireland.'

These were dark ages because gay sex was still a crime right up to the early 1990s and, while prosecutions were rare, the pervasive feeling that what they were doing was illegal maintained an atmosphere of oppression, Finnegan explained.

The change occurred after Maire Geoghan Quinn, the then Justice Minister, announced that the ban would be rescinded. Finnegan said gay men and lesbians were encouraged by the fact that no one either in the Dail or society at large raised any protest. De-criminalisation encouraged the gay community to emerge from the shadows.

'The first Gay Pride march took place in June 1993. There were about 1,000 people taking part in the demonstration and it felt great. We walked down O'Connell Street that Saturday afternoon shouting, "We're Queer, We're here, We're Queer, We're here." There was euphoria about it, a sense of disbelief that we were walking down the main street of Ireland celebrating our sexuality.

'I had just arrived back when these changes were taking place and was astonished at the pace of the change. It just seemed to happen overnight. The most significant event for me, more so than the O'Connell Street parade, was a Gay Pride march through Galway City in July of that year. There were only 150 of us walking through Eyre Square, holding up the traffic, passing by the shoppers and the tourists. I remember little old ladies smiling and waving at us. What it showed was that the average Irish person even in the so-called conservative west of Ireland was tolerant of gay people, regardless of what the Church had to say. And at last we were no longer invisible!'

Chatting with Brian, I am struck by the same sense that I experienced with Ivana Bacik a month earlier: that he is looking back with no sense of nostalgia for times past. The *GCN* editor grew up in a society where homosexuals were either the butt of national jokes (Liam McLiammoir and his partner were known as the 'pets of the nation') or else dismissed as perverts and, even more sinister, a supposed danger to morals and children.

'There was a mass conspiracy of silence. Gay sex didn't officially exist in Ireland. Thank God those days are over,' Finnegan says now.

The fortunes of two gay icons in the new Ireland personify the way that heterosexual Ireland has ignored the imperatives of bishops, cardinals and even popes (the Vatican in 2003 denounced homosexuality as 'evil') and embraced the gay community: the Joycean scholar and Irish senator David Norris and the transvestite television presenter Shirley Temple Bar.

Shortly before Easter 2004, David Norris, a lifelong campaigner for gay rights in the Republic, announced that he would introduce a Bill in the Irish Senate to force the state to recognise gay unions in law. His Bill marks another milestone in the sexual revolution and, surprisingly perhaps, it has provoked little or no reaction from the Irish political class. It will also mark the last political battle of his 35-year career in Irish politics. The openly gay senator stresses, however, that his Bill is not only aimed at protecting the rights of gays and lesbians but also heterosexuals who live with each other but are not formally married.

'In terms of financial benefits such as inheritance rights, gay men, lesbians and unmarried couples are still second-class citizens in this state. So take a gay couple who have been together all of their adult lives. If one of those men dies, his partner at present has no legal rights to inherit his long-term lover's pension. The same is the case with mortgages, where a house cannot be handed over to the lifelong partner if their lover, who is the mortgage holder, were to die. It is a terrible injustice which must be righted,' Norris says.

He points out that there have also been instances where lifelong partners were denied access to their lover while he/she was dying in hospital.

'I have dealt with cases where a long-term lover goes to see his partner and that partner's family ban him from seeing his lover. This is because they are not recognised in law as next-of-kin and so have no rights even on the edge of death.'

In pre-1993 Ireland, such a struggle against these terrible injustices would have caused outrage among the Catholic moral right. But even those who defend traditional Catholic values have given up the fight. They admit that there is no widespread public anger on issues like gay marriage/unions. Whilst the Catholic bishops oppose Norris's legislation, Catholic commentators accept that the issue is likely to be less heated than the controversy over gay marriage in the United States.

Simon Rowe, the editor of the influential *Irish Catholic*, says of the gay union issue: 'It is not going to be a lightning rod for Catholic anger.' He adds: 'In the United States, gay marriage will be a key domestic issue during November's presidential election. I honestly don't think that our politicians, with respect, have the same philosophical rigour to campaign on social issues like this in Ireland. Although the Bill will open up the floodgates to any civil union, it is not an issue that sets people alight the way, say, abortion does.'

The lack of hysteria over gay unions recognised in Irish law reflects the shifting moral landscape of the Republic. Back in the late 1980s, politicians in the Dail were claiming Aids was God's revenge on gay people. Today, a gay Miss Shirley Temple Bar presents the popular prime time *Telebingo* game show on RTE 1. Meanwhile, two of the key characters of Network 2's urban youth-orientated drama *The Big Bow Wow* are a gay Garda detective and his English DJ lover.

Shirley Temple Bar's success is bewildering even to gay writers like Brian Finnegan; her presence on prime-time Irish television unthinkable just over a decade ago.

'Shirley's success shows that people don't really care; in their day-to-day lives they are tolerant. Here we have a drag queen presenting a show that is most popular with little old ladies and housewives, including those living in those conservative rural parts of Ireland. It's just another sign of the incredible change that's happened,' the *GCN* editor reflects.

For David Norris, the new freedom represents a golden age for the Irish gay community.

'I remember when we organised our first discos far back in the 1970s, when homosexuality was still illegal, you saw young gays who were psychologically scarred, hurt and damaged. It's good to leave those days behind.'

If, however, the Irish government decide to block his Bill, the 60-year-old senator vows to come out of semi-retirement for a final fight.

'If the government does obstruct the legislation, there is one battle left – I will take them all the way to the European Court of Human Rights.'

Jeff Dudgeon has already been to the European Court of Human Rights, all the way back in 1981 when he forced the British government to overturn the outlawing of homosexuality in Northern Ireland. North of the border is still a bleaker landscape for lesbians and gay men. Bigotry and hostility towards the gay community is more vocal, ingrained and nasty, especially amongst evangelical Protestant Christians. Just a fortnight after David Norris introduced his groundbreaking Bill, there was an incredible outburst of anti-gay hysteria on the Ulster airwaves. *Talkback* – Radio Ulster's weekday news talk and current affairs show – focused on the prevalence of gay men and lesbians on soap operas like *EastEnders, Coronation Street, Emmerdale* and Radio 4's *The Archers*, which featured a gay kiss involving a homosexual from Northern Ireland. The shock-horror phone calls from concerned citizens, almost all women, reached panic pitch. Callers rang in to denounce gay love as 'evil', 'dirty' and 'perverted'. All this happened, by the way, just days after several gay men were beaten up by homophobic thugs in Derry.

The hostility of evangelical Christians and their political allies on the unionist right is, of course, riddled with hypocrisy. One of the nastiest homophobic incidents I witnessed was when the then Northern Ireland Secretary Peter Mandelson visited Portadown just before the Drumcree Orange Order march in July 2000. As Mandelson entered Carlton Street Orange Hall, hundreds of loyalist extremists harangued the New Labour politician with chants of 'Homo . . . Homo . . . Homo'. I had to repress a smile while standing amidst these brainless bigots. Were they aware that so many bachelor Orangemen and unionist leaders had been closet homosexuals? Were their chants really a case of the loyalist lads protesting too much? This obsession of evangelicals and loyalist extremists with gays and lesbians in the North borders on the pathological; through its vehemence it reveals a toxic cocktail of guilt and self-loathing.

Northern Ireland, however, is no longer as hostile or claustrophobic a place for gay men and lesbians as it was during the years of gay bashing, illegality and the Paisleyite campaigns to 'Save Ulster From Sodomy'. The latter crusade failed thanks to the European Court of Human Rights, which, by 1982, had ruled that the continued outlaw on gay sex in Northern Ireland was itself illegal under EU law. Jeff Dudgeon, the veteran gay-rights activist, who fought to have the law changed all the way to Strasbourg, is, like David Norris in Dublin, optimistic about the future for gay men and lesbians in what is still a deeply conservative and religiously devout society.

Ten years after the 1993 sexual revolution in the Republic, the first ever gay sauna was opened in Belfast. Sex in saunas has now been legalised in Northern Ireland under the Sexual Offences Bill, which finally abolished the crimes of gross indecency and buggery. The Garage sauna is part of a new gay village for central Belfast, located in the city's newspaper district with the gay-owned bar and disco The Kremlin being the centrepiece of this latest development.

Straight boys and girls owe an enormous debt of gratitude to the gay community, which through the darkest days of the Troubles in Belfast kept some semblance of nightlife alive. The gay owners of nightclubs like the Plaza and Delta in Donegall Street threw open their doors to straights as well as gay men and lesbians. The clubs held alternate nights where on Fridays in the Plaza the discos were for gays and on Saturdays mainly for the straights. Even at the mainly gay discos on Fridays in the Plaza, after you warded off the advances of men dressed in pencil skirts, high heels, stockings and tight shirts that revealed false boobs, when the clientele and staff finally worked out that you were straight, there was a high degree of toleration and respect. For that small band of anti-sectarian youth based around the music scene in the '80s, gay clubs were relatively safe places to drink after the pubs closed at 11 p.m., given that they were usually free from the bigoted hordes of spides hell-bent on smashing someone's face in at the end of the night.

As late as the mid-1970s, the Royal Ulster Constabulary was raiding the premises of the gay contact and information group Cara-Friend. In 1975, for example, the RUC arrested 20 members of Cara-Friend and threatened to prosecute them on charges of sodomy. Only the intervention of the Attorney General in London halted these sexual show trials from taking place. Think about it: hundreds of sectarian murders were being committed all over Northern Ireland in the first half of the '70s and yet the RUC devoted some of its scarce manpower and resources to arrest, charge and attempt to convict 20 adults simply on the grounds they were having, or may have been having, anal sex. Almost 30 years later, the Police Service of Northern Ireland has created a liaison unit to work with the gay community and to defend lesbians and gays against homophobic attacks; another small but important measure of how life in Northern Irish society has radically improved for gays.

Each of those sexual minorities – on the one hand struggling for equality and social acceptance and on the other those fighting for justice over the crimes of Church and state – represent a disparate, heterogeneous coalition for freedom. In their individual and different ways, they have wrought a cultural and social regime change in Ireland. Whilst the political establishments North and South remain untouched over the last decade or so, these social movements have transformed the two nations.

The greatest paradox of the Irish sexual revolution involves my former co-religionists. Catholics in the South have essentially become very 'Protestant' in their approach to the directives from Rome-Centre. They now pick and mix their morality as they choose, in an exercise of private conscience. Even their supposedly more conservative brethren in the North are, in ever increasing numbers, using contraception, having sex before marriage and divorcing when marriage breaks down. The morality tales like 'Egdol Lived' no longer shock the flock into submission. Horror stories of raven-haired temptresses turning into Satan or tendentious cinematic images of an androgynous devil suckling a child while Christ is flayed can no longer stop Ireland from swinging.

CHAPTER SIX

The Wealth of Two Nations

Upstairs in a dank and draughty derelict office overlooking Cromac Square at the top of Hamilton Street is where I was sworn into the Official IRA's junior wing. There were Tricolour and Starry Plough flags, the latter the emblem of Irish Labour, draped over an unstable wooden table with only three legs. Behind it on a leather office chair sat a 17-year-old gaunt and pale man, a transparent fringe of moustache on his upper lip and tufts of wispy hair sprouting from his chin; in front of him was a nervous, shaking 11 year old standing bolt upright to attention, with his left hand held upright, repeating an oath that today I cannot remember. After years of chasing after the older boys in stone-throwing ambushes of British Army foot patrols, keeping look-out for gunmen and petrol bombers, walking along the pavements trying in vain to join the parade of menacing teenagers in their dark sunglasses, army jumpers and green and black berets marching through the Markets, I finally thought I was a 'made-man'. It was 1976 and although our 'war' was in reality long over, I believed I was finally enlisting in a secret People's Army that was no longer meant to exist.

It is 2004 and I am seeking out again the man sitting behind the table in that foul building commandeered by the Official Fianna in the

Markets 28 years earlier. On an unseasonably cold May afternoon, the sky is darkening outside the DART train as I travel from Dalkey to Bray, the sagging low-lying rain clouds merging into the grey stillness of the Irish Sea. As the 1.30 p.m. arrival rolls into the station, I notice that on the wall behind Bray Wanderers football stadium someone has daubed in black: 'Class War'.

My stomach lurches at the prospect of meeting my old Fianna inductor after a gap of 12 years. The last time we had spoken was inside the same church where we were both baptised, St Malachy's Chapel in central Belfast. I had come there in 1992 to discuss the latest feud to break out among the breakaway republican factions in the city, a violent power struggle within the extreme Irish People's Liberation Organisation (IPLO). The sanctuary of St Malachy's was the safest place to meet him. I was now a journalist, my old friend one of the chief protagonists in the intra-IPLO battle that would claim five lives.

Now we are reunited on the concourse of Bray railway station and he looks the same as ever, hardly a fleck of grey in his hair after years of imprisonment under the Supergrass system, narrow brushes with death and the trauma of a life in the centre of republican violence. I am half-expecting a hostile reception because of what I wrote about the 1992 feud, as ever treading carefully so as not to provoke any paranoia-induced response, or accusations of siding with the 'other crowd' or working to a British agenda, etc., a common trait of all veteran republicans you meet. The greeting instead is warm and genuine. Stephen 'Bronco' Downey is glad to meet and talk with someone from home.

But I have come here not just to see him but also to revisit his adopted home over these last dozen years, the seaside town on the border between counties Wicklow and Dublin where revolution was once preached along the promenade overlooking the Irish Sea.

In the early 1970s, Bray was one of the favourite destinations in the 'great escape' for Belfast's working-class Catholics every mid-July. So, early in the morning of 12 July 1976, my mother, father, sister and myself walked the short distance from the Markets to the GNR railway station in Great Victoria Street. Although we set off at 8 a.m., the streets around the station were already thronged with Orangemen and their supporters staking out vantage points from which to watch the annual Twelfth parade through the city. We managed to mingle into the crowds and crossed Great Victoria Street before the bands and the Orange marchers arrived.

Inside the grand station there were loyalist bandsmen dressed in assorted uniforms of red, white and blue. Some of them were already drinking from dumpy bottles of Harp and Smithwicks, 'curing' their hangovers from the night before at the bonfires held on the eve of the Twelfth. Others roamed around the platforms looking for Fenians heading for the southbound trains. At the kiosk in the centre of the station, where you could buy the latest edition of the *Amazing Spiderman* and other Marvel comic superheroes, I witnessed at first hand the ugly face of loyalist sectarianism. Whilst queuing up to pay for my Marvel comic and two bottles of lemonade for Cathy and myself, a group of loyalists wearing petrol-blue jumpers and matching blue berets with protruding flower-shaped plumes of cotton dyed red and white started abusing people around the kiosk. The hassle only amounted to a few thugs bumping into elderly Catholic men waiting to be served at the counter and the odd bigoted remark muttered behind the travellers' backs. But outside the kiosk, one of the loyalists got so close to my face that I could smell the stale stench of lager on his breath. He hissed: 'Wee Fenian bastard.' Now I knew why we were leaving for Bray that morning.

We spent the day of the Twelfth roaming around Dublin, paying homage to the heroes of 1916 at the GPO and watching with contempt the Orange march back at home live on television inside a bar off Middle Abbey Street. Then we stayed overnight at a guest house in Talbot Street facing Connolly Station. I remember the walls of the bedroom the four of us shared shaking violently in the night as the late passenger and freight trains roared along the raised rail platform at the back of the B&B, crossing north and south over the Liffey to and fro from Connolly.

The following morning was my mother's birthday and for a treat we went out to Bray by bus from nearby Busáras. For the next three days we stayed in another B&B on a street leading down to the promenade that was lined with amusement arcades, tatty shops selling rock, giant sweety dummies and ice cream as well as novelty items like the plastic piece of fake vomit that I bought and placed at the side of my sister's bed just before she woke. There was also a string of pubs on the seafront, including the Bailey Bar where my parents would take us every evening of the holiday after dinner.

In the '70s, Bray had become a Dundalk-by-the-sea; like the north Louth border town, the resort was a haven for republicans on the run from the North as well as a centre of radical agitation by the warring factions of left-wing republicanism. Seamus Costello, the former IRA man who split from the Officials and created the Irish National Liberation Army, was still an Urban District Councillor in Bray at the time. His estranged comrades in Official Sinn Féin, such as the local doctor John McManus, also had a strong presence in the town. The two rival republican socialist organisations had just emerged from a murderous feud the year before and feelings were still running high in the town. The year after our visit Costello, too, would be dead.

Despite our family's sympathy lying with the Officials, my father maintained a policy of remaining on good personal terms with both sides of this latest divide. In Bray, this meant we were caught in the middle of fierce debates inside the Bailey Bar on the rights and wrongs of the Officials' 1972 ceasefire, the split two years later and the subsequent murders carried out by each faction in 1975. The men we sat and drank with had two things in common: they all preached the imminence of an Irish revolution and almost all of them sported the same droopy moustaches, from which every night of our holiday there dangled droplets of tan-coloured froth from their Guinness. On our second evening, the late James Doherty, a kind gentle giant of a man from Co. Derry, whose brother was later to become the INLA's chief-of-staff, sat with my mum and dad drinking Irish coffees in the Bailey. Quietly he sought to persuade them (in vain) to join/support the INLA's political wing, the Irish Republican Socialist Party (IRSP). Big James, who was generous to Cathy and myself during our short stay, shared Costello's mistaken belief that 'armed struggle' in the North could somehow precipitate revolution in the South.

But today, their dreams of the 'Socialist Republic' have long since faded away; they have proven to be as impermanent and insubstantial as the tan froth melting on the moustaches of all those saloon-bar revolutionaries way back in the Bailey Bar. In the new century, Bray remains a slightly shabby, run-down seaside town, which has seen better days; Bray's environs, however, are among the richest in Ireland.

Two stops north on the DART is Killiney, one of the Republic's most affluent quarters, the 'rock-broker belt' that is home to the likes of Bono and The Edge from U2, Van Morrison and Enya. A couple of days before my reunion with Bronco, I took a drive with friends around this prosperous corner of south County Dublin and north Wicklow. The roads leading to Dalkey village and then Killiney contain echoes of Ireland's colonial past, as we drive along Westminster and Albert roads. On the former route, we spot the chief executive for a multinational mobile phone company in Ireland, who has just bought a cottage for €1,500,000. Further down Albert Road, one of my friends points to a bog-standard semi-detached house with three bedrooms, which he says has just gone on the market for €700,000. As we move on towards Killiney, his wife reminds us of a saying in south Dublin. 'In the late 1980s and '90s, they used to say you would need to win the Irish Lottery to afford to live in Killiney – a million Irish punts would have been enough. Today you would have to win a rollover jackpot in the UK Lotto to afford anything in Killiney,' she says just as we pass by Enya's mini-castle on Victoria Road.

Turning onto Vico Road, where on May Day 2004 Tony Blair sat down to lunch with Bono and his family, we pass by another row of inconsequential cottages. In 1987, these properties would have sold for between 80 to 90,000 Irish punts; today they are likely to go for upwards of €800,000, as not only rock 'n' roll tax exiles from Britain but more than ever the nouveau riche who made a fortune in the Irish economic boom that became known as the Celtic Tiger aspire to settle on Ireland's Riviera.

While on the road, I notice other motorists doing exactly what we are doing on this May morning: cruising around this ultra-fashionable area of south Dublin, star-spotting and secretly dreaming of the break that will land them a place in Killiney. Because that is what the majority of Irish people aspire to: to make enough money to become The Edge or Neil Jordan's next door neighbour, to own the €5 million house with a helipad in the back garden and wake up every day to the vista of the Wicklow Mountains and the sea. These are the real dreams of the Irish bosses and workers alike; not the 'people's control of the means of production, distribution and exchange'. Painful as it may be to write this, the Irish have embraced the revolution – the one started by Margaret Thatcher three years after our family Twelfth holiday to Bray.

I can't bring myself to express these heretical thoughts to Bronco, lest he accuse me of selling out on socialism. When we finally sit in the back of John Doyle's pub, a bar Stephen used to drink in when he was on the run from the British authorities in the 1980s, both of us reminisce. I sip at my Guinness whilst he slurps on his cider and I ask him if he recalls my swearing-in ceremony in Hamilton Street all those years ago.

'There were so many we swore in up there for the Fianna that I lost count,' he confesses as we both try to ward off the sexual advances of a horny Jack Russell who constantly mounts our legs under the table.

And what about socialism and the republic, I ask him. Where did it all go wrong?

Bronco has no answer but rather lists a string of tragedies that afflicted first the Officials and then the IRSP/INLA, all the various deadly divisions and feuds that claimed so many lives, so many victims that we both knew personally. Although we ended up on different sides in this internal struggle – he joined the INLA after being brutalised by a local Official IRA commander two years after the 1975 split, while I stayed a supporter of the Official Sinn Féin and later the Workers Party – we both agree on the utter futility of the feuding and faction fighting. We express particular regret about the death of Thomas 'Ta' Power, shot dead along with another Markets man John O'Reilly at the start of an intra-INLA feud in 1987.

Then he turns to the present generation, who have been fortunate enough not to experience a life like we did under incipient civil war.

'The teenagers today are more interested in spending two hours in the bathroom getting ready for a night out, and that's just the boys. There's a lot of indifference even in the poorest areas down here. Everybody just wants to make money,' Bronco says in a despairing tone.

I inform him that it's exactly the same north of the border. Politics is a minority pursuit and those involved in street fighting in Belfast are motivated by the tribalism and the rivalry of Rangers and Celtic rather than revolution.

Our conversation explores dark corners of our past in the Markets:

the bloodthirsty, the insane, the absurd. The cast list includes Bronco's brother Joe, a Provisional IRA gunman shot dead during a gun battle the day after the Bloody Friday massacre in July 1972; Robert Elliman, an Official IRA internee shot dead by the Provos in 1975; and Stephen's friend Jim Power, who was blown up in front of him whilst transporting a bomb in a paint tin during the 1981 hunger strike.

'I was never sectarian, never,' Bronco protests and personally I believe him. But his protestations are irrelevant. The armed struggle from the outset contained the germ of sectarianism; it unleashed the contagion that spread rapidly across Northern Ireland from the day the Provos decided to launch their 'war of liberation' on a deeply divided society. It was made all the worse by the armed intervention of the INLA. Intention is secondary here. The net result was always going to be disaster. And after that disaster, the survivors have now crawled from the wreckage. That is how I see Stephen and men like him. They have been damaged by what they have done and what they have endured. Their dream has not been and probably never will be realised. All some of them are left with is the residue of basic humanity, of empathy even with one's victims. He is particularly remorseful over the murder of Karen McKeown, a young Protestant missionary from east Belfast whom the INLA gunned down in cold blood during a mad outburst of sectarian revenge in 1982. Bronco was arrested and questioned about the woman's killing. He said he had nothing to do with it and, knowing the man as I have since I was a child, I accept his denial without question. His disgust nearly a quarter of century later has not diminished. It is the chink of light, a spark of humanity flashing in the dark recesses of our shared history.

As we part warmly in Bray Station, Bronco suggests that perhaps he should write his own book about life and death in the Markets during the worst days of the Troubles. I encourage him to do so, to exorcise the ghosts, to get all of this off his chest for good. On the DART train back to central Dublin, underneath the ads for men's Nivea cream and shaving foam (I am reminded of Bronco's remark about the young spending two hours getting ready to go out) and mobile phones, I look up at my fellow passengers. They are a mixed bag of kids from south-side posh schools gabbling away in California-speak, using words like 'whatever' and 'cool, and 'totally'. Close by stand a huddle of Eastern Europeans speaking what could be Russian, who have come to capitalist Ireland from former communist countries for a new life. The North, the Troubles, the dreams of the Socialist Republic, the past of Bronco and myself, mean nothing to either group bunched together on a packed train passing through some of the wealthiest suburbs anywhere in the EU.

More heresies are uttered the next day inside Buswell's Hotel next to the Irish parliament. They fall from the lips of a youthful-looking 43 year old who has become the unofficial spokesman for the new right in Ireland. Paul MacDonnell is the antithesis of all that Bronco stood for. Yet he is a revolutionary in his own right, determined to roll back the state, promote the free market and argue for even more privatisation and de-regulation. His experience of the 1970s was radically different from either Bronco's or mine.

'I remember the '70s as a time of conformism and dullness. To be a businessman was not something you were meant to aspire to. Freedom in parts of life was restricted. There was no consumer choice. The left was in vogue right up to the economic crises of the 1980s. A lot of my generation went to the left back then, so I suppose I was the exception to the rule,' he says in between sips of cappuccino in the bar facing the Dail.

Whilst we read Marx and Lenin, MacDonnell devoured the works of Milton Friedman and Friedrich von Hayek, as well as the pamphlets of Keith Joseph, Margaret Thatcher's personal new-right guru. Paul and I quickly found out, though, that we did share something in common: we are both philosophy graduates. It suddenly strikes me that most of those I have ever met who majored in philosophy and who are in their 30s and 40s share his new-right vision of the world.

Surely, then, he should be delighted at the way Ireland has turned out. The Irish Republic is ranked seventh in the world as the freest economy on the planet, according to the latest Economic Freedom of the World report. Vast swathes of the public sector have been privatised, taxes have been cut, foreign investment has flooded in and prosperity propelled by the free market has soared. Yet MacDonnell refuses to be complacent, believing that Ireland still needs to undergo an intellectual revolution.

'There is still a prevailing view in the Republic that Thatcherism was wrong and that greed is bad. There is a guilt attached to earning money, getting wealth, among official Ireland, especially in the media. There is still a belief that certain institutions like the civil service, for instance, are untouchable,' MacDonnell states with all the ferocity of a true believer.

MacDonnell insists Ireland's economic turnaround, its embrace of the free market, only came about because there was no alternative.

'While in Britain there was an intellectual struggle in the Tory Party before Thatcher came to power, Ireland went the same way only because there was a pragmatic realisation that things couldn't stay the same. Statist culture is still ingrained in Irish society.'

In response to what he sees as the prevalence of that 'statist culture' in Ireland, he has set up the pro-business Atlanticist Open Republic Institute, a think-tank aimed at challenging the left in the battle of ideas. In my former life on the left, I would have hated not only everything MacDonnell stands for but maybe the man himself, such was the intolerance of a Marxist-Leninist cadre. These days, alarmingly, I find myself agreeing with a lot of what he has to say and starting to regard him as the real revolutionary and the old left as the new conservatives.

MacDonnell launches into a passionate argument over his favourite gripe: the transfer or dumping of economic risk.

'Successive Irish governments are dumping risk onto workers in the private sector,' he explains with conviction. 'So the taxpayer has to finance a civil servant throughout his or her life, to ensure that there are no risks, that he/she can't be sacked and that they receive a good pension on retirement. But the civil servant is being supported by a trainee hairdresser through his or her taxes. The trainee hairdresser has no job-for-life guarantees or state-backed pensions. She or he takes the risk for the civil servant. Where is the justice in that?'

His crusade is to shine light into what he calls the 'dark matter of the economic universe', the dumping of risk from the public to the private sector. MacDonnell's thesis is devoid of any class bias or snobbery. If anything, his vision for the Republic is of a classless society in which no interest groups are safe from the cold winds of free-market competition. He even wants to see powerful monopolies like the Law Society broken up and exposed to competitive practices. Again, his arguments are based on a notion of equality and classlessness.

'A couple of years ago, the government de-regulated the taxi industry and broke the monopoly in that business. It has resulted in hundreds more cabs on the streets and lots more consumer choice. But why just pick on the taxi men and women who don't exercise much power in society? They were easy meat for the state compared to big interest groups like the legal profession. If the present government is serious about opening up Irish society to more competition, then they need to de-regulate the Law Society, allow private legal institutes to be set up and create new lawyers, to end the monopoly of control on this business.'

MacDonnell graduated from Trinity College Dublin appropriately enough in 1984, as the literary world debated the legacy of George Orwell's nightmare vision of a totalitarian society and Margaret Thatcher was locked in a real life-and-death battle with Arthur Scargill and the miners. In the same university, around this same period, a group of economists were charting a path for government that would turn Ireland into one of the most successful capitalist economies in the world and throw up an intellectual and electoral challenge to the mainstream Irish left.

Dr Sean Barrett likes to tell jokes at the expense of some of my former comrades. The first one is a reversal of the old Irish Labour slogan at the end of those over-optimistic years of student protest and revolutionary fervour. 'The Seventies will be Socialist,' the Irish Labour Party promised at the end of the 1960s. Labour leftist critics preached similar prophecies, only these were to be brought about not through parliamentary democracy but through either the vehicle of the Provos' armed struggle or a Bolshevik-style revolt of the Irish working class. Both visions failed miserably, which has prompted Dr Barrett to make a prediction of his own: 'In this decade, the Socialists will be in their Seventies'. He also continually delights in pointing to the durable delusions of the Irish left right up until 1989, the year of the Tiananmen Square massacre, the Berlin Wall's fall, Solidarity's victory over the communists in Poland, the Prague Velvet Revolution, the darker, bloodier uprising in Romania.

Rocking back and forward in his leather chair inside a cramped office one floor up on the Arts Block of Trinity College, Dr Barrett refers to a 'relic' from 1989. It is the Institute of Public Relation's annual yearbook for that historic year. Inside are lists of various and disparate voluntary and political organisations in the Republic. They include a listing for the Irish–GDR Friendship Society, of which I was once a member. Dr Barrett bursts out laughing when I tell him this and then reminds me that the IPR book mentions the society's last annual meeting/fundraising event in Dublin. A band called The Train Now Leaving provided entertainment for the pro-East German PR front organisation. The head of economics at Trinity can't contain himself any longer.

'Imagine that, eh? The Train Now Leaving playing for the Ireland–GDR Friendship Society and in the very same year the people of the GDR were leaving in their droves by train to get out of the place, to escape to the West, to get as far away from communism as they could. You couldn't make that one up,' he chuckles while scanning the papers belonging to students who are about to knock on his door.

The two undergraduates who arrive in quick succession at his office, interrupting our chat, embody the new Ireland Dr Barrett has witnessed emerging after years of recession, chronic unemployment and mass emigration. The final-year student is seeking a reference from his tutor for a job in United Airlines. He informs us he already works for the United States carrier and now has to decide whether to enter the business management end of the corporation or pursue a career as a pilot. While at Trinity, he says he managed to earn his pilot's licence. He, like the next student to rap on the door, sees his future either in the US or working for an American corporation. She too has come to seek a reference before jetting off to work in Wall Street this summer.

'You see what I mean?' Dr Barrett says. 'These are the new Irish who are comfortable working anywhere in the world. They don't sit around moaning about their lot but get out there and are determined to make money.'

In the same year as communism's collapse, Dr Barrett was advocating a strong dose of Thatcherite medicine to cure the sick man of Western Europe. By 1989, the Republic was in a dire economic condition, with record unemployment and emigration levels, PAYE taxation at 68 per cent and crippling national debt. He and a cabal of other economists would meet politicians at Dublin's Unicorn Restaurant, where the former would urge the latter to slash personal taxation, reduce public spending and lift taxes on corporations in order to attract foreign investment. Their enemies and friends alike referred to these meetings of minds as 'An Bord Snip' given the intellectuals' penchant for slashing the public sector.

Whilst Dr Barrett and his fellow thinkers were proposing a free-market libertarian solution to the Republic's ills, it seemed ironic during that terminal year for socialism that the Southern Irish left was suddenly on the march. The 1989 national and European elections in the Republic witnessed a surge in support for the Workers Party (the descendants of Official Sinn Féin), with Proinsias De Rossa topping the Euro-poll in Dublin and the Workers Party securing six seats in the Dail. By this time I had abandoned politics for journalism (I believe to this day that reporters and correspondents should, for ethical reasons, not even vote!) and put clear blue distance between myself and my old comrades. Nonetheless, I couldn't conceal my delight at De Rossa's victory and even attended a de facto celebration for him and the six TDs at Club Ui Cadhain, the Workers Party-controlled basement pub just a few yards away from their HQ in Gardiner Place.

Yet 1989 turned out to be the watershed year for the party and the future of socialism in Ireland. Just before De Rossa's triumph, the party's chief pamphleteer Eoghan Harris published an internal paper on the direction the Workers Party should take in the light of glasnost and the imminent death of communism. Harris started his 'Necessity of Social Democracy' in 1988 and ended it just before the slaughter on Tiananmen Square. The essential thrust of Harris's polemic was that Marxism was obsolete, particularly because of its suppression of the individual in favour of the collective. The most telling aspect of this brief but earth-shaking document was the section Harris labelled 'The Primacy of the Person'.

> Socialism said that politics was about the collective, about society, about the proletariat, about any number greater than one. And in 1989, the people of Europe, for the second time in 200 years, told us that was not so, and that politics is always about the person. The individual is the whole point of history.

Therein lies the overarching theme of this book, of my personal journey, of the struggle between the freedom of the individual and the desire for collective justice. 'The necessity of social democracy' – published in a series of pamphlets entitled *The Wealth of the Nation* –

hammered a stake through the heart of the ideology I grew up with, undermining the long-held view that class loyalty superseded being true to oneself.

Harris's advice to the Workers Party was to ditch Marxist-Leninism and embrace social democracy. His counsel was not heeded, so he resigned, his supporters were expelled and the party staggered on until 1992, when it finally split and the majority faction formed Democratic Left. The greatest irony of this latest division in the various mutations of the original Sinn Féin movement was that, although there wasn't a window broken or a shot fired, it turned out to be the most damaging of all the ruptures afflicting the republican left tradition in Ireland.

Ostensibly, the reason for the schism was the continued existence of the Official IRA and the accusations by the likes of De Rossa and current Irish Labour leader Pat Rabbitte that there was a Marxist 'kitchen cabinet' operating inside the party. The underlying factor, though, for the Workers Party's fragmentation was the refusal to recognise a fundamental reality – that the very people the left sought to liberate had abandoned many of the left's values and goals. The peoples of Eastern Europe had swept away the communist vanguard that had ruled supposedly on behalf of the working class. The peoples of Eastern Europe, and two years later the Soviet Union itself, rather than embrace a Trotskyist workers' republic or a Eurocommunist alternative à la Italia, voted instead to reverse the allegedly immutable route map of history. They supported a return to capitalism and the free market. Given a choice between freedom and state socialism, the peoples who lived under communist regimes opted for the former. Harris's prophecy, penned and printed even before the massacre of students in Beijing, turned out to be deadly accurate.

Other intellectuals across Dublin were also preparing the entire people of the Republic for these new uncertain post-Cold War times. Whilst the rational left engaged in an ideological and ultimately disastrous quarrel normally the preserve of the Trotskyists and Maoist grouplets in the Irish capital, the intellectual right were marshalling their forces, influencing government policy and affecting a real social revolution in the Republic. Even Charles J. Haughey, the charismatic and highly controversial Fianna Fail leader, survivor of the arms trial of 1969 in which he stood accused of arming the fledgling Provisional

IRA, the embodiment of corrupt corporatist Ireland, was being won over to the cause of free-market liberalism.

'We used to hold discussions with Ray McSharry [the future European Commissioner] and through him urged Charlie to stop acting the maggot, to start freeing the taxpayer and relinquishing state controls,' Dr Barrett recalls.

The Trinity College economist is adamant that the political truce declared by Alan Dukes in 1989, when the Fine Gael leader said he would support his party's historic enemies in Fianna Fail in their bid to bring down the national debt and reduce unemployment, was crucial to the success of the new economic programme. Within a decade, Ireland experienced an astonishing turnaround, with double-digit growth, record employment, net immigration into the state, unprecedented wealth levels and the country moving from a net recipient to a net contributor to EU funds. Dr Barrett is convinced that the underpinning philosophy of this reversal of national fortune can be summed up in one word: freedom.

The evidence for Dr Barrett's thesis is compelling and hard to argue against. The Republic is now ranked as either the fourth- or fifth-largest economy in the world, according to the OECD, a position it used to occupy at the end of the nineteenth century when Dublin was the second city of the British Empire, and Ireland, through Belfast, built liner ships such as the doomed *Titanic*. The contrasts between the Republic of '89, before the privatisation of the Irish state sector got underway, and the early twenty-first century are illuminating. At the beginning of the 1990s, the average cost of a return flight on the Dublin to London route was 218 Irish punts; today you can fly on the same journey for €34 to several alternative destinations in and around the UK capital. The opening up of the airline industry, pioneered by Dr Barrett's most famous student, the Ryanair boss Michael O'Leary, has turned the Dublin to London air corridor into the second-biggest inter-city airline route on the planet. The de-regulation of the bus industry has also transformed the lives of thousands of ordinary Irish people. In 1980, for instance, there was one state-owned bus route operating between Dublin and Galway; today, thanks to bus privatisation, there are thirty-four coaches carrying passengers between the two cities every day. Tax cuts have also proved immensely popular and electorally rewarding for the Fianna Fail–Progressive Democrat coalition that has dominated Irish politics since 1997. Personal taxation of the average PAYE worker was 68 per cent at the start of the 1990s; it is now running at a rate of about 42 per cent. Irish entrepreneurs are admired and feared by their competitors the world over. They own large chunks of the British racehorse industry, as well as most of Manchester United, and they are buying up vast amounts of property in central London.

They are already starting to 'colonise' the new nations of the EU, with the Irish becoming the single largest foreign property-owners in countries like Hungary. Every week in the property sections of the *Irish Times* and the *Sunday Independent* there are advertisements enticing homeowners who have suddenly found themselves with tens of thousands of euros to invest from the equity on their houses to buy up in places like Hungary and Bulgaria. Companies such as www.BulgarianDreams.com and magazines directed at Irish investors buying property in Budapest are thriving. Meanwhile, even on the traditional tourist destinations such as the Costa del Sol, the Irish have, in a rapidly short period of time, displaced the British and Germans as the principal investors in property. In Nerja, for instance, one of the jewels of southern Spain, Irish people seeking to buy their dream home in the sun have already replaced the British as the number-one investors in the Andalusian town.

The best measure of the soaring Irish property rates can be gauged every Thursday in the *Irish Times'* property section. On page two of the supplement, the paper prints 'Take Five', a weekly comparison between an individual property in Ireland and what you can buy for the same price at four different locations around the world. On 13 May 2004, 'Take Five' used a mid-terrace house requiring refurbishment on Dublin's South Circular Road as an example. It went on the market for €700,000 but will be sold for more than that. For the same price, an investor could buy a seventeenth-century villa in Lunigiana, Italy, with a country-style kitchen, en suite bathrooms off all five bedrooms, a swimming pool and mountain view. For around the same price as the mid-terrace house in south Dublin you could also purchase a five-bedroom farmhouse in the French Côte D'Azure with a separate guest apartment and 9,000 square metres of landscaped ground. No wonder so many of the Irish nouveau riche are buying abroad, their migration nicknamed 'the flight of the Wild Golden Geese'.

Back at home, the physical transformation not only of Dublin but also provincial towns and villages all over Ireland has been staggering. Up until the completion of the LUAS light rail/tram system, the capital itself resembled a vast building site. Walking down thoroughfares such as Middle Abbey Street, you can stop and listen to the legions of workers laying down the tramlines. There you will hear a babble of languages from around the planet – Chinese, Russian, Romanian, Polish, Czech, Malay and even the odd smattering of English. Once-neglected corners of the city are coming back to life, such as the area between the Royal Canal and Connolly Station. This new development at Crosbies Yard is offering one-bedroom apartments from €270,000 upwards and two-bedroom apartments for over €320,000. There was a time not very long ago when the idea of young professionals settling in and around Connolly Station would have been treated as a joke. In the new Dublin of exorbitant property prices and land pressure, however, the advertisement in the *Sunday Independent* (25 April 2004) for Crosbies Yard warns buyers that 'Demand around this area is very high so these are likely to be snapped up quickly'. The name of the development, the ad-writer reminds potential buyers, is taken from Paddy Crosbie, the songwriter who penned the sugary sentimental tune 'The School Around the Corner'.

In the first quarter of 2004, the average price of a non-new-build house in Dublin according to estate agents Gunne Residential was just over €500,000. Dublin 6 – the areas of Rathmines, Rathgar and Ranelagh popular with lawyers and young entrepreneurs – recorded the highest figure outside the luxury millionaires' rows of Killiney and Dalkey. Non-new-build homes in Dublin 6 in the same period were on average close to €800,000. Those economists and commentators who predicted an end to the boom back in 2002 have been proved entirely wrong.

There is nothing sentimental about the new Celtic man and woman. They have not only changed the physical landscape of their capital city but also unfashionable towns and provincial cities. East-coast towns such as Drogheda and Dundalk have become virtual suburbs of Dublin, with younger or first-time buyers who are unable to afford a house or apartment in the capital settling instead in Co. Louth's two main population centres. The soaring cost of property in Drogheda and Dundalk has even convinced some first-time buyers to look for a home across the border in Northern Ireland. Newry Chamber of Commerce has noted an influx of homeowners from Dublin who now prefer to commute on the one-hour journey south for work and return to the border town in what is officially UK territory in the evenings. Newry, too, is enjoying a mini-boom thanks to the spillover from the Irish economic miracle. Sainsbury's branch in Newry recorded the highest sales figures for anywhere in the UK over Christmas 2003, thanks in large part to the thousands of Southern shoppers who flocked north to buy their food and drink for the festive season. The queues outside the supermarket's wine store on Newry's Quays shopping centre grew so long at one stage that the company had to employ extra security guards to police and control the crowds of Southerners spending their euros in Northern Ireland.

He will not like the nomenclature but Mick Wallace is New Celtic Man personified. A somewhat different unconventional capitalist compared to Sean Barrett's most famous student Michael O'Leary, Wallace is a self-made millionaire builder who started out in business at the end of the 1980s when the Republic was mired in recession, with thousands of the country's youngest, brightest and best leaving for Europe and North America. That segment of Dublin city centre that he now owns was once a rundown, neglected niche in the capital. The area running from Jervis Street (where the hospital for the city's heroin addicts once stood) in a straight line towards the Liffey was occupied by a string of huckster shops and rundown antique outlets. Today it has been transformed into Quartiere Bloom, Dublin's new Italian quarter, with trendy wine bars, cafés, shops selling delicacies and fine wines from Italy, as well as several luxury apartments each costing around €650,000 above seven business units.

Wallace's eclectic tastes reflect the internationalism and strong attachment to Europe among the Irish entrepreneurial class. His journey from small-time builder touring Italy in a Hi-Ace during the 1990 World Cup to owner of Dublin's Italian quarter is symbolic of the turnaround in Southern Irish economic fortunes. The 48-year-old builder who grew his construction company during the 1990s became so enchanted with Italy he decided to bring a little piece of the *Bel Paese* back home.

In between poring over documents and answering phone calls inside his office over the Liffey side entrance to Quartiere Bloom, Wallace explained his company's philosophy: 'Live hard, work hard, play hard'. Every weekend he leaves Dublin for Milan and takes in a home game at the San Siro or the Stadio Della Alpi. After catching a Juventus, Inter or AC Milan match, Wallace drives off into the Piedmontese countryside to check on his newly acquired vineyard at Cortemilia.

'It's in a lovely spot overlooking a valley,' he enthuses as the windows of his office rattle from the vibrations of the traffic on the Liffey's Quays. 'I bought it a year and a half ago and now we have to replant and clear the land. Ultimately, I want to bring this wine back to Ireland and sell it.'

This unconventional shaggy blond-haired builder, who dresses like a heavy rock fan, is the antithesis of the clichéd/offensive image of the meat-and-two-veg, Guinness-swilling Paddy working on the building sites and motorways of Britain. What drives him on is the quest for quality workmanship instead of just getting the job done on time. What sustains him is a thirst for the finer things in life.

'When I started out, I was determined to get a reputation for our company as being proper and honest. A lot of builders in this city get away with poor workmanship just to make a quick buck. I am not in this just for making money, although that's important; it's the quality of the work that I'm interested in as well.'

His drive for quality goes beyond an insistence that building contracts around the city (one of their biggest clients is Dublin Corporation) are carried out to the highest standards of craftsmanship. He believes that standards in the food and wine outlets of Dublin also need to be raised considerably.

'This city is full of restaurants but I wouldn't call the wine or food in them top class. When I go over to Italy, I'm astonished by the high quality and large number of restaurants and wine bars on offer even in a small area of Piedmont. Ninety-five per cent of the wine on offer in Ireland is not fit to be in a glass; but there is a market here for really good wine and food and I intend to fill that gap.'

The wine bar Wallace owns downstairs is stocked with labels from all over Italy, 75 per cent of the bottles originating in the Piedmont region. He has even 'imported' Italian staff from Rome and other cities to guide the discerning Irish customer towards the finer wines and food.

In London and other metropolitan cities of Europe, Quartiere Bloom would quickly evolve into a yuppie ghetto, which is something Wallace is determined to avoid.

'I would like to get a spillover from the pubs and clubs in Temple Bar. I hate Temple Bar but I think people, ordinary people, should be given a choice of finer things – they are not just for the yuppies,' Wallace adds.

Our conversation is interrupted by the arrival of a young Polish man in his early 20s armed with a CV and a list of questions. It is the eve of EU Accession Day, when on 1 May 2004, ten new states, including Poland, entered the European Union. The Pole plonks his CV on Wallace's desk and explains that he has worked in Ireland for years as a builder. He even offers Wallace the services of six of his compatriots, all plasterers, who have worked on a number of building projects in Dublin. As I listen to the two of them – the successful Irish builder, the ambitious young Pole – I imagine that discussions like that must have been commonplace in London, Munich, New York and Boston during the 1980s, only with desperate young Irish men and women offering their services to English, German and American employers. This informal job interview above the Italianate archways and slickly designed bars of Quartiere Bloom is another physical manifestation of that turnaround in Irish economic fortunes.

Blunt and to the point, Wallace tells this new arrival: 'We give everyone a try but at the minute I'm not looking for plasterers. But I'll take a look at your CV.' Then the two men shake hands and the energetic, job-seeking Pole heads out of the office. Wallace is impressed. He points out of the window towards the bronze plaque announcing the opening of Quartiere Bloom.

'There are names on that plaque from 17 different countries who worked for me. They include men from Albania and Romania. I like the Eastern Europeans' attitude to work. They don't mind getting stuck in and learning new things. I have one Albanian guy working for me who started in our company when he was just 17. Now he is in charge of 20 other men as their foreman. Most of the Eastern European workers arrive here in Ireland relatively unskilled and uneducated, but they prove themselves, they demonstrate that they can adapt very quickly.'

Wallace recoils from the new xenophobia taking root throughout the Republic and the rising resentment towards foreign workers. Instead, he welcomes them into the new Ireland and sees their presence as necessary to maintain growth and prosperity.

On one level, he is an unusual entrepreneur. He adopts radical causes such as the No to Nice referendum campaign and sponsors anti-racist projects like the multinational Dublin side Sport Against Racism Ireland. Nonetheless, Sean Barrett would still be proud of him and his evolution, particularly the fact that Wallace started out wanting to work in the public sector as a teacher (he has a teaching degree from University College Dublin) but decided instead to follow his father into the building trade. From the closed-shop world of Irish education, where teaching unions have the power and influence to prevent successive Irish governments from printing league tables of school performances, to the cut-throat world of construction. Truly this man is another son of the Celtic Tiger.

One of the negative by-products of the Irish boom has been the emergence of a newly acquired national smugness, which cuts across all social and class boundaries. It comes to the fore whenever the issue of the cost of Irish reunification is raised. The argument of traditional nationalists is that the Republic is now a marginally wealthier society than Britain and, therefore, could afford to absorb the one and a half million citizens of Northern Ireland. Paradoxically, the Republic's unbounded success is used by hardline unionists as a fear factor, to scare their own electorate into believing that British perfidy and Irish expansionism will soon push them into a unitary state.

Shortly before he died, I went to see Ernest Baird, one of the leaders of the now defunct Vanguard movement, a former ally-turned-opponent of the Ulster Unionist chief David Trimble. We sat together in the headquarters of Baird's chemist dispensary business in Belfast's Donegall Pass. When I suggested that his and the Democratic Unionist Party's prophecies about an encroaching United Ireland were paranoid and out of touch with economic reality, Baird bit back sharply.

'I deal with them fellows in the South on a daily basis in business. And I'm telling you and the unionist people, they are no mugs. The old idea that the South is just a society made up of farmers riding around in carts pulled by donkeys is dead. Them fellows down south could take us over if they wanted to.'

Baird's backhanded compliment to the Irish entrepreneurial class can be taken a little too far, however. Economists on both sides of the Irish border estimate that the shock of absorbing the North would be so great that the Irish economic boom would, in all probability, burst. When Gerry Adams delivered his first-ever talk to the Dublin Chamber of Commerce just after Easter 2004, the Sinn Féin president was challenged from the floor about who would pay for the annual £36 billion subvention Britain pumps into Northern Ireland every year. All Adams could come up with was a glib, intangible response: 'The Irish People – that's who.'

Whether 'the Irish People' south of the border would be prepared to massively increase their taxes to ensure every man, woman and child in Northern Ireland still received their annual £2,000-per-head subsidy is debateable. Germany is still reeling from the crippling cost of absorbing the communist east from 1990. According to economists, the shock for the Republic taking on the North would be even greater than the German experience.

Graham Gudgin, a Belfast-based economist who runs a consultancy firm advising local businesses on new economic trends, estimates that, given Ireland's much lower population compared to Germany, the shock of unity would be five times greater in the Republic than it was in the old western Federal Republic. Moreover, the two economies on the island of Ireland remain hugely different and divergent.

'Northern Ireland is fully integrated into the UK economy. From a Northern perspective, only 8 per cent of trade and goods are exchanged with the Republic whereas it's 33 per cent between Northern Ireland and the rest of the UK. There are two entirely different systems between the North and the South. Far more money is spent on our National Health Service in Northern Ireland than on the Southern health system. The Republic still operates a corporatist model of the economy, where the trade unions sit down with governments to work out national wage agreements – that has long been a thing of the past in the whole of the UK. Trade unions in Northern Ireland sit on a few quangos but they don't have any real national power. There is less resistance to privatisation in the UK, including Northern Ireland, than in the Republic, where the big public-sector unions are still powerful. But, paradoxically, the public sector in the North is still much larger than the South,' Gudgin says.

The greatest barrier to economic fusion, he adds, however, is the existence of two currencies on the island of Ireland. Signs of euro-creep may be obvious all over Northern Ireland – from the thousands of BT phone boxes with yellow bands on top that indicate customers can use both euro and sterling, to the growing number of ATM machines dispensing the euro in Northern city centres and railway stations. The idea, however, that the presence of the euro in UK territory will act as a catalyst to unification is ludicrous, Gudgin warns.

'The Republic is operating inside an entirely different economic zone from Britain and Northern Ireland. The UK maintains control over its interest rates while the Republic, when joining the euro, handed the levers over to Frankfurt. Given the British government's diffidence over entering the euro-zone and getting rid of sterling, the notion that you can fuse two economies with entirely different currencies and interest-rate regimes is absurd.'

The economist's office overlooks a property in south Belfast that points to the other main problem to beset any future unification: security. Just across the road from Gudgin's consultancy is a multi-million-pound block of luxury flats whose front and sides have been defaced with sectarian graffiti. 'Nationalists Out' and 'Republican Spies' are among the slogans that have been daubed on the lower end of two entrances to the apartments. Those responsible for the hate slogans come from the nearby loyalist Sandy Row and Village areas, where, in the spring of 2004, an anti-foreigner/nationalist hate campaign erupted. The Protestant residents alleged that someone inside the flats flaunted an Irish Tricolour at Sandy Row, one of the original loyalist heartlands of Belfast. Whatever the veracity of that claim, the protest marches and sectarian/racist graffiti were symptoms of a general malaise afflicting inner-city Protestant Belfast. At the root of this was a belief that Southern property developers have been and still are buying hundreds of homes at knockdown prices in urban loyalist strongholds and flooding these areas with foreign workers, nurses and even nationalist students. Even that ultimate stronghold of

Ulster Loyalism, the Shankill Road, has not been immune from this Southern-backed spending spree. Although Dublin-based estate agents refuse, for obvious reasons, to speak publicly about their investments in Protestant Belfast, it is now widely accepted that Southern property investors own at least 500 homes and flats in the Greater Shankill area, a social fact unthinkable just a few years ago. If a modest trend in the Southern ownership of property in Belfast can bring people onto the streets (no matter how ill thought out and immoral their cause might seem), imagine the reaction to an announcement that the two states were about to merge.

Dr Gudgin's scepticism about Irish unity through economic fusion has to be viewed with the knowledge that, up until the collapse of power sharing in 2001, the economist worked as an adviser to Ulster Unionist leader David Trimble. He has an 'interest' that he has always openly declared.

Other prominent economists in the Republic, however, concur with his thesis that the financial costs of merging the two economies would destroy the South's boom and wreck the social-democratic, welfarist infrastructure of the North. Sean Barrett goes as far as to implore the British not to abandon sterling for the euro. He blames the Republic's inflation after euro-entry on tagging the South's economy to other EU countries like France and Germany who have yet to, in his mind, reform adequately like Ireland did in the early 1990s.

One of the intellectual architects of the Irish economic miracle has hit upon an unspoken truth throughout nationalist Ireland. He describes the Good Friday Agreement peace deal as the 'optimum settlement'. In other words, the pact that brought about power-sharing at Stormont *within* the UK, that created checks and balances to protect the rights of a growing Catholic minority in the North and set up symbolic cross-border bodies whose powers are nominal and impact on ordinary lives is negligible, is as far as the Republic is prepared to push it. Peace, stability and fairness for Catholics in the North rather than the reclamation of the Fourth Green Field is the desired polity not only of the political establishment but the majority of the Republic's population. There may be an emotional, historically-based yearning for a unitary state (which comes to the fore at 11 o'clock in the pub when the drink is flowing and the traditional ballads are rousing) but, according to hard-headed economists like Dr Barrett, there is little desire to pay the cataclysmic costs – financial and in terms of security – of merger.

From the 1970s onwards, the Irish left was torn asunder over how it approached the Northern Ireland question. It divided broadly into two schools of thought. The first, which drew its inspiration from the new intellectual challenge to nationalist foundation myths in the universities and colleges, came to the conclusion not only that socialism could never be advanced through the barrel of a gun but also that there was a moral and democratic imperative to accept that Ulster Protestants had a right to say no to Irish unity. Any attempt to force the Protestants against their will into a United Ireland, socialist or capitalist, would create an unbridgeable chasm within the Northern working class and lead eventually to civil war. The other school casually dismissed unionism as 'false consciousness', imagining that Protestant workers would come to their senses once the British announced a declaration to withdraw from Northern Ireland. In places like Bray, this divergence of ideas broke up old friendships and alliances; in places like Belfast, it led to kneecappings and murder.

In the Republic by 1977, the battle of ideas had already been won by the first school of socialism. Even in Bray, Seamus Costello's home town where he sat on the Urban District Council, the revisionist left had displaced the old republican left as the coming political force. In the '77 general election, the year of Jack Lynch and Fianna Fail's majority government triumph, Costello faced his old comrades in Official Sinn Féin/the Workers Party (SFWP). SFWP's candidate, the local doctor John McManus, got several hundred votes more than the IRSP's founder, a straw in the wind for the future success of the former party. Just a few months after the election, Seamus Costello was shot dead by the Official IRA in Dublin, his assassination an act of revenge for the INLA murder two years earlier of the Officials' commander in Belfast's Lower Falls, Billy McMillen, a republican veteran whom my mother once worked for in an election in Northern Ireland eleven years earlier.

One of those in Bray who stood by the new revisionist left in the '70s was a recently qualified young architect and one-time student radical, Liz McManus. She had married Dr McManus and later replaced him as SFWP's candidate for the Wicklow constituency.

Thirty years on, she is deputy leader of the Irish Labour Party, a TD for Wicklow and one of the most recognised faces in and outside the Dail.

I arrange to meet her exactly a week after my return to Bray and the pub chat with Bronco Downey. We sit down to coffee in the new annexe building to the left of Leinster House, where government ministers, opposition front-bench spokesmen and women and journalists mill about. In her 50s, she is still a strikingly handsome woman, with beautifully sculpted cheekbones and a slender figure. She knows there is only one question I have come to ask her: whatever happened to Irish socialism?

Before she answers, we both reminisce about Bray in the '70s and the presence of the left in the town.

'Wicklow has always been a microcosm of Irish society,' she says with one eye on the giant TV screens beaming back a debate on the floor of the Dail. 'There is Bray with its working-class run-down estates, isolated villages in the mountains where the rural poor live, housing schemes in towns like Arklow with a growing drug problem, as well as the millionaire houses and the big country estates. It is Ireland in miniature.'

I return to my main question by re-framing it: haven't the Irish working class themselves abandoned socialism and the left? Like any good politician, Liz's answer is a yes and a no.

'Look at the contributions that the left has made to Ireland. We pushed forward the liberal agenda from the early 1970s. I remember as late as 1979 working for John in the local elections when Fianna Fail tried to make an issue out of our support for family planning. Back then, Fianna Fail was opposed to any form of family planning; we were on our own standing up for women's rights. It didn't stop him getting elected and it showed that the people had moved on.

'The left also changed the landscape regarding Northern Ireland. We fought for a more pluralist attitude towards the North instead of reclaiming the Fourth Green Field. Much of what was contained in the Good Friday Agreement 20 years later was what we campaigned for – such as the principle of consent in Northern Ireland.'

She even claims that the recent prosperity in the South is founded on the social-democratic partnership of national wage agreements between the trade unions, business and government. There is a degree of truth in her assertion, as industrial stability has been one of the attractions for foreign capital flowing into Ireland.

Her Labour Party, however, as Liz herself confirms, will not dare increase corporation tax on the multinationals based in Ireland. The Republic has the lowest corporation taxes in Western Europe; Labour knows that to hike the rates up would drive away the foreign companies that have generated the biggest boom in Irish history.

We part as she gets ready for Labour's annual James Connolly commemoration at the statue dedicated to the executed hero of 1916 facing Liberty Hall, the HQ of the trade union movement from where the Marxist rebel led his Irish Citizens Army to the GPO on that fateful Easter Monday morning. Like Bronco and all others to emerge from the republican left tradition, Liz and her comrades claim lineage from Connolly. For the last three decades, the Irish left in all its multi-faceted forms, Stalinist, Eurocommunist, Trotskyist, social democratic, have fought over the remains of the Edinburgh-born socialist like a fraction-prone family arguing over the estate of a lost loved one. In the 1970s, this dispute turned murderous; we who survived those dark times can be thankful at least that these arguments are now conducted on a more civilised basis.

Two ex-members of SFWP, Liz and Pat Rabbitte, now lead the Labour Party. The mainstream Labour movement has finally absorbed this small but intellectually and socially influential strain of the republican left tradition. This tradition championed what were once unpopular and electorally dangerous positions to hold: the abolition of Articles 2 and 3 of the Republic's constitution (the old imperative to seize back Northern Ireland), the separation of Church and state and the primacy of individual conscience.

Here, in relation to the quest for a socialist republic (the secular religion of my youth and student days), then lies the greatest paradox of all. The left championed the rights of the individual against the overweening power of the Roman Catholic Church. Liz is right: they were the pioneers who campaigned for the availability of contraception, for the right to divorce, to ensure women got equal pay with men, to decriminalise gay sex, to change Ireland from a virtual theocracy into an open European society. Yet, in doing so, they also created the conditions in which globalised consumer capitalism could thrive. Paul MacDonnell and his Open Republic Institute – the intellectual nemesis of Liz McManus and her comrades – has touched on a painful truth after all. Ireland does indeed owe the rational left a great deal; they did, in fact, invent the grammar of personal freedom in Ireland; but the liberty the people opted for had no room in it for either state socialism or the Workers' Republic.

CHAPTER SEVEN

Sicily Without the Sun

Jimmy Guerin holds the mobile phone close to my ear so I too can listen in on this bizarre conversation. He is talking to a self-confessed Dublin criminal; the subject of their chat is the purchase of a gun.

'We're in St Stephen's Green,' Jimmy informs the gangster. 'How quickly could you get the piece to us?'

The phone crackles and the sound of a thick Dublin accent breaks through the airwaves: 'I could be there in half an hour but it'll cost you €350,' the man on the other end of the line tells us.

Suddenly Jimmy starts shouting down the phone, apologising for being unable to hear the caller, pretending the line is breaking up.

'I'll call you later,' Jimmy promises and then closes the palm-sized silver phone.

He takes a sup of coffee, then flicks the mobile open again and dials another number, this time in search of foreign women for sex.

'Hello, there,' Jimmy says. 'I've a friend with me from Northern Ireland who wants a girl for the evening. How quickly could I get one?'

This man tells us he could get one in 20 minutes, or, if we prefer, we can log online instead to www.irishescorts.com and there will be an endless string of women of all nationalities available. Jimmy again makes his excuse about a crackly connection and terminates the call.

183

In the space of half an hour, I could have bought a handgun and hired a trafficked woman for the day, Jimmy says. Welcome to twenty-first-century Dublin!

It is one month to the eighth anniversary of the death of Jimmy's sister Veronica, the journalist murdered on the orders of drugs barons and the subject/heroine of a Hollywood movie starring Cate Blanchett. After Veronica was assassinated in cold blood on 26 June 1996, the Irish government was forced to confront the criminal underworld in Dublin. The public outcry over Veronica's death prompted the then liberal-left Rainbow Coalition government to hunt down major crime lords in the Irish capital. The Irish state set up a Criminal Assets Bureau (CAB), which would eventually be used to seize millions in cash, property, businesses and luxury items such as top-of-the-range cars from Dublin's fantastically wealthy gangsters. The CAB became a permanent monument to Veronica's memory and in the first few years after her killing, the bureau seized tens of millions of euros' worth of assets from criminal gangs. The pressure on the crime bosses became so intense that many, such as George 'The Penguin' Mitchell, left the Republic altogether, secreting their riches abroad and running their empires by remote control from the Spanish Costas or Amsterdam.

The standard wisdom is that Veronica did not die in vain; that her death shook the Irish establishment out of its torpor, rousing them from their complacency regarding the crime gangs and propelling the state into an outright confrontation with the gangsters. The social impact of her murder has been compared to the deaths of the Italian investigating magistrates Paolo Borsellino and Giovanni Falcone in 1992. The Mafia murdered the two state lawyers within three months of each other, blowing Falcone, his wife and three bodyguards to pieces in a massive bomb near Palermo Airport on 23 May; then, on 19 July, Cosa Nostra assassins placed a car bomb outside Borsellino's mother's house, killing him and five bodyguards.

The assassinations of the two anti-Mafia judges marked a significant escalation in the war between Cosa Nostra and the Italian republic. The bombing also provoked massive public outrage, with millions of ordinary people marching in the streets of Italian towns and cities to demonstrate their opposition to the Sicilian crime organisation.

For a brief period after Veronica Guerin's death, it appeared that the Falcone–Borsellino revolution had come to the Irish Republic. A wave of national protests and subsequent government action engulfed Dublin's gangland. Veronica's two killers, Paul Ward and Brian Meehan, were put behind bars for life, while the drugs baron who ordered her murder, John Gilligan, was jailed for 28 years.

Her death was meant to mark a watershed in the Republic. It would be the pivotal moment at which the Irish state woke up to the threat to its authority and took on Irish Crime Inc. But Jimmy Guerin buys none of this: 'If you take the year of Veronica's death as a base line and compare the Ireland of then to the Ireland of now, I would say crime and drugs are 50 per cent worse, at least,' he says.

'If Veronica could come back to us, even as a ghost, I don't think she would be surprised by what's happened since her death at all. The gangs are back and they are younger, nastier and better organised than they were when Veronica was shot.'

And Jimmy should know. Since the start of the new century, he has been writing about and helping to expose the new crime gangs, the teeth of the Hydra slain after Veronica's murder that have now become a virtual underground army, undermining the authority of the Irish state. The crime gangs are back with a vengeance and the dark side of the Irish boom now casts a long shadow over the Republic's recent phenomenal economic success.

Veronica Guerin – the movie – premiered in Dublin in early summer 2003 and had the blessing of the murdered reporter's family. The Guerin family circle said they were 'very happy and proud' about the way Cate Blanchett had portrayed Veronica. Her loved ones were content that the film would help lay to rest a poisonous whispering campaign against Veronica, which started when she was first shot and wounded on Gilligan's orders in 1995. Several reporters, who spend a disproportionate amount of time greasing up to politicians in the Irish parliament, put out rumours that Veronica had arranged for criminals to shoot her in order to boost her public profile in the Republic. This toxic game of Chinese whispers, played out a year before her murder, only highlights the warped and misplaced priorities of sections of the Irish media who look for transgressions in the lives of those dedicated to shining light in dark corners while doing nothing themselves to seek out and expose real criminals committing real crime.

A fortnight after *Veronica Guerin* was unveiled in Dublin in front of the likes of Bono from U2 and Ronan Keating, three men died in separate gangland wars in Dublin and Limerick. There are currently thirteen rival criminal gangs operating in every quarter of Dublin, almost all of which make huge profits from the peddling of Ecstasy, speed, cocaine, heroin and now crack. All of them are far more volatile and ultra-violent than even the old gangs controlled by the likes of master Irish criminal Martin 'The General' Cahill (also the subject of a Hollywood movie), according to Jimmy Guerin.

In between our phone calls to gunrunners, drug dealers and criminals who traffic women from Eastern Europe, Africa and South America, we discuss the similarities between Veronica's legacy and the impact of the Falcone and Borsellino murders. Is Ireland as bad as Mafia-blighted Italy? Has the Republic then become a Sicily without the sun? Jimmy Guerin, who buried his sister and then took up her fight, offers up a startling answer.

'Is Ireland Sicily without the sun? I'd say it's worse than that. Even with Cosa Nostra, there are warped ethics at work. Almost like an underground army, there are limits and boundaries they impose. They impose rules and regulations on their members. From what I know about the Dublin gangs, there are no rules or boundaries. These gangsters fear no one and show no loyalty to each other. There is no mechanism to stop them going to war with one another, no mediation process to stop people being killed. And they will kill you at will. They kill anybody who stands in their way, even low-grade drug dealers have been shot dead if they tread on the turf of big gangs like the Westies up in Blanchardstown.'

A few hours after meeting Jimmy Guerin, I cross the River Liffey and try to test out his theory that Dublin is awash with cheap, easily available illegal firearms. Through a community worker in the North Inner City, one of my oldest and most loyal friends, we contact a local criminal gang and ask to buy a sawn-off shotgun. Posing as robbers, we explain to them in a pub that the sawn-off will be used for a post office raid. They say they won't sell us the weapon but instead can offer it for rent. For 24 hours we can have a sawn-off shotgun and the price for hire is just €50. Instead, in the ignoble tradition of tabloid journalism, we make our excuses and leave the bar.

Veronica Guerin's death was the result of her repeated exposure of the drugs barons who, in the mid-1990s, were flooding the Republic with Ecstasy, cocaine and heroin. When she was murdered in 1996, there were 7,000 registered heroin addicts in Dublin but four years later that figure had more than doubled to 16,000; it is still rising. By the beginning of the twenty-first century, the country with the fastest growth in Europe also had the youngest population of heroin addicts in the EU, according to a report from Brussels on Continental drug abuse in 2000.

There is evidence all across Dublin of the seemingly insoluble heroin crisis, even in those parts of the city centre that can attract tourists. Outside St Paul's Catholic Church on Arran Quay along the River Liffey, almost every morning there are signs of the constant detritus from the homeless heroin addicts who seek sanctuary inside the railings of the boarded-up chapel. St Paul's was the first Catholic Church opened in a main street anywhere in Ireland after the Duke of Wellington introduced Catholic Emancipation in 1829. It was the place of worship where Eamon de Valera, the founding father of the Irish Republic, got married. Now closed, its steps provide a sleeping place for the desperate inner-city addicts without a bed for the night.

Just before the area was gentrified, there was a disused cottage-style house five minutes' walk from Dublin's International Financial Services Centre, where some of the largest global banking corporations have relocated. The building in Seville Place was predicted to fetch up to half a million Irish punts when it eventually went on the market. In the meantime, however, it was used as a 'shooting gallery' for the north inner-city heroin addicts, who left their used syringes, burnt spoons and blood-soaked bandages strewn throughout the generally squalid house.

Outside the centre of Dublin, areas under the shadow of gangs like the Westies in Blanchardstown have become ravaged by drug abuse. Local community worker Seamus McDonagh, who runs a sports and training club aimed at preventing the next generation becoming hooked on heroin, has produced a report which found that 80 per cent of teenagers in the Corduff area of west Dublin had taken drugs. McDonagh, a radical socialist who campaigned for Irish workers' rights while working in England during the 1960s and '70s, is visibly worn down by the impact of the heroin crisis.

'There are instances on this estate of kids as young as eleven experimenting with heroin, smoking the drug rather than injecting it. I've been working with this problem for more than ten years and the kids we refer to methadone and counselling programmes are getting younger all the time.'

Seamus brought me to meet one of the addicts on the Corduff estate, Paul, who has been injecting heroin since he was 14. Paul tells me that there is one boy in the area dealing for one of the gangs who is only 14. Paul himself had been forced off a methadone programme for getting involved in a shooting incident outside the James Connolly hospital in the west of the city. Losing access to methadone was his 'punishment' for re-involvement in crime.

'I was doing all right until they forced me off the programme. Now I'm back on the smack again, back at square one.'

Corduff is one of the most depressing places in the Republic and on several visits over the late 1990s and first few years of the twenty-first century it has always reminded me of war-torn estates in the North during the worst days of the Troubles. There are boarded-up houses, knots of menacing teenagers hanging around corners and outside the doors of known dealers, graffiti and mounds of rubbish discarded everywhere.

Perhaps, though, there is one place even more soul destroying than the squalid misery of Corduff, somewhere far beyond west Dublin, located in the Republic's third-largest city, Limerick. In the winter of 2003, a small deprived corner of Limerick was turned into a war zone, with armed police and troops patrolling the sink estates housing around 10,000 people, trying to prevent more death and destruction in one of the nastiest gangland wars the state had ever experienced.

The Island is surrounded on all sides by the River Shannon and is home to some of the city's most violent criminal gangs. Limerick used to be nicknamed 'stab city' because of its reputation for disputes being settled with knives. By February 2003, however, 'stab city' was fast becoming 'AK city', as the local criminals replaced machetes and Stanley knives with Kalashnikovs and pistols as the new favoured weapons of gang warfare.

The war on the Island centred on two criminal families, the Ryans and the Keanes, who were once friends but fell out in 1999. For four years, the dispute between them bubbled just beneath the surface, occasionally rising up in an outburst of violent confrontations and murder. In 2000, Kieran Keane shot dead Eddie Ryan snr while he was drinking in the Moose pub in Limerick's Cathedral Street. Keane had become paranoid about Ryan's new links with other criminals in south-west Ireland, including a third crime family who, it later emerged, were actually manipulating the feud between the former friends. From 2000 up to 2003, the Gardai estimate that there were 40 violent incidents involving both families. In one episode a girl was attacked by several women and had her face slashed with a Stanley knife. The feud even spilt into the local school playground, with brawls between children belonging to the rival families. All of this was watched over by the third gang, whose plan was to allow the two families to wipe each other out, allowing them to take control of Limerick's drug and extortion trades.

Although ostensibly a local affair, the Keane–Ryan feud also demonstrates the pan-European nature of Irish criminality even amongst relatively low-level, low-life, unsophisticated gangs like the Limerick mafia. As in *The Godfather*, there was a larger design to the squalid turf war. The third family, who fomented the 2003 feud, have extensive links to big English criminals involved in fencing stolen goods in the West Midlands, mainly valuable antiques from country estates in the west of Ireland, as well as the smuggling and supply of Class A drugs between the Republic and Britain. Irish Crime Inc., even in a small regional city of Limerick, has gone global.

If, as Paul MacDonnell insists, the transfer of risk is the dark matter of the economic universe then tax evasion and top-level corruption are also part of the dark side of the Irish boom. There are two sets of criminals robbing the futures of tens of thousands of Irish people. There are, of course, the criminal overlords who have survived and prospered despite the post-Veronica Guerin backlash. But then there are also the white-collar criminals who siphoned off the profits from publicly owned enterprises put up for privatisation and who avoided paying tax even when the Republic was bankrupt and running to the International Monetary Fund for urgent assistance. The latter have stolen far more money from the state than the likes of the Westies or John Gilligan's gang could ever dream of. Yet, unlike the drugs barons, these white-collar gangsters have, to date, not served a single day in prison.

The revelation that a corrupt 'golden circle' was operating at the highest levels of Irish society to deceive the taxman and rob the state of millions that could have been used to build hospitals and schools, and alleviate the social ills of recession, all began with a cocaine-snorting tycoon and an American hooker in a Florida hotel room.

When the multi-millionaire Ben Dunne was arrested in 1992 for creating a disturbance at a hotel in Orlando, no one could ever have imagined that it would eventually expose a web of deceit spun by some of the richest and most powerful figures in Ireland. High after snorting an ounce of coke, Dunne was taken into custody, charged, fined and ordered to attend an addiction clinic. On his ignominious return to the Republic, a bitter boardroom battle ensued over control of the Dunnes Stores business, which pitted Ben Dunne against other members of his family. Although the family row was settled, with Ben Dunne receiving a large pay-off to quit the firm, fresh allegations about his business dealings started to rise to the surface. It first emerged that a Fine Gael Minister in the Rainbow Coalition government, Michael Lowry, had a house extension built thanks to Dunne's largesse; Lowry was later forced to resign. Then a far more important political figure became caught in the fall-out over the Dunnes' feud, none other than former Prime Minister Charles J. Haughey.

Haughey had borrowed up to two million Irish punts from Dunne to fund his lavish lifestyle and his taste in yachts, fine wines, silk shirts imported directly from Paris and numerous other luxuries, all enjoyed while the then Taoiseach lectured the Irish people on the need for the nation to tighten its collective belt.

The revelation about back-handers from businessmen was bad enough, but the fact that the golden circle, including Haughey, was also avoiding tax through a cleverly constructed scam provoked national outrage on the same scale as the public's revulsion over Veronica Guerin's murder. A series of public tribunals unveiled the existence of an offshore bank, Ansbacher Cayman, which would become synonymous with the corruption, graft and outright criminality of that golden circle.

Ansbacher's chairman was the late Des Traynor, a man known as a 'walking bank' and a close personal friend of Charles Haughey. Since the 1970s, Traynor had used the Cayman Islands-based bank to channel extremely wealthy Irish citizens' money abroad, often legally, but in some high-profile cases without the tax authorities ever knowing anything about it. Traynor ran what was effectively a money-laundering operation for rich friends and associates. Anyone wanting to conceal profits and earnings from the Irish taxman simply gave the money to Traynor, who deposited it in the Cayman Islands, where it earned undeclared interest. And if the tax dodgers wanted to spend the money, they used another clever ruse devised by Traynor: he would arrange a loan back in Dublin, which would be secretly guaranteed by the hidden money out in Cayman. This meant the client didn't have to explain to tax inspectors how the cash was obtained. As an extra bonus, the interest charged on the Dublin loan from Traynor could be then used as a legitimate business tax-deductible expense.

It took five years, more costly tribunals, legal challenges by depositors all the way to Ireland's Supreme Court and a 10,000-page document to reveal the names of the tax dodgers. The list was a Who's Who of Irish society, with doctors, dentists, airline pilots and even a primary school teacher appearing.

Cynics in Dublin used to quip (and probably still do) that beyond Newland Cross on the Naas dual carriageway on the western edge of the Irish capital nobody paid tax. For three decades, through boom and bust, urban PAYE workers felt that they alone were shouldering the tax burden and paying for the public services of the state. It is now clear that from the early 1970s, millionaire business leaders, ranchers, beef barons, hoteliers, horse breeders and friends of the Irish political establishment *were* avoiding paying tax. What made this scam so galling for PAYE urban workers was that while they were being lectured on the need for financial prudence, the people doing the lecturing were themselves ripping off the state.

At the time Des Traynor was running the 'Ansbacher' scheme, PAYE workers were paying half of their entire income to the Irish Exchequer. Even as late as the mid-1990s, the average Irish PAYE worker was being taxed at 48 per cent. Given the extra payments on social welfare and at one stage a Youth Levy – a tax aimed at funding job-creation schemes specifically for the young unemployed – this meant the taxman was taking 60 per cent of Irish PAYE workers' salaries. Even today, with the economy still booming, Irish workers are still paying more tax than almost every other EU counterpart, with the exception of Denmark. Unlike Denmark, however, the Republic does not have a cradle-to-grave welfare system; unlike the Danes, the Southern Irish do not enjoy free health care.

In contrast to the immediate aftermath of Veronica's death, however

– when the state acted rapidly to set up the CAB and started hunting down the crime bosses – in the wake of the Ansbacher scandal, the Irish government announced that no one would go to jail or face prosecution over the tax-evasion scam that had robbed the public of hundreds of millions in desperately needed revenue. But the even more astonishing thing about this most important of all the corruption scandals highlighted in the late 1990s and early twenty-first century has been the absence of any serious political fall-out. The two major parties in the Republic, Fine Gael and, more critically, Fianna Fail, emerged relatively unscathed from the disgrace of Ansbacher. Michael Lowry even got re-elected to the Dail, standing as an Independent, while Fianna Fail was returned to government just a month before the publication of the Ansbacher report.

On a superficial level, some of the one-time 'Masters of the Irish Universe' appear to have fallen from grace with the same velocity as Wall Street yuppie Sherman McCoy in Tom Wolfe's satire on 1980s greed-obsessed America *The Bonfire of the Vanities*. The Flood Tribunal (yet to run its full course) into planning corruption and the seedy back-door deals between builders and politicians in Dublin has led to the humbling of the once powerful and ebullient. Take Ray Burke, for example, the former Communications and later Foreign Affairs Minister in Fianna Fail-led governments of the late 1980s and early '90s. In his former life, Burke was the scourge of RTE broadcasters and an outspoken critic of the left. It was his bullying that led indirectly, for instance, to the end of the RTE political and social satire radio show *Scrap Saturday*, the programme that first made Dermot Morgan (later Father Ted) a household name in the Republic and which every week cruelly lampooned Burke's boss, Charlie Haughey. Burke relished the role of Charles Haughey's rottweiler, launching blistering attacks across the floor of the Irish parliament on Labour Party TDs like Pat Rabbitte and Eamon Gilmore, reminding the duo of their past associations with the Marxist Workers Party, labelling them during one debate as 'the children of Ceausescu'.

These days, Ray Burke is a much quieter man. The initial 150-page Flood report ruled in the autumn of 2001 that Burke had received corrupt payments from a range of Irish builders. Mr Justice Flood also found that during his time as Minister of Communications in the late 1980s, Burke made decisions on broadcasting that were not in the public interest. That is, he was given money, while a Minister, by Oliver Barry, the owner of Century Radio, then vying to become a major rival to RTE. Moreover, Mr Justice Flood concluded that Burke and 14 other people had 'obstructed and hindered' the work of his tribunal into corruption and illegal re-zoning.

More incredible was the sight of Gardai officers from the Criminal Assets Bureau raiding Burke's home in October 2002. The CAB, the agency initially founded to target rich criminals like John Gilligan, is still investigating allegations that the former Foreign Minister obtained illegal payments from builders to have land re-zoned in north Dublin. The state did seize Burke's house, worth more than €2 million, as part of the CAB investigation, but so far the ex-Cabinet Minister has yet to serve a day in jail. This one-time mouthpiece for Haughey and boot boy for the hardline nationalist wing of Fianna Fail has found solace in exile – in Oxfordshire, England, to be precise.

In any other liberal democracy, Burke's arrest would have been an earthshaking event for the political establishment. Try to imagine the political implications for Tony Blair or George Bush if a former British Labour Cabinet Minister or member of the White House staff was declared guilty of corruption by one of the most respected judges in the UK or the United States. In the last decaying days of John Major's administration, the Tories were fatally wounded by a series of corruption allegations concerning Jonathan Aitken's stay at the Paris Ritz, courtesy of Mohammed Al Fayed, and the sleazy back-handers of Neil Hamilton and co. However, the amount of money these Tory politicians received in the cash-for-questions and Ritz scandals pales into utter insignificance compared with the millions the likes of Ray Burke and his equally disgraced Fianna Fail colleague and part-time jailbird Liam Lawlor pocketed illegally from certain figures in the Irish construction industry.

Even today, the era of Burke and Lawlor's dodgy dealings with the builders marks the lives of ordinary Irish citizens in the Republic. By holding on to and speculating on the land that back in the late 1980s was desperately needed to cope with Dublin's rising population, the builders were able to make hundreds of millions in profits thanks to inflated market prices. Irish economists suggest that this is one of the main reasons why Dublin is one of the most expensive places to buy a house anywhere in the industrialised world. Not only, therefore, did the corruption of Burke, Lawlor et al. rob the Irish Exchequer of millions needed to fund public services, by midway through the first decade of the twenty-first century it also resulted in young first-time buyers being unable to get a foothold on the property ladder in Dublin.

Back in 1979, tens of thousands of PAYE workers took to Dublin's streets marching through the capital in protest against the punitive and unfair tax regime. A quarter of a century later and little has changed in terms of political power. As of 2004, Fianna Fail – the party most tainted with corruption – has been in power for 18 out of the last 20 years. The promised revolution in Irish politics, the re-alignment on left–right lines, has not materialised. Despite the publication of the Ansbacher report and the deluge of dirt cascading from all the other tribunals like Flood into planning corruption across Dublin, the golden circle's political allies have regrouped, re-scrubbed themselves and still hold office today.

Fianna Fail, and to a far lesser degree Fine Gael, have long had overlapping interests with many in the golden circle, yet they remain the two immutable dominant forces of Southern Irish political life. Public anger over rich tax evaders and their political chums was evident before and after the Ansbacher revelations, but voting patterns do not as yet suggest this anger is being translated into a radical transformation of the political landscape. So how, then, do we account for this conundrum?

Part of the answer lies in the national psyche, in a deeply ingrained distrust of the centre and an admiration for those who rebel against authority – all part of a throwback to the colonial era when 'The Castle' (Britain's seat of security authority in pre-1921 Ireland) was to be at all costs tricked, conned, defied and eventually undermined.

There are underlying subtle connections here between the political apathy towards the tax dodgers and the sneaking regard for the master criminal. Martin 'The General' Cahill, the Dublin criminal mastermind, was not without his admirers before and after his assassination in 1994. Cahill's derring-do, his audacious bank and jewellery heists, were the stuff of legend in the capital. Urban myths sprang up around The General regarding his allegedly frugal lifestyle (he didn't drink, for instance), his personal disdain for drugs and his supposed generosity to the poor. This Robin Hood image belies the fact that Cahill was a ruthless and murderous criminal whose empire brought misery to thousands of the most deprived and vulnerable. And isn't it highly apposite, when one thinks about the toleration for tax scammers, that one of Cahill's innocent victims happened to be a tax inspector who lost his legs in a booby-trap car-bombing the General had organised simply because this dedicated civil servant was tracking the criminal's assets?

State servants, whether they are police officers, tax inspectors or other civic-minded officials, are often painted in a negative light by the Republic's legions of 'sneaking regarders'. Despite 83 years of independence from Britain, the authority of a democratic state is still treated as if it is some interfering, alien presence and its servants defamed as collaborating 'Castle Catholics'. Terrorists and criminals, on the other hand, enjoy the status of daring outlaws: they are the 'boys' forever slipping out of authority's clammy grasp, like Celtic versions of the Dukes of Hazzard. That these state employees are in reality collecting revenue to pay for cancer treatment, the education of children, the care of the elderly, the creation of jobs for the unemployed, the upkeep of roads, rail networks, public lighting, sewage and other utilities, all of which mark out a civilised society, has not dented the image of the outlaw and the cute hoor, the criminal and the stroke-merchant, as the likeable rogues of the Republic.

There is one political party hoping to exploit the Southern public's disgust with established parties and the corruption at the heart of Irish democracy. It is currently led by the most popular politician in the Republic, is the fastest growing party in the state, the most successful recruiting force on college campuses and, compared to its rivals, is lean, mean and ideologically motivated. Sinn Féin, the IRA's political wing, is the coming party of the twenty-first-century Republic.

Yet while Sinn Féin condemns the established order over its links to the golden circle, it remains the richest party not only on the island of Ireland but also across the British Isles, using a bottomless war chest for its campaigns funded partially through criminality.

If the average Irish voter, particularly in the South, wants to get a glimpse into a future Ireland run by Sinn Féin, then all they need to do is visit west Belfast, the home base of party president Gerry Adams.

And if they look close enough, they will see that behind all the agit-prop murals and propaganda slogans lies a micro-society that has mutated into the closest thing in Western Europe to a one-party state.

That Sinn Féin and the IRA command mass support in west Belfast is beyond doubt. That they maltreat, isolate, demonise and intimidate the minority in the constituency who don't agree with them is also unquestionable.

Tommy Gorman is a living legend of Belfast republicanism. On 17 January 1972, along with six other prisoners, he took part in a daring escape from the *Maidstone* prison ship moored off the city's Lough. Gorman covered himself in butter, to ward off the cold of the water, and boot polish, to conceal himself from the British Army searchlights scanning the water for the escapees. After taking 20 minutes to swim to shore in freezing conditions wearing only his underpants, he eventually made his way to McEntee's pub off Cromac Street in the Markets and was offered help by a friendly barman. Gorman was given the keys to a Ford Cortina and drove off towards the Republic with the British Army and the Royal Ulster Constabulary in hot pursuit. I can still remember the Markets that night of the escape, with British helicopters flying low above the houses, more searchlights trained on our streets and foot patrols pounding the pavements, banging on doors, raiding homes and pubs looking for the seven men who had swum to freedom. When Gorman and his fellow prisoners turned up a few days later to recount their break-out at a news conference in Dublin, they entered republican folklore. I recall even the Official IRA supporters in the Markets singing the praises of the 'Magnificent Seven' for their ingenuity, stamina and courage in breaking free from the *Maidstone* – a hated symbol of British military misrule in the North.

Gorman later returned to Northern Ireland and became a leading light in the engineering department of the Provisional IRA's Belfast Brigade, which was responsible for the near destruction of central Belfast in the 1970s. He dedicated his entire life to the cause of a united socialist Irish Republic and, although I am absolutely convinced that his 'war' set back that goal for decades if not centuries, Gorman remains one of the true believers, someone who genuinely felt he was fighting in a just struggle.

Today he is not just a disappointed man but an angry one too. Gorman is one of the few west Belfast republicans who will speak

uncomfortable truths, the most important being that the settlement
Sinn Féin and the IRA opted for in Easter 1998 was a partitionist one.
He agrees that Provisional republicans have come to accept what their
hated rivals in the Officials concluded way back in the 1970s, namely
the principle of unionist consent for a united Ireland. Even at the time
of the first IRA ceasefire ten years ago, a joke was doing the rounds of
west Belfast and other republican redoubts in the North.

Q: What's the difference between the Stickies and the Provos?

A: Twenty years.

A plain speaker with a gruff tone, Gorman accepts that the 'war' is
over and, to his credit, continually implores young republicans not to
join up and engage in the violent campaigns of terror groups like the
Continuity IRA or the Real IRA. Gorman will not, however, join in
the game of verbal and mental gymnastics that the Sinn Féin leadership
has put the Irish republican base through. He will not pretend that
entering a Stormont Assembly in 1998 and a power-sharing executive
with unionists would somehow create a dynamic towards Irish unity.
Gorman has been around republican politics long enough to know that
Sinn Féin's recognition of the agreement was, in turn, recognition of
the reality of partition.

What really angers Gorman, however, has been the use and direction
of the 'army' he joined in 1970, the Provisional IRA, to suppress
dissent and debate. For republican veterans like him and his comrade,
the former-prisoner-turned-writer Anthony McIntyre, the popular
guerrilla army has evolved into a 'Rafia'.

If anywhere on the island of Ireland can be called 'Sicily without the
sun' it is west Belfast. The parallels between the fortunes of Cosa
Nostra and the IRA are startling. Both organisations claim historic
lineage to the blood sacrifice of their forefathers in the war for national
unification. In Sicily, the feudal militias from which the Mafia emerged
provided the front-line troops for Garibaldi in his struggle with the
Neapolitan army and the liberation of the island from Bourbon
tyranny. The *Risorgimento* and the Easter Rising are equally important
in terms of national renewal. Both movements are linked by a common
religion and a shared experience in political uprisings.

During the 1970s, successive British ministers tried to dredge up the
Mafia analogy to undermine popular support for paramilitary groups
on both sides of the sectarian divide. But their use of the Mafia slur did

not work on the republican community. In the '70s and '80s, life for the average IRA volunteer was frugal, financially unrewarding and extremely dangerous: for the leadership and membership were alike. By and large, in contrast to the Ulster loyalists, they did not steal from their own people or exploit their base.

The situation today is very different, and one of the major prices that Ulster society has paid for the peace process is the British government turning a blind eye to non-terrorist criminality by the paramilitaries. The upshot has been the creation of a new class of republicans, the 'Tiofchaid Armanis'. Gorman uses the sartorial analogy to contrast the republican leadership during the 'war' and the peace process.

'There was a time when they, the leading figures, looked like us. They wore the same clothes, drank in the same pubs, lived in the same houses, worked in the same low-paid jobs when they weren't on the run.'

The price of speaking out against this new elite can be fatal, as Real IRA member Joe O'Connor found out when, after clashing with senior Provisionals, he was shot dead near his Ballymurphy home in October 2000. Another sanction is communal ostracism, as Anthony McIntyre and his partner Carrie Twomey endured just days after the O'Connor killing, when a Sinn Féin-organised picket protested outside their house simply because the couple pointed the finger at the IRA for murdering the dissident. Their friend Tommy Gorman suffered another penalty for publicly criticising the party line. He lost his job.

'One of the ways they operate social control is through employment. The IRA controls, through its proxies, thousands of jobs, both public and private, in west Belfast. If you don't toe the line, you won't get a job; and if you do get a job, you are paid your wages in one of their social clubs, where you will spend your money and make them even richer. At the start of 2000, I lost a job I had with an ex-prisoners' welfare group because an ally of Sinn Féin warned the funders that I was a dissident and said that I should be dropped before more public money was given to the group. So I was let go purely because I spoke out about the direction in which Sinn Féin was going.'

Gorman and McIntyre reel off the names of various senior republicans who have become extremely wealthy over the last ten years of relative peace. The names are familiar to anyone with a background or interest in Belfast republicanism. This new elite own mini-shopping centres in the west of the city, houses worth over £150,000, a slice of the Blackmountain the size of 18 acres, property in the west of Ireland – particularly counties Donegal and Sligo – and one former IRA finance officer from south Down even owns a casino in Antigua, the duo claim.

The template for this new empire was forged by their old rivals in the Official IRA, some of whose leading cadres amassed fortunes in building-site tax scams, racketeering and a sophisticated international fake-currency operation. Gorman and McIntyre contend that their former comrades in the Provisionals have, however, far exceeded the Officials in terms of rackets and scams.

'They [Sinn Féin] are the richest party not only in Ireland or these islands but I would say in Europe,' Gorman emphasises.

The ex-IRA volunteers estimate conservatively that in west Belfast the movement is able to raise around £20 million per annum. Much but not all of this huge sum is re-directed into Sinn Féin's highly competent, unrivalled organisational machine.

Republicans, unlike loyalists, steer clear of drug dealing, regarding it as socially and electorally damaging. A report, however, in the spring of 2004 by the British government's Organised Crime Task Force shed light on exactly how the republican movement finances itself. Cross-border smuggling, illicit cigarette dealing, diesel washing, money laundering and duty and VAT fraud, it said, were the main sources of finance. The investigation found that one in five cigarettes sold in Northern Ireland is smuggled and is providing income to the main terrorist organisations. Almost a third of all smuggled tobacco seized by UK Customs was netted in Northern Ireland – 88.5 million in 2001–02 out of a UK total of 2.6 billion cigarettes.

The same report also highlighted the production and distribution of smuggled alcohol, which includes homemade vodka known to the working class of west Belfast as 'Chuckie Vodka'. It is distilled in south Armagh under the control of IRA commander Thomas 'Slab' Murphy, the multi-millionaire border smuggler whose farm straddles the frontier. Two years ago, the Garda Siochana and Irish Customs officials thought they had smashed the illegal vodka racket after they raided a massive distillation plant in south Armagh. Within weeks, Murphy's men were able to set up an alternative distillery in another part of the region over which they have de facto control.

If west Belfast, where all aspects of life are dominated by the Sinn Féin–IRA movement, resembles Palermo, south Armagh is akin to rural Sicily, with 'Slab' Murphy the undisputed Capo de tutti Capos of the region. He has personal control of a fuel-smuggling operation that nets millions for the movement. The Irish government estimate that Murphy himself is worth £20 million. The money is raised through buying cheap central heating oil and 'washing' it with dangerous chemicals that turn it from green to red. The by-product of this process is a highly toxic waste, which is dumped at night far away from the Southfork-style mansions with their four-wheel-drive jeeps parked outside – all belonging to the leaders of the south Armagh brigade. Between the autumn of 2003 and spring 2004, the clandestine toxic dumping almost destroyed the entire water supply of north Louth. If it hadn't been for the quick actions of environmental officers and the Gardai, people in the region would have been drinking bottled water for the next decade. None of this embarrasses the articulate, energetic Sinn Féin politicians on either side of the south Armagh/north Louth region, who capitalise on, among other things, environmental and health issues!

The Organised Crime Task Force dossier estimated that the smuggling of cigarettes, illicit booze and fuel (all sources of PIRA income) is costing the British Exchequer somewhere between £1.7 billion and £2.7 billion per annum. At a superficial level, these losses are hardly a cause of concern for the average working-class nationalist. Some may even regard the scams as a neat way of depriving the hated British imperialists of revenue. What they tend to overlook, however, is that during the brief period of power-sharing government between 1999 and 2001 (punctuated by unionist walk-outs), Sinn Féin held the posts of health and education in the administration. During her tenure as Health Minister, Sinn Féin's Bairbre de Brun chaired a conference aimed at drastically cutting the number of people smoking in Northern Ireland. Her anti-smoking campaign was launched even while her party was making huge sums of money through its grass-roots members and supporters flooding constituencies like west Belfast with smuggled cigarettes.

Most staggering of all is that virtually no one either in the media or political life, North or South, was willing to point out this obvious contradiction. A Sinn Féin minister was imploring people to stop smoking on health and economic grounds yet no one noticed that her party's coffers were boosted via its military wing from the vast sale of cigarettes that brought no tax revenue into the NHS or other public bodies. In any other democratic society, the electorate would be alerted to and vote against a political party guilty of such glaring hypocrisy. But in peace-process Northern Ireland, anything goes as long as the paramilitaries remain on ceasefire. The terror leaders, so long as they are not bombing the City of London or Dublin, remain virtually untouchable. And the electoral fortunes of their political allies continue to rise. In the 2004 elections, de Brun was elected to one of Northern Ireland's three seats to the European Parliament at the expense of the SDLP.

Most astonishing of all is that whilst the majority of the Irish people indicate their belief through opinion poll after opinion poll that the IRA is involved in crime and that Gerry Adams is one of the Provisionals' paramilitary leaders (despite his constant denials), the Sinn Féin president also remains the most popular politician in the Republic. His popularity in the South even rubs off on those Sinn Féin politicians photographed beside him. Adams was omnipresent in the Republic's 2004 European elections, standing beside Sinn Féin candidate Mary Lou McDonald at every available photo opportunity. The magic seemed to work, as McDonald was comfortably elected to the European Parliament despite Sinn Féin sustaining a barrage of criticism from Irish government ministers about the party's armed fundraising wing.

In a bizarre way, the Republic's love affair with Adams mirrors its ambiguity regarding Charlie Haughey. The disgraced former Taoiseach still has his own legion of admirers and 'sneaking regarders', even though they are well aware of his tax scams, strokes and schemes, his hypocrisy and his venality. To draw another parallel with Italy, the electorate are well aware of the charges of corruption levelled at Silvio Berlusconi but this has not halted the forward march of the television tycoon's Forza Italia party. Like Haughey, Berlusconi, despite all his flaws, is seen as a man of action, a born leader, a brazen personification of the nation at its most truculent and powerful.

There is yet another similarity here between Ireland and Sicily: like Cosa Nostra, a disturbingly large number of Irish people also believe that the IRA are honourable men. This belief is strongest in areas like west Belfast, where Sinn Féin and IRA propaganda is swallowed whole without question or doubt.

Whilst the CAB in the Republic has stripped the likes of John Gilligan of their ill-gotten gains, it has never been allowed to move against the likes of 'Slab' Murphy. There have been incremental measures aimed at trimming his estimated €60 million empire of fear. But the south Armagh smuggler remains among the richest criminals anywhere in the UK and Ireland, and in a 2004 *Sunday Times* survey, Murphy was ranked ninth in a hierarchy of the wealthiest UK-based crime bosses.

Gorman and McIntyre's criticisms come from inside the republican family, which is why they are so deeply despised in the top ranks of Sinn Féin. Yet can they explain the enduring popularity and support Sinn Féin enjoys in places like west Belfast? The 'Rafia' may be a recognised fact of life in republican strongholds but its existence has not damaged Sinn Féin, as the party's vote in the North continues to climb.

'Sometimes it baffles me why the people in west Belfast don't rebel and stop voting for the Shinners,' Gorman confesses. 'I have friends who are IRA volunteers and they get £20 a week for whatever work they do for the organisation. There is blind loyalty even though their commanders and middle rankers are getting £300 per week. That's the most depressing thing of all. They don't question what's going on, either through fear of physical attack or being socially excluded or not getting a job.'

McIntyre then repeats his favourite mantra: 'If Gerry Adams told the rank and file to turn up outside his house on Monday morning, hand over their dole money, speak Swahili and wear PSNI uniforms, they would do it.'

The main reason why the majority in west Belfast are not prepared to rock the boat is the overwhelming desire for the IRA ceasefire and the peace process to remain intact. Even republican sceptics like McIntrye and Gorman accept that the imperative of peace is paramount for most nationalist and republican voters. Martin McGuinness and Gerry Adams have 'delivered' the IRA. In reality, they (Adams and McGuinness), as members of the Army Council, steered the Provos out of the armed struggle cul-de-sac. As long as the Sinn

Féin leadership can maintain that cessation in the absence of any credible republican alternative, the party's electoral support will not be significantly dented.

For anyone who grew up with the Provos through the '70s and '80s, this collective acquiescence is puzzling. Throughout that period, the average Provisional I would meet in the street was fired up with a deep sense of anti-authoritarianism. They hated the state. They wanted to destroy it. Their passionate desire to pull down society bordered on the pathological. They were prepared to risk their own lives and the lives of others in the name of the 'cause'. They were, as the Israeli author Amos Oz has noted about any fanatic, more interested in you than yourself. So what an incredible turnaround, then, from those days of rebellion to the new era of passive acceptance. The most fascinating thing to note about Anthony McIntyre and Tommy Gorman is that they are on their own; they are isolated figures acting the role of the precocious little boy who suddenly notices that the Emperor has no clothes. Perhaps that is what defeat of the traditional republican stance through secret discussion, the toleration of criminality, the creation of a social system of collectivism breeds: stoicism and apathy. What was once the most recalcitrant constituency in Britain or Ireland has ended up becoming, paradoxically, the most docile.

A benign interpretation of west Belfast would be to draw a parallel with Red Bologna and the other Communist Party-dominated cities of Italy during the Cold War. In the PCI strongholds, the communists won popular support by turning their municipalities into models of good government. The Eurocommunists of the PCI had a philosophy, 'the creation of space', in which all aspects of life, the economy, culture, education, sport and so on, were marked with the party's stamp. In the Italy of Christian Democrat corruption and collusion with the Mafia, the 'red belt', with its efficiency, fairness and absence of graft, provided a positive example to voters.

The truer, more accurate parallel, though, is still with Sicily, given the network of criminality, patronage, nepotism and latent terror extant in west Belfast. The old PCI did not back up their polity with arms. Nor did the Italian communists finance their machine with the proceeds of crime. Furthermore, the leaders of the 'red belt' practised a policy of toleration and openness; unlike the Provisionals, whose reaction to any dissent is to intimidate, slander, assault and even murder their critics, depending on what they can get away with at any given time. In the two republican strongholds of west Belfast and south Armagh, one-party rule is intertwined with an all-encompassing criminal enterprise, all of which is a far cry from the utopia envisaged by the likes of Tommy Gorman.

The Sicilian sub-culture of 'Omerta', the imposition of collective silence on an entire community, permeates areas like west Belfast and south Armagh. It was no coincidence that Jean McConville, a widow with ten children, was seized from her west Belfast home and then transported to the south Armagh/north Louth region in 1972, from where she would never return. For more than 20 years, an Omerta descended on the Lower Falls/Divis Flats area of west Belfast regarding Jean's fate. Because she was labelled a 'tout' or informer (simply for tending to a British soldier wounded outside her flat), her orphaned children were isolated and humiliated by large sections of the Catholic community around them. When the IRA finally admitted it had killed her, and then, after years of campaigning by her family, Jean's 'disappeared' body turned up on Templetown Beach in the Cooley Peninsula in 2003, her neighbours were given a chance to publicly atone.

Yet when Jean was finally given a Christian burial 31 years after the IRA put a bullet into her brain, the community silently rallied around the killers rather than the victim. Only a handful of locals turned out on a bleak October Saturday morning to pay their respects. The majority of the mourners were members of the McConville family circle and journalists who had worked with her daughter Helen McKendry for over a decade to raise the issue of Jean's disappearance, as well as some 'outsiders', both Protestant and Catholic, from beyond west Belfast. I remember standing outside St Paul's Chapel on the Falls Road (the same church from which my uncle Emmanuel was buried, another victim of the IRA, who accused him of being an informer) that morning when Jean McConville was finally laid to rest. Like my uncle's funeral 16 years earlier, relatively few people from the locality turned out to show any solidarity with Jean's loved ones. Maybe this was partly because so many in their 'community' had participated in the last days of Jean McConville.

The inquest into her death sheds small rays of light into this dark affair in the history of the Troubles. Evidence was given that 28 armed masked men and women abducted Jean, tearing her away from her screaming children, putting a gun to one of her boys' heads on the day she disappeared: 28 people! Consider that double the number, possibly treble, helped the gang, either by the provision of safe houses or simply keeping watch in case of British Army or RUC patrols, to drag Jean away from her home and kids. Let us say 50 people had direct or indirect roles in her initial disappearance. Several hundred more, through family relationships, word of mouth, street gossip, would have known about the woman's fate. None of them ever offered a scrap of information to her children as to her whereabouts over the next three decades. Instead, several of them spread poisonous rumours that she had run off with a British soldier and abandoned her kids. Others, many years later, even taunted Helen with laughter and cruel, sardonic smiles.

The silence and the absence of a majority of Jean's neighbours at her funeral spoke volumes about the IRA's grip on the constituency. By failing to turn up, the people were sending out a message as chilling as the signals transmitted in the closed world of Cosa Nostra-dominated Sicily. What happened to Jean on that dark December day in the bloodiest year of Ulster's Troubles could be 'understood', 'explained', even 'justified'. Their silence, their absence from her final journey merely confirmed this.

The enduring presence of gangland culture in the Republic and the ever-expanding empire of paramilitary criminality in the North is spreading a cancer that threatens to undermine both states on the island. Parallel societies have been created on either side of the border. There may indeed be a surface world of soaring property prices, near-full employment, conspicuous consumption, garish displays of wealth in towns and cities exuding phenomenal prosperity. Beneath, however, is an underworld where all the basics of post-modern living – the DVD player and the PlayStation for the kids, the designer gear for the teenagers, the narcotics, the tobacco and the alcohol for the adults wanting to escape from the drudgery of their lives – can be provided at cheaper-than-market prices by the gangs and illegal armies who can use their position as owners of the means of production, distribution and exchange to shape the everyday existence of the Irish underclass. The people, of course, gladly acquiesce in this black economy, regarding the evasion of VAT and other duties as small victories over the state, particularly when the government in the North happens to be regarded by one side as a foreign one.

An underground society, no matter how mired in criminality or corruption, also provides useful shortcuts for the poor not only to those must-have consumer goods but also more esoteric things like justice. Over the last 30 years, the paramilitaries, both loyalist and republican, have been able to short-circuit the justice system in Northern Ireland and to a lesser extent in the Republic. Instead of going through the laborious process of reporting a crime to the police, hoping that detectives will choose to act against known criminals in their area, then waiting for the courts to put the accused through due process and finally impose a prison sentence that may not even reflect the gravity of the original crime, people in areas like west Belfast can gain access to a form of instant justice. In a matter of 24 hours, the IRA or UVF punishment squad can speed up the complaint against the joyrider, the petty thief, the street-corner thug, the local drug dealer and sex offender, to the point of 'instant consumer satisfaction'. Just as the paramilitaries and their criminal sub-contractors can provide the knock-off PlayStation or the latest Hollywood hit on fake DVD at Christmas, so for the whole of the year they can offer a swift and brutal form of justice that eschews such irritants as legal defence, statutory rights and a right to appeal. That is why there is no outcry in working-class communities over the kneecappings and the beatings. Although these practices have never solved the underlying causes of crime and anti-social behaviour in these areas, they remain popular. The left in Britain would label this subversion of justice and law as vigilantism; sections of the Irish left instead excuse or contextualise it as 'people's courts' and 'popular justice'.

All the chambers of this very Irish-specific underworld – paramilitary empire, gangland and golden circle – are interlinked by a series of passages built from the sub-cultural substance of modern Ireland. Irish traditional tolerance of, often admiration for, the outlaw, the rogue, the anti-establishment character, provides the raw material for that base. Even the most exposed of the golden circle in the early 1990s, like the beef baron Larry Goodman, can portray themselves as the little guy pitted against the goliath. During the Beef Tribunal inquiry into links between his corporation and Fianna Fail and Fine Gael politicians, Larry Goodman had the audacity to describe himself as a victim of the establishment, the establishment here being the so-called liberal media clustered around Dublin 4. Berlusconi plays the same trick in Italy, portraying himself as the enemy of the bureaucrats and meddling left-wing-biased magistrates, the go-getting people's champion against big government. The Italian Prime Minister has been dogged by allegations that his Forza Italia party in Sicily has had links with Cosa Nostra; the former Taoiseach and a côterie of hardline nationalists in Fianna Fail face the court of history for meddling in the republican movement *circa* 1969–70, encouraging the split that gave rise to the Provos and even arming the nascent terror group. The similarities between Sicily-with-sun and Sicily-without are indeed uncanny.

There are no Falcones or Borsellinos around in the Republic or Northern Ireland willing to take on and dismantle this interlocking sub-culture of crime and corruption. Only a few Irish journalists such as the second potential victim after Veronica Guerin on John Gilligan's hit list back in 1996, the crime reporter Paul Williams, are left to carry out the perilous task of forcing an otherwise indifferent public to gaze into the darker corners of twenty-first-century Ireland. While the boom goes on in the South, and the North continues to enjoy a 'peace dividend', the middle classes on either side of the border are safe in their ignorance of the underworld. Not only perhaps ignorance but also indulgence. In a section of the Irish bourgeoisie, particularly among its young, it has recently become hip and fashionable to demonstrate overt support for the IRA's political wing. It is regarded even in Dublin 4 itself as the height of 'cool' to be seen photographed with Martin McGuinness and Gerry Adams, the whiff of cordite they give off as socially alluring as the quaff of bubbly or the snort of coke.

As long as the good times roll on, there is little chance of the Irish underworld rising up to intersect with the surface world above. A downturn in Irish economic fortunes, however, a recession on the scale of the early to mid-1980s, would create the circumstances for one of the three underworld forces, Sinn Féin and the IRA, to build an electoral base that could threaten the very existence of the two states on this island. If that scenario ever emerged, those who oppose the Provos, including some of their former disgruntled members, would be forced to take the Tommy Gorman option. But instead of jumping off the ship like the 'Magnificent Seven' in 1972, they would be clamouring to get on board boats to escape in the other direction from the island they call home.

CHAPTER EIGHT

The British Presence

Every Sunday morning I encounter the 'British presence' in Ireland in a dialogue with the dead.

There are no armed soldiers or stern-faced men in bowler hats and sashes or lines of Union Jacks, but simply gravestones, shrivelled and withered poppy wreaths, the odd insignia with crown above harp and the regimental badges of long since defunct military units; only ghosts whose fates follow the trajectories of rebellions, riots, political crises, world wars and civil conflicts over the last three centuries.

My companions through the four seasons are teenage Orange bandsmen, British Army captains, Spitfire pilots, Royal Ulster Constabulary officers and Naval reservists. They all lie at rest in a graveyard on the south side of Belfast, which commands a panoramic view of the city. Knockbreda Cemetery is divided into two zones, with the upper half close to the local Anglican church and home to tombstones containing the remains of men, women and children from the eighteenth century onwards. My weekly walk up Church Road, through the newer half of the cemetery towards the church, ends at the old stone wall where, if you look north beneath the mountains of Belfast, you can clearly see, even in the winter gloom, the main combat zones of the Troubles in the distance: north and west Belfast with their housing estates and tower blocks alongside local landmarks like the black façade of the Mater Hospital or the sprawling complex of the Royal Victoria wedged between the M1 motorway and the Falls Road.

The cemetery is a time capsule, a place of peace and reflection coexisting beside the roar of twenty-first-century commerce. One of the busiest roads in Northern Ireland, the traffic-clogged Ormeau, runs parallel to it; Sainsbury's and Forestside Shopping Centre are just a stone's throw away.

The place is also physical history, providing lessons from the past amid the tombs and the graves of the departed. The oldest resting places are the most imposing and impressive: 12-foot ivy-covered gothic tombs with spikes and pepper-pot-shaped urns protruding from the top. They contain the great and the good from eighteenth-century Belfast, such as Thomas Greg Esq., 'who departed this life in the 10 day of January in the year of our Lord 1796 aged 75 years'. Relatives of Thomas Greg are also entombed there, all of whom died between 1796 and 1830, having lived through momentous times in Irish, British and world history: the 1798 United Irish Rebellion, the 1801 Act of Union, the Napoleonic Wars, Catholic Emancipation in 1829, the Great Reform Act four years later.

Directly behind Thomas Greg's tomb, up against one of the sides of the stone wall surrounding the cemetery, is the grave of one Robert Henry McDowell. The epitaph on his gravestone is a reminder that disputes over Orange marches, territorial struggles and violent counter-protests were not invented in the 1990s in places like Drumcree.

'Erected by the members of the Purdys Burn flute band as a token of respect to the memory of Robert Henry McDowell Aged 17 years who met his death by an attack on the band in Belfast on 11th September 1880.'

Amid the forest of stones containing the surnames of Protestant Ulster – McIlveen, Bell, Harbison, Crooks, Oxer, Neil, Nixon – are the resting places and memorial tablets to soldiers who fought and died in the Great War. They include 'Harry "Chappy" Lynass, 2nd Lieutenant Royal Irish Rifles, killed in France 2nd September 1916, aged 20', who is commemorated on the gravestone dedicated to his father, who died just six months before the First World War broke out.

Even below, in the modern end of the graveyard, with its giant tree that casts a permanent shadow beneath a mop of branches and leaves, there are other little corners of personal tragedy colliding with great world events. One of the most touching epitaphs is dedicated to a young fighter pilot from Northern Ireland shot down during the Battle of Britain. It begins with his wartime serial number 816023 and is dedicated to the memory of 'Sergeant P.C. Hanna, Pilot, Royal Air Force, Auxiliary Air Force, 3rd September 1940, aged 23'. And then it ends with a quote from the scriptures: 'Lord of life, be ours Thy crown, life for evermore.'

In a neatly maintained memorial garden to the left of the church is a brown bench erected by the mother of a victim from Ulster's last conflict. On 18 July 1991, gunmen from the Irish People's Liberation Organisation ran into McMaster's DIY shop in Belfast's Church Lane and shot dead John McMaster at point-blank range. The terrorists' excuse for murdering this defenceless shopkeeper was that he had served in the Royal Naval Reserve, which had been deployed earlier that year in the first Gulf War to eject Saddam Hussein's forces from Kuwait. McMaster was a popular character in Belfast's commercial centre, a man known to be extremely helpful, courteous and tolerant to all those who used his store, regardless of class or creed. Sitting as I often do on the seat dedicated to his memory (the church nearby was where he worshipped), the words of the man who ordered and organised that squalid murder still chill my blood.

'Our friends in the Middle East will note this,' said Jimmy Brown. I feel not only chilled but also angry because I knew the IPLO leader who offered up such a pathetic reason, such a ridiculous rationale, for the death of a decent man. Jimmy Brown sat in the living room of a house in the Lower Falls area a day or two afterwards and without irony, let alone regret, sought to justify the McMaster murder. For Brown, the 'British presence' meant imperial conquest, whether in Ireland, Kuwait or Iraq. For him, John McMaster was just 'collateral damage' (to borrow a phrase in vogue at the time of the 1991 Gulf War) in Brown's grand march towards the Irish Marxist revolution, a utopian experiment that ended not in the Workers' Republic but rather in a series of feuds and murderous turf wars that would result in the IPLO leader's own death just under a year after the shopkeeper's murder.

Haunted by the loss of my own grandfather in the Second World War, drowned in a U-boat attack on his Atlantic convoy, I often find myself standing over these memorials, imagining how these men, mostly young, met their end and sometimes whispering not so much a prayer but a few words of tribute and remembrance.

There are cemeteries like this one scattered all over Ireland, North and South, which within them house the remains or memorials to people killed in the service of Britain. One of my favourite is located on an incline overlooking Killybegs Harbour in the churchyard of St John's Church of Ireland. Among the gravestones is a tablet dedicated to a Private Thomas Chestnutt, who was killed in action on the Somme in 1916 while serving with the Royal Inniskillings. On all my visits to the Co. Donegal fishing port over the last 19 years I have seen virtually no one inspecting the gravestones or laying flowers or poppies at the site dedicated to Thomas Chestnutt's memory.

We who were born into the Irish, Catholic, nationalist, republican tradition of this island were only ever shown one side of what the 'British presence' in Ireland actually meant. The soldiers with the boot polish rubbed onto their faces kicking down our doors and tearing up the floorboards, holding my family and me under house arrest, slamming their armoured personnel carriers into the front of our home – this was 'the British presence', not the 900,000 plus Protestants in the North who insist they were and are British, nor the clandestine Brits (or 'West Brits', as nationalist Ireland labels them so contemptuously) who submerged their tradition in the official Ireland of Eamon de Valera's constitution with its stress on the Gaelic and the Catholic.

If nationalist Ireland wants to understand what it really means to be British on this island, they should come to places like Knockbreda Cemetery. For it is here where that sense of service to the British state is so evident, through the unbroken lineage of loyalty, from the young bandsman beaten to death in a Belfast street during the Home Rule Crisis, to the 20-year-old officer killed in the fields of France, to the fighter pilot shot down defending not only Britain but the free world at a time when Hitler and his war machine looked invincible. If genuine national reconciliation is ever to take place on a 32-county basis, it could begin with history classes in these Protestant resting places.

That sense of service to the British Crown is coloured by another collectively held notion, the sense of siege, that universal feeling of embattlement. It is most pronounced at the edge of the Union, in the Protestant redoubts closest to the Irish Republic. One such place is the Fountain estate, the last unionist area on Derry's west bank where local Protestants will tell you that they are still under siege 315 years after the loyalist residents defended the old city from Jacobite forces.

The Fountain is a quadrant of houses surrounded on three sides by 30-ft fences and the city's ancient walls that withstood Jacobite bombardments in 1689. Only 300 men, women and children remain on the estate and the single street of terraced houses between the River Foyle and Derry's old citadel. They are clinging on to this historic quarter of Protestant Ulster by their fingertips, a dwindling, ageing population, uncertain if there will still be a unionist presence on the western side of the Foyle over the next few decades.

Derry city centre is enjoying the peace dividend and the overspill from the boom across the border. UK retail giants are flocking into the city's commercial heart, and new hotels, restaurants, pubs and nightclubs are opening. On a late spring afternoon, with the sun shining and shoppers thronging the streets, Derry appears more like a Celtic Tiger boom town in the Republic than a geo-politically divided one in Northern Ireland. It may have been the city where the Troubles officially started in 1969, with the Bogside residents resisting the incursions of the B Specials, and the civil rights movement capturing the imagination of the world with their demands to defeat unionist misrule. But it is also the city where the Troubles were brought to a close, where Martin McGuinness held secret talks with MI5 officers to transmit the message to the British government that the IRA wanted to bring the 'war' to an end, and where the 'Derry experiment' (a phrase coined by author and leading authority on the IRA, Ed Moloney) was tried out, i.e. an absence of bombings in the commercial district, a winding down of IRA activity and a back-channel of secret dialogue between the Provos and the British.

For the residents of the Fountain, however, there is neither boom nor peace dividend; they do not share with the rest of the people on the city side that infectious optimism and confidence that Derry outwardly exudes. Such is the fear of retribution, of being singled out, that all of the adult men you speak to from the Fountain will only allow you to quote their Christian names.

Like one of the original Apprentice Boys who locked the gates at the start of the 1689 siege, Alex closes a gate every night leading to Derry's walls, still attempting to defend a Protestant bastion. If the Bishop Street Without entrance is left open after dark, young nationalists from the Bogside have easy access to the wall overlooking the Fountain estate, a handy vantage point from which to fire missiles into the area. On the evening I arrive to accompany Alex and his friend and neighbour Peter around the walls, fireworks explode on the other side of the fence as the almost nightly ritual of stone throwing, petrol bombing and general intimidation begins. Before closing the gate at the tower in Bishop Street Without, which is in sight of a British Army spy post, Alex explains that he was a 'blow-in', an outsider who moved from a rural part of Co. Derry, which was itself plagued with sectarian strife, into the west bank loyalist enclave.

'I moved into the Fountain in 1985 and, despite ceasefires and peace processes, life hasn't improved much. There are constant attacks on homes in the estate. Just last week there were two separate attacks, one at 7.30 p.m. and another at 9 p.m.'

He is fingering an orange-coloured mobile phone with a picture of a Glasgow Rangers player urinating on a Celtic shirt on the screen. Alex is wearing a Rangers shirt today. Would he be safe wearing the Rangers colours in Derry city centre? Peter frowns and then interrupts our conversation: 'A 14-year-old girl from the Fountain was walking through the Richmond shopping centre just a few hundred yards away from here a couple of weeks ago. A grown man spotted last season's red-and-white striped Rangers away kit sticking out of the girl's coat. He pulled the girl to the ground, kicked her and told her he didn't "want to see that fucking shit here again". The child told us later that the security men in the centre didn't intervene and none of the other shoppers went to her help.'

Alex nods his head and recounts an incident just before Easter involving his English girlfriend, yards from the Fountain and close to the city's courthouse.

'My girlfriend was walking along a street near the courthouse with my four-year-old son. It was a quarter past two in the afternoon and she was set upon by a group of nationalist teenagers. They called her "an Orange bastard" and told her they were going to burn her out. That's not an unusual story when our people go into the city centre,' he says bitterly.

The most dangerous periods for residents of the Fountain occur at the weekends, when the pubs on the nationalist side of the fence and walls empty, and when Celtic or the Republic of Ireland games are screened live on television.

'When Celtic won the Scottish Cup in May, they came out of the pubs and lobbed their beer glasses over the fence. I've lived on the Fountain all my life and it's always been like this. The weekend stone throwing, the constant bombardment goes on despite ceasefires, Good Friday Agreements or whatever else,' Peter says.

These stories are uncannily similar to conversations I have had with Catholics living in loyalist-dominated towns on the east Antrim coast, such as Larne and Carrickfergus, who had to put up with a lifetime of sometimes petty, often menacing, humiliations and threats. Listening to the Fountain Protestants' complaints about certain times of the year being the most precarious for them, I was propelled backwards in time to my own childhood, to the years 1975 and '76 when I spent my summers at a play scheme for children in the Upper Ormeau area. We played with Protestant kids from streets around Haypark, Ava and Haywood avenues for the last week in June and the first week in July. After that they would disappear from sight, preferring to hang around the bonfire the older loyalist boys were building on the Annadale embankment beside the flats complex overlooking the River Lagan. They didn't want to be seen hanging around with young Catholics during the period when their Protestantism and loyalism was on open display.

When the red, white and blue bunting was strewn across lamp-posts around the streets of Ballynafeigh, they acted like warning lights. These weeks were the ones when you were most likely to be beaten up or picked on by loyalist youths, even while your part-time, 50 weeks-a-year, Protestant 'friends' looked on from afar.

July, a month of freedom from school, of sunshine and summer schemes, was also the most precarious month for Catholics living in areas dominated by Protestants, though it could throw up moments of deep absurdity and hilarious stupidity. A decade on from my annual trip to the Holy Rosary summer scheme, I was sitting drinking cider in the back kitchen of George Dobbin's house on the eve of the Orange Twelfth. George played the drums in one of my bands of the early 1980s and had invited the group up for drinks to escape the interminable boredom and danger of the Eleventh night. Around midnight, we heard a commotion in the back entry to George's house in Fernwood Street. We looked out through the curtains and saw a circle of highly inebriated loyalists of all ages kicking what appeared to be a man lying on the ground. After a few minutes, the gang broke off from their victim and charged down the entry towards a loyalist band hall/social club, probably in search of more sustenance. George crept outside to check on their quarry. He called us out as well and when he reached the 'body', it turned out to be an effigy of the Pope with a yellow plastic traffic light you find at either end of zebra crossings used as the Pontiff's head. Grown men had spent five minutes kicking and punching a makeshift doll!

Back in 2004, despite the prevalence of CCTV cameras and British Army listening and surveillance posts on the walls, Peter and Alex believe the security forces have given up defending them. He claims that no one from the Bogside or other areas surrounding the Fountain has been prosecuted through the use of CCTV evidence for the attacks. Now that the British Army's 'war' with the Provisional IRA is over, the men argue that the military are not going to risk antagonising republicans by going after those who attack the Fountain. If they are right (and they have good grounds to be suspicious), this polity represents a metaphor for all unionists in Northern Ireland. The British government's, and thus its armed forces', first priority regarding the troublesome Province is to make peace with the organisation capable of sending soldiers back to Britain in wooden boxes and bombing the City of London. The loyalists of Londonderry, particularly those hemmed in on the west bank, are of far less consideration and concern to Whitehall.

In 1689, the besieged loyalists who held out for months under cannon and musket fire, as well as the constant threat of famine and disease, were finally relieved by a fleet of Williamite ships raised from the Protestants' supporters and allies in London. Three centuries and a bit later there are no more rescuers arriving from London to lift the new siege. Derry/Londonderry's loyalists have become expendable.

As the sky darkens and the air turns cooler, we walk through the remaining few streets of the Fountain past a wall mural dedicated to the breaking of the boom blocking the Foyle in 1689 and the eventual lifting of the siege. More fireworks explode from beyond the perimeter fence like distant rolls of thunder. Around the corner from another mural with the words painted in white on a black background: – 'LONDONDERRY West Bank Loyalists Still under siege NO SURRENDER' – a woman comes to the door and barks out the name of a child. It is time to come indoors. The fireworks are alarms, portents of trouble to come. Which indeed it did, 48 hours after my visit, when the Fountain came under attack once more from bottles, bricks and paint bombs, the loyalists retaliating with petrol bombs hurled towards Catholic homes in Bishop Street Without.

Later we skirt the edge of the estate under the shadow of the church wall behind which sits St Columb's Church of Ireland Cathedral. Between the houses and this part of the historic walls is a line of trees in full bloom, with birds twittering in the upper branches. Yet even nature is deployed here as a protective screen for the Fountain. Peter points up at the tree tops and tells me that Derry City Council proposed to fell the trees a year ago in order that tourists tramping around the outer perimeter of the seventeenth-century walls could have a better view. The people in the Fountain objected, arguing that the trees provided perfect camouflage/cover between a row of Protestant houses and the ramparts of the walls. After vigorous protests, the trees stayed in place.

Both Peter and Alex would never consider going into the city centre for a pint or a meal after 5 p.m. Once darkness falls, the commercial and social heart of the city is a no-go area for the Fountain's residents. There are only three places they feel safe to socialise in, all within a minute's walk from their enclave: the Apprentice Boys Memorial Hall at the edge of the walls overlooking the republican Bogside, the Talk of the Town pub and the Northern Counties club. The latter has a 'for sale' sign over its giant front-door entrance at Bishop Street Within. Once a gentleman's club for the Anglo-Irish gentry, this 9,000 sq ft of Britishness set down in the middle of a predominantly Irish nationalist city is, at the time of writing, on the market. Steeped in a pro-Union ethos, the Northern Counties is another disappearing symbol of the 'British presence' on the west bank. There is an atmosphere of faded Raj about the building, with its billiard room, dining halls with three giant chandeliers still hanging from the ceiling, the Victorian-style tiled toilets and washbasins, the servants' quarters and the sepia photographs framed in black of old 'Irish' regiments of the British Army hung around the walls.

Peter and Alex sit chatting with me in an upstairs function room with a portrait of a recently crowned Queen circa 1953 on one side and an oil painting depicting the 36th Ulster Division going over the top on the first day of the Battle of the Somme on the other. During the Second World War, the Northern Counties operated as an officers' mess. After the conflict, it became a social club for the city's unionist elite but the exodus of Protestants from the west side of the Foyle led to dwindling membership, ironically opening up the club to the loyalist working class who remained in and around the Fountain.

The sale of the Northern Counties follows a pattern of retreat amongst Derry's Protestants that has seen churches, schools and sports clubs either closed for good or relocated to the east bank of the Foyle. This is part of the slow but inexorable re-partition of Ireland, the re-drawing of the border established in 1920–21. The loyalist slogan 'No Surrender' was first patented along the walls during the siege of 1689. Today, only the few penned in around the Fountain are following that battle cry. The Protestant middle class has long since regrouped across the Foyle, even moving into the Co. Derry hinterland and to unionist-dominated towns like Coleraine. The strategy of voluntary surrender to re-settle eastwards has replaced No Surrender. Only the Protestant proletariat is left behind to lock the gates, scan the walls for incursions and fly the colours of the British presence.

As I leave the club through one of the last wooden swing doors still in use in Ireland, with Peter and Alex alongside, I suddenly shudder with a burst of cold. Just before I clambered up a rotten staircase to the servants' quarters, the barman had warned me that there was a ghost of an old British Army major haunting the upper floor. Had the major made contact with me as I left the Northern Counties for the last time or was I experiencing that peculiar frisson associated with time-travel, of passing back from a world pre-1921, never mind pre-1969, into another hurtling into a future where there is no room for Peter and Alex, let alone the officers and gentlemen of the 'club'?

On leaving the Fountain that evening, I notice graffiti scrawled on the nationalist side close to the fence surrounding the Protestant enclave. 'Huns Out' (Huns being slang for Protestants), it reads and 'Start Swimming'. Republicans in Derry insist the attacks on the area are not organised but are instead the work of young thugs. Loyalists are merely excluding themselves from the city's social life, the republicans contend. I think back to a conversation with a former IRA prisoner in a Derry pub close to the Bogside a day after the Ulster Defence Association slaughtered six Catholics and one Protestant across the Foyle in the village of Greysteel in October 1993, retaliation for the Provo bomb on Belfast's Shankill Road that killed nine Protestants a week earlier.

'We could have gone into the Fountain at any time and shot it up to revenge the people of Greysteel, but the republican movement didn't,' he told me in a solemn, self-righteous tone. 'The IRA is not sectarian.'

Neither Peter nor any other Protestant on the estate buys that line; as they know only too well, there are other ways to drive them out of the west bank. As far as he and all the others I meet are concerned, the frequent sorties launched at the Fountain are all part of a campaign to turn the west bank into a loyalist-free zone.

'You see, they want us out. They want us to get out of here and make us swim across the Foyle to the Waterside. And as for this city's boom, well, it stops at the walls.'

A two-and-a-half hour drive south-east takes me to another loyalist outpost of the Union where there is that same palpable paranoia, the sense of exclusion and encirclement you detect even in the air of the Fountain. Shandon Park lies on the northern edge of Newry, another border boomtown also enjoying the benefits of Southern spending power.

Newry, a traditional frontier market town dominated on one side by the Cooley Peninsula and on the other by the mountain range of south Armagh, became a city in 2003. Although its urban status came about thanks to the Queen's Golden Jubilee year (an ironic twist of fate that tickles the local loyalists), Newry, like Derry, is very much an Irish provincial city. The tills of Newry's shops, including those of the UK retail giants like Sainsbury's and Marks and Spencer, accept both sterling and euros, as do most of the pubs, clubs and hotels.

Up in Shandon Park, the locals say they do not partake in Newry's boom out of fear and a sense of alienation. They claim that after 5 p.m., an invisible curtain is drawn across the Belfast Road beside the PSNI station. Beyond this dividing line, particularly after dark, the Protestants of Newry have decided they shall not pass.

Unsurprisingly, few of the men, especially the younger ones, are prepared to give you their real names, in this case even their Christian names must not be mentioned.

Twenty-year-old 'Keith' is typical. He says he would never dream of going for a drink or meal in Newry city centre after dark. His fears sound exactly like the ones that are so prevalent among the last loyalists of Derry's west bank.

'I know some friends who went to a nightclub in Newry a few weeks ago and they were singled out and beaten up because they are Protestants. You wouldn't go down there after dark. Instead, all the teenagers and people in their 20s go north to Banbridge. It's only half an hour up the dual carriageway and we feel safer there,' he says.

We are sitting around a table inside the Mourne Country Hotel, which faces onto the front of the Belfast Road. Across the room are a group of rowdy but good-natured Irish travellers who at one stage approach one of the local Protestants ordering Coca-Cola and Fanta from the bar. 'Will Armagh win the championship this year, boss?' one of the drunken travellers, a guest at a wedding in the room next door, asks. The young Protestant nursing four bottles in his arms shrugs his shoulders. He hasn't a clue. Ulster Protestants do not follow the fortunes of Armagh or any other county playing Gaelic sports; some even view the Gaelic Athletic Association with suspicion and hostility. That little cameo at the bar, the sports question lost in translation, says as much about the two worlds of unionists and nationalists as volumes of academic studies and forests of journalistic reportage.

The only one amongst the group of Shandon Park residents prepared to offer his full name is a man with little to lose: 81-year-old William McKeague. He is a former Ulster Unionist councillor on Newry and Mourne District Council. What angers him most is that nationalists in Newry tend to deny there is any problem at all regarding Protestant alienation.

'They say we are excluding ourselves, but our young people feel threatened in the centre; and every time there is an Orange Parade, Sinn Féin stages protests.'

William claims that any outward display of Britishness in this republican stronghold, where the writ of the IRA's south Armagh brigade runs large, is not tolerated.

'Despite all that, I'm staying put in Shandon Park. They will have to take me out in a box,' he says, banging his walking stick on the bar-room floor.

Outside it is a beautiful warm evening, the late spring sunshine lighting up the top of the mountain south-west of Shandon Park. Pristine Union Jacks and Red Hand of Ulster flags flap gently in the breeze on lamp-posts all the way from the roundabout marking the beginning of Newry right down to the invisible curtain at the PSNI base, where these symbols of the British presence suddenly stop. Keith takes me for a tour around Shandon Park, a journey that takes about three minutes from the Belfast Road to the northern end of the Protestant street. There is the odd piece of graffiti dedicated to the Ulster Volunteer Force and its youth wing, the YCV, but apart from these paramilitary initials scratched onto a telephone box and a pole the estate is litter-free, with neatly mowed front gardens. Keith looks up towards Camlough Mountain in the near distance, a British Army spy station perched on its summit. Almost everyone in south Armagh wants military installations like this one looking down upon the home village of IRA hunger striker Raymond McCreesh torn down. They call it 'de-militarisation'; the loyalists of Shandon Park, however, regard such moves as another sign of retreat and eventual British withdrawal.

'Seeing that base up there gives the Protestants of Newry and south Armagh some assurance, a feeling of security,' Keith adds.

There are about 200 people living in Shandon Park. It, too, is an ageing population. The young see their future north in Banbridge or beyond, in Northern Ireland's other new city, Lisburn. Their eventual flight will also redraw the geo-sectarian map, pushing the frontier with the Republic closer to the Protestant-dominated areas of Antrim and east and north Down. Like their co-religionists in the Fountain, through their own fear and isolation they are playing their part in the re-partition of Ireland.

The Fountain and Shandon Park are outposts of the Union, but even in its heart, insecurity and doubt over the future also reign. For 35 years, the Shankill Road has been one of the two major war zones of Western Europe, the other being its geographic nemesis over on the Falls. Despite familial links with the Shankill through my maternal grandmother, it was always a place that instilled fear during the Troubles. On my first visit to the road with punk friends in 1978, I remember my knees were knocking while I travelled inside the cab of a UVF-controlled black taxi up the Shankill to an old girlfriend's house. On this same road at this very time, the Shankill Butchers gang were prowling the north inner city seeking out Catholics to abduct, torture and murder. Passing narrow streets, I experienced flashes in my brain from news reports, the grim and grey images of bodies covered in sheets being found up entries, the victims with their throats slashed and horrific wounds on their corpses. Today, even after countless trips to interview the next generation of loyalist killers such as members of Johnny Adair's 'C Company', I still find myself slightly worried about not returning, of being recognised as a Taig.

That sense of a threat around every corner, among every little group of men or teenagers on the street, returned on an early June evening just before the 60th anniversary of D-Day. As I stood pressing the buzzer to the door of the local Ulster Unionist Party office, with no one answering my call, a little knot of young men were coming towards me. My heart was beating faster the closer they came forward and just before they passed by, the door was pulled open by Shankill UUP councillor Chris McGimpsey. He had arranged for a representative gathering of men and women from the Greater Shankill to speak with me, to discuss where the world-famous loyalist stronghold now stood in the twenty-first century.

In an upstairs room, there was a fug of cigarette smoke and the clink of bottles of vodka and Stella Artois being taken out of white plastic bags. Six people were talking, their conversation solely concerned with the forthcoming D-Day events. At least four of these Shankill Road residents had served in the British Army. The daughter of the chairwoman, Maggie Fitzgerald, later came into the office; she was preparing for an entrance exam into the British military. Through the toxic clouds of exhaled smoke, amid the slurping of booze, that sense of siege and service so evident on Derry's west bank and the northern Protestant fringe of Newry once again became apparent.

Besides the talk about where they would be on D-Day (some were heading for Normandy's beaches, others to smaller local services at memorial gardens all over Belfast), this little group were also discussing the forthcoming European elections. Chris McGimpsey was asking for help to rap on doors, distribute leaflets, ferry pensioners to polling stations and staff election booths. The other woman in the room,

Violet Black, interrupted McGimpsey to remind him she would not be canvassing the Lower Shankill. She was one of hundreds of families driven from their homes in the Lower Shankill estate during the murderous feud between the UDA and UVF in late August 2000. Members of Adair's 'C Company' fired makeshift bombs constructed from Chinese firecrackers and ball bearings at Black's home, forcing her and her partner, both regarded by Mad Dog as 'unreliable', out for good.

McGimpsey has kept repeating that the internal loyalist war has probably inflicted more damage in the space of a few weeks on the Shankill than the IRA managed to do over three decades. Violet Black, a painfully thin, pale woman, who is evidently very ill but still chain-smoking, agrees with that theory.

'I will never return to that area. I don't even like going down to the doctors near the estate because of the way "they" look at you. It's as if you don't belong down there. You shouldn't be there.'

'They' used to be the republicans, the Fenians, the Taigs. Nowadays, with the Shankill still divided into two paramilitary-controlled zones of influence – the UDA in the lower end of the road, the UVF in the middle and upper part of the loyalist heartland – 'they' has come to mean whatever side of the invisible line on the road the other loyalist faction resides.

One of her old neighbours, a former soldier in the defunct Ulster Defence Regiment, reminds us all about a telling scene during the 2000 feud: UVF-controlled black taxis crossing through the peace line at Northumberland Street to the republican Falls Road en route to the city centre rather than risking driving down the Shankill past the UDA-dominated estate at the bottom end of the road.

'That made me sick, totally sick. Protestants feeling safer on the Falls Road than the Shankill, passing down there with the IRA's approval,' Billy says bitterly, refusing to give his surname, worried even now about his identity many years after retirement from the British Army.

Billy is bitter about many things: the seemingly never-ending demands from nationalists for public inquiries into disputed killings by the state, the fact that so many Catholics vote for the IRA's political wing, the presence of Provos at protests against loyalist parades from the Shankill into the city centre, the belief that it is all going the republicans' way.

When I challenge him on that latter point and argue that in fact
Sinn Féin's entrance into Stormont marks a major ideological retreat by
the Provos, Billy, bulging out of a tight-fitting Rangers home jersey,
retorts with a series of what-abouteries all the way from the burning of
Bombay Street in 1969 (Billy claims the IRA attacked Protestants first
along that infamous interface) to the Bloody Sunday Inquiry, which he
says is a waste of time because '13 terrorists' were shot dead by the
Parachute Regiment. The 'Fenians' (his word) are in general wiping the
floor with the two main unionist parties.

There is a self-defeating logic to his arguments, a suspicion that if
Gerry Adams says the republican community is winning then they
must be winning. I try to explain to him that this is not actually the
case, to take him through the back-flips and the 360-degree turns
Adams has put his organisation through. Billy sees none of this. The
Provos are still at war for him no matter what I say and Tony Blair is
ready and willing to do anything to keep the IRA on board the peace
train.

'Tell me why then your people keep voting for them animals,' Billy
asks. I assume 'them animals' means Sinn Féin, who would
subsequently defeat the SDLP's candidate Martin Morgan in the June
2004 European election.

We are not even speaking the same language by this stage. I cannot
understand let alone sympathise with 'my people' who vote for the
IRA's political allies, but they are not voting for 'animals' either.
Misguided, arrogant and fanatical maybe, but not 'animals'; nor do I
feel that they are 'my people', i.e. the entire Catholic community. I
wonder if Billy is listening as I try once more to rationalise Sinn Féin's
rise and in particular the way the party has stolen the SDLP's moderate
clothes.

The only dissenting voice to speak out against all this pessimism
turns out to be from Ballyclare, although he holds associate
membership of the Shankill branch. Unlike the others, Jim Fee has
travelled throughout the Republic and knows that the Southern
population want peace and stability in the North not the conquest of
the Fourth Green Field.

'The last opinion poll in Northern Ireland showed that 20 per cent
of Catholics support the Union. If the Union is to survive in the long
run, we need to reach out to that crucial 20 per cent, as their votes in

a future referendum will be vital,' Fee implores his fellow unionists. 'Our new battle is for hearts and minds. We unionists need to take religion out of our politics, to make the Union attractive to everyone. Saying "No Surrender" is not enough.'

Some eyes roll up to the ceiling as Fee expounds his secular brand of unionism, although no one in the room challenges his thesis . . . at least in front of me.

As the beers go down, the vodka is knocked back and more cigarettes are lit, the talk turns to the loyalist paramilitaries outside, whose presence is evident in a UVF mural at the top of the street – the UVF being one of the many groups who have appointed themselves defenders of the Shankill Road.

'I don't know how much more "defending" this community can stand,' McGimpsey says as the two women reminisce about the way the Shankill Road was once united in the face of the IRA threat. Their pining for a supposed golden age when Shankill loyalists and unionists stood together suddenly reminds me of a remark I heard over and over again while on various trips to Israel and the West Bank during the 1990s.

'If the Arabs make peace with us, then we will turn on each other,' was the constant refrain of politicians, soldiers and academics right down from the Lebanese border to the Negev Desert. Something similar is already happening in the dead centre of Protestant Ulster. Throughout May 2004, the UVF and smaller LVF fought out the fourth feud within loyalism since 1996. One man was killed and several families were forced out of their east Belfast homes. This latest feud even touched the lives of those living in the most prosperous unionist part of Northern Ireland, north Down. At the height of the UVF onslaught to drive out the LVF, British Army checkpoints were set up on the main approach roads to Bangor, a seaside town relatively unscathed by IRA violence during the Troubles. The unprecedented sight of armed troops manning roadblocks in the richest unionist quarter of the north was a powerful sign of the times, a symbol of the role reversal between loyalists and republicans since the peace process: the Protestants at war with each other, separated by troops they are loyal to; the Catholics at ease and confident about what lies ahead in the coming years.

Just as the bottles are cleared away and the fug of smoke evaporates in the night air once the door is finally wedged open, Maggie Fitzgerald leaves us with one disturbing claim.

'This is hard to believe but a lot of the young men in their late teens and early 20s would love to have the "war" back again. Even my son, who doesn't like the UDA, says the IRA only came to the negotiating table because Johnny Adair and his mates were shooting and terrorising the republican community. I'm telling you, they really want to get back at it, that's what's frightening,' she says.

There is silence in the room for a second and then McGimpsey gets up to offer me a lift across to south Belfast, that other world across the River Lagan far beyond the experiences of the Shankill and the Falls. The depressing atmosphere of the office off the Shankill Road follows us into the front of McGimpsey's four-wheel-drive jeep. Seven months earlier, McGimpsey suffered his own private humiliation on the Shankill. He has been a renowned hard-working councillor for 15 years, risking his own life during the UVF–UDA feud to rescue families from the Lower Shankill estate during the Adair faction's orgy of intimidation. When the November 2003 Assembly elections were called, he believed he stood a good chance of taking the last west Belfast seat from Sinn Féin. Protestant apathy in the previous Assembly elections of 1998 had given Sinn Féin four out of the five seats, meaning there was no unionist representation from the Shankill at Stormont. The Protestants of the Shankill did, however, turn out this time around, only to elect Diane Dodds, a relative unknown from Ian Paisley's DUP. Her stunning triumph summed up the surge of support for the DUP and the unionist people's rejection of the Good Friday Agreement.

McGimpsey is still suffering from unionist in-fighting, having just failed to get elected as Deputy Lord Mayor of Belfast for 2004–5 because he could not secure the support in City Hall of either the DUP or the UVF's political wing, the PUP. These double-blows in the space of six months reflect the mood of the Shankill and more generally Protestant Ulster's move away from the rational unionism articulated by McGimpsey for three decades.

The irony is that the DUP are starting to sound more secular and potentially moderate; they too are stealing the clothes of their rival party, in this case the Ulster Unionists. The DUP may eventually enter government with Sinn Féin, the party Paisley once vowed to smash.

Again, the parallels with Israel are striking. Only a few years ago, Ariel Sharon urged Jews to 'seize the hilltops' so that no Israeli government could ever again shut down settlements on the West Bank and Gaza. As I write, Sharon is busy engineering a vote in his cabinet that will allow the Israeli Defence Forces to pull out from Gaza and relocate hardline Jewish settlers into Israel proper. The question for Northern Ireland is: will Paisley or his political heirs do a Sharon?

Physical traces of the British presence are still visible south of the border even after eight and a half decades of experiments to engineer the Celtic Soul. On an Indian summer's morning in mid-September 2003, I came across remnants of British rule in Ireland while in the presence of a group of Ulster Protestant pensioners. They were staying in the Royal Marine Hotel overlooking Dun Laoghaire harbour, having travelled down from the North free of charge on the railway courtesy of the Irish government's travel scheme for OAPs. The old symbols of Ireland under the Empire were all around for them to see: the green-and-gold-coloured monument to Queen Victoria; the RNLI flag; the memorial stones to courageous seamen who died while on a doomed rescue mission at the end of the nineteenth century; and the models of HMS *Victory* encased in glass inside one of the local yacht clubs, with mini Union flags stuck on both stem and stern.

Perhaps the pensioners felt at home here amid all these reminders of Britishness, in the place they used to call Kingstown. Watching the blue-rinse and beige-jacket brigade taking tea on the lawn that morning, I was struck by this thought: if all unionists in the north were given free travel passes to the Republic, they might come to realise that the Southern nation is not ready and waiting to surge north and absorb their Province, that they have their own complicated social and economic problems to deal with.

For Dun Laoghaire was not simply an open-air museum for nostalgic loyalists pining for a pre-Partition/Independence arcadia. The area directly facing these Northern OAPs provided them with a perfect microcosm of the twenty-first-century Republic. Contiguous to the garden where the pensioners and I sat enjoying mid-morning tea is a small park sometimes used by the local alcoholics and drug addicts. As we sat in the sunspot near the front of the hotel, three winos were having a row, screaming incoherently at each other in the park. Just beyond this little group was a young mother who had pushed a pram with a baby inside it towards a park bench. I leaned over a hedge and watched her as she sat down, fished what looked like a metal box containing a geometry set out of a handbag, took out a syringe and then banged up what must have been heroin, judging by the colour of the liquid.

A few hundred yards beyond this pathetic little group was the harbour with, among the forest of radio masts and boats bobbing in the water, a new yacht worth €300,000, bought as a birthday present for the son of a local property owner. To the right of the young addict and the drunks were a row of apartments costing between €1 and €2 million, while to the left the DART station was packed with African, Asian and Eastern European workers waiting for trains to take them into Dublin. Directly across from the station, office workers were enjoying elevenses in Itsa Bagel, the bagels actually flown in fresh overnight from New York City. Conspicuous consumption living side by side with the losers in the Republic's casino economy, all within touching distance of one another.

This social kaleidoscope encapsulated the true concerns of the Republic's people: crime, drugs, astronomically high property prices, immigration and an inflationary economy. Ulster, the border, the Six Counties, the Troubles were and are far removed from the priorities of the office workers, the foreign commuters, the mother hooked on heroin and the booze-ravaged men in Dun Laoghaire on that glorious early autumn morning. Did the Northern pensioners catch a glimpse of these socially revealing tableaux? Did any of these geriatric tourists take the message back home that Southerners are too preoccupied with their own domestic problems and challenges to spend time and effort reclaiming the 'lost territory' of the Six Counties?

Yet the Republic's attitude to the British presence in their state is ambiguous and at times deeply hypocritical. In early 2004, the British Council published a report that seemed to confirm Southern Ireland's deepening love affair with the Old Enemy. It was launched with an ironic sense of place and timing. The survey came out just as the Bloody Sunday Tribunal in Derry was winding to a close; the slaughter of 13 unarmed Irish citizens by the Parachute Regiment being the nadir in post-war relations between Britain and Ireland. The location of the launch was also historically apposite – the British Embassy in

Dublin's Ballsbridge. Three decades earlier, angry protestors had burned down the old Embassy in the aftermath of the Bloody Sunday killings. (The revulsion in nationalist and republican Ireland over Bloody Sunday was widespread and deep. I remember standing with my mother in Cromac Square near Belfast city centre at the Republican Clubs bookstall holding pages containing white stickers with shamrocks and the number 13 on them – to mark the death count – and being astonished that even anti-republican, pious daily communicants were running to get these badges to slap onto their lapels. As we stood handing out the Bloody Sunday stickers, Paul McCartney's song 'Give Ireland Back to the Irish' was blaring from a hi-fi behind us.)

The *Through Irish Eyes* report of 2004 revealed how the icons of British popular culture have played a key role in strengthening the bonds between the Republic and Britain. Seventy-six per cent of Irish people described themselves as 'well disposed' to Britain. Among the main reasons why this culture shift occurred were David Beckham, Del Boy, David Brent from *The Office*, *Coronation Street*, the Premiership and the A to Z list of celebrities who occupy the pages of *Hello!* and *OK*. Even the negative aspects of British life that irritated the Irish in this survey were illuminating. They included the Western world's nuclear dustbin, Sellafield, English soccer hooligans and the British public and tabloid's obsessive fawning over a family of German origin whose matriarch sits on the British throne. What was most fascinating about *Through Irish Eyes*, though, was the absence of the Northern Ireland question from the top list of all those factors that turn the Irish off the British. Unionists take note!

There are estimated to be more than 300,000 people in the Republic with a British background. They include thousands who hold UK passports, as well as a larger number who were born in Britain or have at least one British parent. In the furore over race and immigration inflamed by the Irish government's 2004 referendum on citizenship, the fact was lost that the British in Ireland constitute the largest foreign minority.

Many of the forgotten Brits, like Robin Bury, spent their formative years across the Irish Sea before coming to settle in Ireland. While Irish culture and sport have cross-fertilised British, men like Bury insist the official attitude to the British presence is still inherently hostile. The

60-year-old retired Protestant schoolteacher felt so strongly about this attitude that he established the Reform Movement. Since it was formed after the Good Friday Agreement was signed, it has campaigned for the anti-British aspects of Southern Irish society to be challenged and eradicated. Reform's demands include a new Irish constitution devoid of any references to Gaelic and Catholic; the end of the Irish language as a compulsory part of education and a pre-requisite to entry into the civil service; the Republic's entrance into the British Commonwealth; and the right of anyone in Ireland to apply for a British passport.

Bury also lives among the old vestiges of the British presence in Dun Laoghaire, spending his retirement years arguing through the media that this tradition be resurrected and respected in the Republic.

'They [the British in Ireland] are still very nervous about raising their heads in the Republic. People only talk about their tradition behind closed doors. It only comes out on Remembrance Sunday, for example, or at times of major wartime commemorations like the current D-Day celebrations. In border areas of the Republic, it is manifested through the Orange Order and latterly the Ulster-Scots movement. But for 51 weeks of the year, bar a few exceptions, the British tradition in the Republic keeps its head way down,' Bury contends.

He cites the ambivalence about English soccer in the Republic as an example of the Irish's Janus-like attitude towards our nearest neighbour and those living in Ireland who see themselves as part of the British tradition. There is widespread glee when the English national soccer side endures humiliation on foreign fields; ABE – Anybody But England – is as intense over here as ABU – Anybody But United – is across the Irish Sea. Yet the same ABEs who will support any side in the world playing England also worship English soccer heroes like David Beckham, Michael Owen, Steven Gerrard, Wayne Rooney and Paul Scholes, etc. Even saloon-bar republicans are ambivalent about England and the English. On the morning of Manchester United's 1999 Treble-winning triumph, the final against Bayern Munich in Barcelona, I had to share a mercifully short bus journey from Heuston to Connolly Station with two drunken men singing pro-IRA ballads. They sat in the back of the bus slurring the words of 'The Boys of the Old Brigade' as the vehicle stopped and started along Dublin's quays. I kept my back to them for the whole of the journey until the bus halted at Busáras. The two songbirds then got up, swished past me and alighted. They were both wearing Manchester United away strips.

Ambivalence about the Brits extends beyond sport into other areas of life, including the Royal Family. When Queen Elizabeth II was crowned in 1953, the main cinemas in Dublin city centre broadcast live coverage of the coronation at Westminster Abbey. The thousands who came down to O'Connell Street and other major thoroughfares in central Dublin had to run a gauntlet of republican demonstrations, and in some cases the IRA actually closed down cinemas showing the coronation. Twenty-eight years later, when the Queen's son married Lady Diana Spencer, central Dublin was virtually deserted as the Irish public tuned in to watch the royal wedding of the century on television. When Diana's funeral was broadcast, the streets of Dublin were even more desolate as the entire Irish nation watched Britain's final salute to its 'People's Princess'.

In his Nobel Peace Prize acceptance speech on 10 December 1998, David Trimble, then Northern Ireland's First Minister, admitted that between 1921 and the suspension of Stormont 51 years later, unionists had turned Ulster into a 'cold house for Catholics'. To which those 'left behind' in the South after Partition counter-charge that de Valera's constitution made Eire and then the Republic into a cold house for Protestants and unionists. When he was trying to woo unionism to consider a United Ireland in the early 1980s, Charles Haughey made a speech informing Ulster Protestants that they would be amazed at the generosity of the Irish state; that the Republic would move heaven and earth to accommodate the unionists. To which Ian Paisley replied wittily with the tale of the spider and the fly.

'Come into my parlour said the spider to the fly, it's the nicest little parlour you ever did spy . . . well, let me tell you, Mr Haughey, the Ulster people are too fly to fall for you,' Paisley bellowed to his whooping, sniggering band of supporters during one of his 1981 Carson Trail rallies.

The majority of unionists I have met no longer regard the South as a predatory entity, the perception of the republican spider enticing the unionist fly into his web no longer prevails. Even the bitterly disillusioned unionists in Chris McGimpsey's office all admitted that they do not believe that the Republic is ready to pounce on them any time soon.

The UK, meanwhile, is not so much a 'cold house' for unionists but rather a rickety, unstable and awkwardly shaped construct in which many of them no longer feel wanted. For the rest of the UK household, Northern Ireland is the unwelcome annexe to the main edifice, an unsightly adjunct that somewhat spoils the view. Since 1997, the grand architect now in charge, Tony Blair, has sought to redesign the building in the style of the twenty-first century. He would gladly dispense with this troublesome outhouse with its squabbling tenants and quaint 'uncool Britannia' customs. However, Blair is bound by the deeds of the house, which stipulate that he cannot dispense with the dwellers outside the main house until they agree to go. Moreover, it is unclear if the only alternative accommodation available is the Irish Republic.

So what should those who want to stay part of the larger entity do to keep a permanent roof over their heads? One solution is to be found on the Hill of Howth, where unionism's staunchest ally in the Republic resides. Later on the same morning that I took tea with the Protestant OAPs from the North overlooking Dun Laoghaire port on that Indian summer's day in late September 2003, I travelled to the northern terminus of the DART. Around lunchtime I was met at Howth station by Maire Mac an tSaoi and taken to the hill on a landmass protruding into the Irish Sea. We hadn't met since her stepdaughter Kate died of a brain haemorrhage five years earlier at her home in Dublin. I was one of many mourners paying their respects to the then Editorial Director of Poolbeg Press. Kate had overseen the editing of *UVF*, a book I had co-written with my friend Jim Cusack the year before, detailing the history of the loyalist terrorist movement. Unlike many in the Republic, Kate had a real breadth of knowledge and a depth of concern for Northern Ireland. In that she followed the example of her father, Conor Cruise O'Brien.

In his memoir dedicated to Kate's memory, O'Brien dropped a bombshell on many of the unionists who respect and admire him. O'Brien's lifelong opposition to the IRA and revanchist nationalism has transformed him into something of a unionist hero in the North and therefore a hate-figure for republicans on either side of the border. His pro-unionism stance even led him in 1998 to oppose the Good Friday Agreement and ally himself with Ian Paisley. This latter decision disillusioned many of O'Brien's long-standing admirers in the Republic, such as the peace campaigner Chris Hudson, who later acted as a go-between for the Irish government and the UVF in the build-up to the loyalist ceasefire. Hudson and a raft of other Southern revisionists had backed David Trimble's attempt at historic compromise with Sinn Féin and the IRA. O'Brien's alliance with the Paisley unionists was too much for these secularists in the Republic who had once drawn inspiration from the 'Cruiser's' writings.

But just seven months after the Good Friday Agreement was signed, O'Brien had something alarming to tell the anti-agreement unionist camp. In an extract from *Memoir* published in *The Observer*, he argued that unionists should now abandon the UK altogether and link up with the Irish Republic. What he termed the 'ex-unionists' should then cut a deal with the Irish state that would ensure they exercised huge political clout in the Dail. The 900,000-plus unionist community, O'Brien mused, was but a small and inconsequential fraction of the entire UK population. In a unified Ireland, though, this voting bloc's strength in a populace of four million would have far greater influence in an Irish parliament. No future Irish government, O'Brien concluded, could be formed without the votes of the 'ex-unionists'. They would in effect be the permanent king-makers of every future Irish administration. The Union, in his own words, had become a trap for the unionists. His advice was for them to move next door and forget about Blair's UK.

His panacea for unionist existential uncertainty caused deep embarrassment to Bob McCartney, the leader of O'Brien's UK Unionist Party (UKUP), whose *raison d'être* was to prevent the outcome of Irish unity.

I came to the Hill of Howth curious to know if, five years later, the 'Cruiser' still held to his controversial thesis, especially since he is still the UKUP's honorary president. I found him pottering around the kitchen of his home, with its windows looking out towards the lighthouse on Howth Head. I sat sipping more tea as the sun beat down and turned the back of the O'Brien residence into a greenhouse. Shuffling towards me with his right hand outstretched, books on every wall around him, he apologised that he did not have adequate time to chat. I had one hour. He was busy completing a biography of George Washington.

'How can any Irish government say no to the unionists if they offer to enter a unitary state?' O'Brien asks. 'If they turned them down, it would mean the end of any chance of a United Ireland. Once they went in, all the advantages would tend to be for the unionists. They would be able to provide the opposition parties with a permanent coalition partner. They could keep Fianna Fail out of power and prevent Sinn Féin/IRA from getting its hands on government.'

O'Brien's wish to see the unionists absorbed in a unified Ireland has as much to do with his concern for the survival of democracy in the Republic as it has for the Protestants north of the border. His 'ex-unionists' in the Dail would dilute the dominance of his old enemies in Fianna Fail, whilst halting the inexorable rise of Sinn Féin. Moreover, the presence of an Ulster Protestant voting bloc would also challenge the authority of the Catholic Church in the Republic because, in order to placate the unionists, the Irish government that negotiated a unity-package would be forced to remove Catholicism's 'special position' in the Constitution. In a stroke, Irish politics would undergo a real revolution.

Other unionists and those trying to preserve the British tradition dismiss O'Brien's counsel as outlandish and unrealistic. Robin Bury has even gone as far as questioning the Cruiser's sanity, claiming Ireland's senior man of letters is 'a cracked man advocating a cracked idea'. Most of Chris McGimpsey's colleagues refuse to consider O'Brien's vision at all, with Maggie Fitzgerald pointing to her heart and saying: 'Being British is not about money or feeling secure. It's in here.'

These protests, though, ignore the precarious position unionists find themselves in at the start of this new century. Sinn Féin's electoral advance looks irreversible, the brightest and best of unionist youth is opting to study at British universities and remain there after graduation, and if only a small but significant minority of the Ulster Protestant middle class ever opted in the next ten to twenty years to vote for Irish unity in a future referendum, unionism would be forced into a United Ireland from a position of weakness.

When he talks about the 'ex-unionists' holding the balance of power in a future united republic, there is a twinkle in O'Brien's eye. Any original thinker has to be prepared to think the unthinkable, to generate fresh ideas, to challenge the status quo, to undermine orthodoxy. O'Brien has been placed on the intellectual rack over the last 35 years for his heresies. He is well used to the opprobrium and the insults. For those of us who have fought to stop the Provisional IRA maiming and murdering in our name, to break the mould of Irish politics, to combat the excessive influence of the Catholic Church on our personal lives, O'Brien's plan has some real merit and attraction. Since Partition, nationalist Ireland has been dominated by three forces – Fianna Fail, the Roman Catholic Church and the IRA. At various times in history the interests of this triumvirate have overlapped and intersected, but their power and influence has, since Partition onwards, seemed unassailable. The arrival of almost a million Protestants from the North in a newly unified state would mark a tectonic shift that would shake the ground beneath power structures that have cast such a withering shadow across this island for so long. Fianna Fail could be put permanently out of office if the 'ex-unionist' king-makers link up with Fine Gael and Labour; to accommodate the Ulster Protestants, the unique Catholic character of the state would have to be diluted and the IRA's justification for its very existence would disappear overnight.

O'Brien's panacea for unionist uncertainty in the North contains the greatest irony of all for the South. The dream of a secular, pluralist and terrorist-free Republic is at last realisable if and when the unionists heed O'Brien's advice. As we sat in his house at the very edge of the Irish world, looking out towards the lighthouse on Ireland's Eye and at the shimmering horizon beyond which lies the English coast, I realised that O'Brien's controversial thesis is, in essence, a patriotic one. This assertion will undoubtedly raise the heckles of his enemies North and South, especially those that have branded him with the 'West Brit' slur for so long. The return of the British presence in such large numbers would radically transform every aspect of life in the Republic. It would ensure the state never falls into the hands of a party with a private army. In addition, it would finally lift the siege that has trapped the Ulster Protestant imagination for centuries, a vice that will eventually undermine its influence in the world. The most important revolution in Irish history begins the day the unionists become 'ex-unionists'.

Epilogue

Two demonstrations separated by 15 months: one in Belfast, the other in Dublin. The same old familiar slogans and faces, the same battle cries of revolution.

It is early March 2003 outside Belfast City Hall and thousands have flocked to the city centre to protest against George Bush and Tony Blair's decision to invade Iraq. The usual suspects have turned up to demonstrate and denounce 'US and British Imperialism'. To my right are some of my old comrades in the Workers Party standing side-by-side with their old enemies in Sinn Féin. I spot some ex-acquaintances from my brief flirtation with Militant Tendency, now the Socialist Party. The Derry socialist, journalist and veteran of many radical causes through 35 years Eamon McCann takes to the podium and informs the people there that this may not be the biggest crowd to have gathered at City Hall but it is certainly the best. McCann launches into one of his 'no-blood-for-oil' tirades. Even my friend, the author and broadcaster Malachi O'Doherty has turned up to support the 'peace movement'.

I stand surreptitiously at the edge of this protest feeling like a spy at the heart of the enemy's camp because I am no longer on the same side as these people.

A group of peaceniks wearing mock chemical warfare kits sits down to block traffic in Wellington Place and engineer a confrontation with the Police Service of Northern Ireland. The majority of the protestors are furious because the demonstration was meant to be peaceful and dignified, timed, as it was, to coincide with a visit by George Bush to Hillsborough just outside Belfast. No one around, however, points out the irony of men dressed up in masks and white boiler suits protesting over a war to overthrow one of the worst mass murderers of our time. Nor does anyone I argue with seem to realise that on the very same day, the Kurds of northern Iraq are celebrating the supposed demise of one of Saddam Hussein's most ruthless killers.

In Kurdish regions of Iraq, they were holding picnics on the graves of their loved ones inside cemeteries for the dead of Halabja. They thought they had something to celebrate: the death at the hands of British forces in Basra of one of their chief tormentors, the man known as Chemical Ali. Saddam's cousin had planned and executed the mass gassing of 5,000 Kurdish men, women and children at Halabja in 1988.

In the Shia south, they too thought they had something to cheer about. Chemical Ali was the key organiser of the Ba'athist regime's brutal suppression of the uprising in Basra shortly after the first Gulf War, a rebellion shamelessly encouraged and then abandoned by George Bush's father. During the regime's operation to seize back Basra, Chemical Ali dispatched troops to the edge of the city and dressed them up in chemical warfare suits and gas masks – like the ones worn by the radical peaceniks halting traffic outside the City Hall. When the citizens of Basra saw those soldiers scattering white powder around the approaches to the city, knowing Chemical Ali's reputation in Kurdistan, there was widespread panic. Human rights organisations later reported that this incident of mass psychological intimidation was crucial in terrifying the recalcitrant Shia population into submission.

As the PSNI dragged the comical radicals off the street, I wondered what the newly liberated Shia and Kurds would have thought of these young Irish peace protestors decked out in mock chemical warfare suits, proclaiming, in the name of Iraqis, that there should be no war to topple Saddam Hussein's gangster regime.

What was on display outside City Hall that day was a compound of, to use the columnist Christopher Hitchens' denunciation of the mass peace marches across the Western world against the war, 'the silly led by the sinister'. There were genuine pacifists holding up banners who simply believed that war was not the way to settle international disputes any more. Although, by their logic then, it would apparently have been better to surrender to Adolf Hitler in 1939 rather than fight back with a war of annihilation against the Nazis. Behind the legions of the young and the ignorant-of-Iraq lay the hard left of both Stalinist and Trotskyist strains. There were men and women here, some of whom I know, who had never forgiven the West for winning the Cold War. Many of them, though not all, had pushed the illusion during the Troubles that the IRA was waging essentially an anti-imperialist struggle that should be given, to recall the greatest oxymoron in leftists' vocabulary, 'critical support'. Some even got the notion into their head that they could be the intellectual vanguard of a 'broad anti-imperialist front', as if the control-freak Provos would ever relinquish leadership of any kind to a cadre of middle-class, former-student radical Rip Van Winkles who went to sleep in 1968 and on awakening kept thinking that capitalism's endgame was near.

Tired and depressed from all the usual rhetoric, I broke off from the peace demo with one thought in my mind. If the leaders of America and Britain heeded the demands of the masses that turned out across the free world not to attack Iraq, the Ba'ath Party dictatorship would remain in power in Baghdad. So no matter how much they said they despised the Iraqi tyranny, the protest was objectively part of the 'Saddam Hussein Preservation Society'. With the same arrogance they had exuded during the Bosnia crisis, when they opposed US intervention to stop Serbian fascists slaughtering the Muslims of the former Yugoslavia, the Irish left was essentially telling the people of Iraq they had no right to be free from Saddam if it meant the Americans coming to their rescue. They used to say the same thing to the peoples of Eastern Europe under communism, even after 1989 when the citizens of Berlin, Warsaw, Prague, Budapest and Bucharest turned their backs on socialism and opted for a return to capitalism, thus disproving Karl Marx's linear theory of history moving inexorably forward in neat stages.

The peaceniks and the Irish left in general are right about one thing on Iraq: it is the defining issue for my generation. But whereas many on the left, particularly those old enough to have chanted the name of

Ho Chi Minh outside the US Consulate in Belfast or the American Embassy in Dublin, treat Iraq like a new Vietnam, I view the war as a moral challenge to all democrats and liberals in free societies. Never mind the WMDs or lack of them, nor the tendentious claim about a link between the 11 September hijackers and Saddam's government. There was and is a moral case for supporting the war. It is based on the old idea that it is better to light one candle than stand there and curse the darkness. Yes, of course, there are nasty, brutal regimes still intact across the planet, both right wing and left wing, that equally deserve to be invaded or overthrown. But at the start of 2003 there was a chance, a very real one, for the opponents of a tyrannical ruler, Saddam Hussein, to seize a historic opportunity and change the regime. The problem remains that the only effective method of reaching that goal was through the United States military and their allies, the British. This is why almost all of my former comrades opposed the war and then, having failed to stop it going ahead, now revert to supporting what is obscenely labelled 'the Resistance', in reality a vile and opportunistic cabal of Ba'ath loyalists, jihadists and sectarian militias. Due to their perverse hatred of all things American, the Irish left wants this 'Resistance' to succeed both in fomenting religious and ethnic civil war and to eject the Western allies from Iraq. This delight in destruction, even if it means the mass murder of Shia pilgrims by jihadist bombers, is both amoral and wanton. Rather than support free elections, the creation of an open media, the elevation of women to political power and the creation of a non-sectarian federal constitution, the Irish left and their comrades in Britain by and large march side by side with Islamofascists whose own agenda is to plunge Iraq and most of the world back into the Middle Ages. In Ireland and other democracies, this means Marxists and medievalist bigots parading together, the '68ers who linked the struggle of the proletariat with the battles of equality for gays and women now sharing platforms with men (only in the main men!) who preach a doctrine of hatred towards homosexuals as well as the enslavement of half of humanity: truly the Grand March of history has a taken a sharp turn down a very dark and narrow pathway.

Fifteen months on from that other epiphany at Belfast City Hall and I was standing on the north side of the Liffey, near the Capel Street Bridge, watching another demonstration. Across the river, around a thousand protestors carrying flags and banners, and walking to the beat of several drummers, were making their way from the city centre to Sean McDermott Bridge near Hueston Station. This was as far as they could go due to the presence of thousands of Gardai officers blocking their route up to Phoenix Park. The largest security operation in the history of the Republic cost around €15 million and was used to protect all the prime ministers and presidents from the European Union gathered in Dublin to welcome the entry of ten new states into the EU.

Among the demonstrators still denouncing 'US imperialism', the occupation of Iraq and that new font of all evils in the world, globalisation, was a small group from the Communist Party of Ireland (CPI). The CPI, along with the Workers Party, was among the most fervent pro-Soviet parties anywhere in the Western world during the Cold War. Many of the CPI cadres still hanker after the 'good old days' and yearn for a return of the Soviet Union. Standing right beside me were two young new Europeans who were to become EU citizens on May Day 2004. Born before the Berlin Wall came down, while communism still reigned thanks to the Soviet Army divisions in his native Poland, Krzysztof Cydzik was enjoying Europe's new dawn. He had no understanding or sympathy with the rag-tag anti-globalisation army across the river, including the 'comrades' who used to come to Poland and tell Krzysztof and his fellow Poles that they were lucky to be living under socialism.

'Why are they protesting about Europe getting bigger?' he asked as the chants and the cries echoed on both sides of the Liffey.

A qualified accountant, the 27-year-old native of Poznan knew his life was about to undergo its own revolution.

'For the last two years I have been working illegally in Ireland but now I don't need a work permit anymore. I am a European citizen. I can work legally now.'

Standing beside him, the flag of her native Slovakia flapping in the wind along with all the other 25 nations of the EU, Luba Cabajova expressed indifference towards the demonstration.

'It doesn't matter to me. I just can't believe it. I only came to Dublin to work two months ago and now I'm legally entitled to stay here and earn money. That's all that matters. It's a great day.'

When I finally crossed the new Millennium bridge to join the protestors, all those hopes of the two young Eastern Europeans I had just met in a bar on the Liffey half an hour earlier dominated my thoughts. It was May Day – the most sacred day in the international left's calendar – but I found myself sympathising only with the young Pole and Slovak who came into the world under the Red Star and Hammer and Sickle but who were now excited over the fact that their two nations had just joined the largest capitalist club on the planet. This was their day, no matter how much the disparate and confused factions of the Irish left sullenly protested.

At home there remains one issue alone that continues to keep me awake at night – Northern Ireland. As I write, the radio news reports confirm that my former co-religionists have just elected a Sinn Féin candidate to Europe. By a massive majority, the Catholics in the North of Ireland have also rejected Martin Morgan of the moderate Social Democrat and Labour Party. Morgan has just lost the seat held since 1979 by John Hume, his party haemorrhaging over 100,000 votes compared to the last Euro-election in 1999. There appears to be no way back for the party. They have entered a period of terminal decline. Throughout the Troubles the SDLP never broke a window let alone harmed a single human being. Sinn Féin, on the other hand, has the blood of thousands on its hands. For three and a half decades it has been the political wing of the Provisional IRA. They were the people that brought you the abduction and murder of Jean McConville, Bloody Friday, the La Mon firebomb massacre, the Birmingham pub bombs, Claudy, Enniskillen and a whole litany of other killings. That they have stopped killing Irish and British citizens in the name of the Republic is a welcome development. That the Northern nationalist electorate can ignore the commitment to democracy, peace and decency shown over the years of terror and atrocity by the SDLP is equally shocking and depressing.

The news from the South is the same: Sinn Féin surges all over the Republic. Despite months of revelations and investigations in the Irish media about the party's links to IRA crime rackets, Southern voters support Sinn Féin in record numbers and, it seems, feel no discomfort over the continued existence of the party's armed wing.

Frank O'Connor used to compare the Irish to Orpheus, whose tendency to look back behind him whilst escaping from the Underworld lost him the love of his life. The Irish, O'Connor complained, also tended to constantly turn back to the past instead of looking forward into the future. The election results of 14 June 2004 make it clear that the Irish have eschewed their Orpheus-complex. In greater numbers than ever before they are now a nation of amnesiacs. The Provisionals' blood-soaked history is not important any more to voters from Wexford to west Belfast, Waterford to Derry's west bank. In his masterpiece novel on totalitarianism, *The Book of Laughter and Forgetting*, Milan Kundera said that the struggle of man against power is the struggle against forgetting. In Ireland, that struggle has been lost. History is being re-written in the manner of Orwell's Ministry of Truth. The 'armed struggle' is no longer about a violent insurrection to bring about a United Ireland but rather a logical extension of the civil rights struggles of the '60s, with Catholics only taking up arms in self-defence and as part of a drive towards 'equality'. The Troubles are re-packaged as a series of milestones of nationalist pain – the burning of Bombay Street, Internment, Bloody Sunday, the Dublin/Monaghan bombs, the hunger strike, the murder of Pat Finucane, the peace process and the Good Friday Agreement. No one asks what the Sinn Féin leadership did during the 'war'. To do so is to risk being branded an 'enemy' of the peace process. Indeed, one Dublin-based correspondent with barely concealed Sinn Féin sympathies has even drawn up a list of those reporters and commentators he believes are none too keen on the current situation in Northern Ireland. They are, to use his own acronym, 'Japs' – Journalists Against the Peace Process.

Gerry Adams and Martin McGuinness, meanwhile, have been awarded the status of pop stars, North and South, in nationalist Ireland. Their presence on the canvass anywhere on this island (excluding the loyalist redoubts in the North) is enough to harvest votes even for the most mediocre and intellectually hollow party candidate. Nuns and housewives on doorsteps throughout both states rush to hold Adams' hand. Even descendants of the Anglo-Irish Ascendancy put up posters in their country houses of the Sinn Féin president's wolfish visage. Is it really that fanciful to imagine Adams being sworn in at Phoenix Park as President of Ireland in the autumn of 2011?

Politically, I no longer have a home to go to; all my colours have merged into an indistinguishable blur. Iraq has finished off my alignment to the broad left in Ireland. Perhaps in the near future I may no longer have a physical home to live in either. Northern Ireland is now a society pulling itself apart. The results of the Euro elections underline again that there is a large majority of people living around me who detest one another because of religious and national allegiances. Six years ago the architects of the Good Friday Agreement promised us peace, power-sharing and a society, to use David Trimble's own words at the time, 'at ease with itself'. The audit of the agreement is not a convincing one. Their voters have sacked the main architects of the peace deal – the Ulster Unionists and the SDLP. The extremist parties, Sinn Féin and Ian Paisley's Democratic Unionists, are in the ascendance over the moderates; their leads over their respective rivals now look unassailable. The physical divisions in the actual 'war zones' of the Troubles seem immutable, human contact between people on either side of these barriers a rarity.

Nor am I at ease with the society I still live in. As I sign off, my children have just arrived back from a visit to my father-in-law, who was discharged from hospital today after six months of care. I watch Lauren, seven, and Ellen, aged three, limp wearily into the house too tired even to come running into my office for a goodnight hug and kiss. I ponder on their future here. Do I really want them to grow up in a community that is becoming increasingly divided on crude sectarian lines? Would they be better off in another society elsewhere that is truly at ease with itself?

The Ireland of the twenty-first century is certainly a freer place to be than it was in the frenetic murderous years of the '70s or the recession-hit, doom-laden '80s. The Irish people enjoy more freedom today than any other generation in our history. But in the north-east corner of this island there remains a deep well of poisonous bitterness and mistrust that threatens at any time to bubble up to the surface and engulf the Province in a tide of blood. For the men and women that waged a terrorist war on Northern society, the armed struggle may be over, but within that pool of hatred and division there lies the ever-present danger of 'war by other means'.

When Charles J. Haughey visited Belfast as President of the European Union in 1990, he was greeted by a mass demonstration of unionists outside the city's Europa Hotel. Inside the heavily guarded hotel, Haughey delivered a speech on the necessity for pan-European cooperation and economic integration on the island of Ireland. During a question-and-answer session in the main conference hall, Haughey was given a planted query from an SDLP member in the audience. What, the party hack enquired of the soon to be disgraced Taoiseach, was his message to the young people of Northern Ireland? Ed Moloney – the world's greatest authority on the IRA – leaned over and barked out loud: 'The advice is to get the fuck out!' Fourteen years on, Moloney's advice still sounds like the best option for those in Northern Ireland who have eschewed sectarian labels and politics. 'Get the fuck out!' will be the epitaph of the Alternative Ulster generation and all those who have followed their example.

List of Abbreviations

BAOR – British Army of the Rhine
CAB – Criminal Assets Bureau
CIRA – Continuity IRA
CPI – Communist Party of Ireland
DUP – Democratic Unionist Party
EU – European Union
FDJ – Free German Youth
GDR – German Democratic Republic
IDYM – Irish Democratic Youth Movement
INLA – Irish National Liberation Army
IPLO – Irish People's Liberation Organisation
IRSP – Irish Republican Socialist Party
NIUP – Northern Ireland Unionist Party
OIRA – Official IRA
PCI – Italian Communist Party
PIRA – Provisional IRA
PSNI – Police Service of Northern Ireland
PUP – Progressive Unionist Party
SARI – Sport Against Racism in Ireland
SDLP – Social Democratic and Labour Party

SED – Socialist Unity Party of Germany
SFWP – Sinn Féin Workers Party
SOCA – Survivors of Child Abuse
UDA – Ulster Defence Association
UKUP – United Kingdom Unionist Party
UTE – Up the Erps
UTP – Up the Provos
UTS – Up the Sticks
UUP – Ulster Unionist Party
YCV – Young Citizens Volunteers

Bibliography

Acheson, Alan, *A History of the Church of Ireland: 1691–2001*, Columba Press, 2002

Allen, Keiran, *The Celtic Tiger: The Myth of Social Partnership in Ireland*, Manchester University Press, 2000

Allen, Nicholas and Kelly, Aaron, *The Cities of Belfast*, Four Courts Press, 2003

Bairner, Alan, *Sport, Nationalism and Globalization*, State University of New York Press, 2001

Beattie, Geoffrey, *We Are The People: Journeys Through The Heart of Protestant Ulster*, Mandarin, 1992

Collins, Stephen, *The Power Game: Fianna Fail Since Lemass*, O'Brien Press, 2000

Cruise O'Brien, Conor, *Memoir*, Profile Books, 1998

Dickie, John, *Cosa Nostra: A History of The Sicilian Mafia*, Hodder and Stoughton, 2004

Elliott, Marianne, *The Catholics of Ulster*, Penguin, 2000

English, Richard and Morrison Skelly, Joseph (eds), *Ideas Matter: Essays in Honour of Conor Cruise O'Brien*, Poolbeg Press, 1998

Fanning, Bryan, *Racism and Social Change in the Republic of Ireland*, Manchester University Press, 2002

Foster, R.F., *The Irish Story: Telling Tales and Making It Up in Ireland*, Penguin, 2001

Galvin, Anthony, *Family Feud: Gangland Limerick Exposed*, Hodder Headline Ireland, 2003

Girvin, Brian, *From Union to Union: Nationalism, Democracy and Religion in Ireland – Act of Union to EU*, Gill and Macmillan, 2002

Goodhead, Giles, *Us v Them: Journeys to the World's Greatest Football Derbies*, Penguin/Viking, 2003

Hourihane, Ann Marie, *She Moves Through the Boom*, Sitric Books, 2000

Keena, Colm, *The Ansbacher Conspiracy*, Gill and Macmillan, 2003

Kennedy, Finola, *Cottage to Creche: Family Change in Ireland*, Institute of Public Administration, 2001

Herrigan, Gene and Brennan, Pat, *This Great Little Nation: A-Z of Irish Scandals & Controversies*, Gill and Macmillan, 1999

Kuper, Simon, *Football Against the Enemy*, Phoenix, 1999

Madden, Andrew, *Altar Boy: A Story of Life After Abuse*, Penguin Ireland, 2003

O'Connell, Michael, *Changed Utterly: Ireland and the New Irish Psyche*, Liffey Press, 2001

O'Doherty, Malachi, *I Was a Teenage Catholic*, Marino Books, 2003

O'Doherty, Malachi, *The Trouble With Guns: Republican Strategy and the Provisional IRA*, Blackstaff Press, 1998

O'Leary, Olivia, *Politicians And Other Animals*, O'Brien Press, 2004

O'Neill, Sean and Trelford, Guy, *It makes you want to Spit! – The definitive Guide to Punk in Northern Ireland*, Reekus Records, 2003

O'Toole, Fintan, *After the Ball*, New Island Books, 2003

Stille, Alexander, *Excellent Cadavers: The Mafia and the Death of the First Italian Republic*, Vintage, 1996

Williams, Paul, *Crime Lords*, Merlin Publishing, 2003

Studies: Racism and Community, Winter 2002

Index